CW01272826

HOW IDEAS ARE BORN
ILLUSTRATORS ON CREATIVE PROCESSES

HOAKI

C/ Ausiàs March, 128
08013 Barcelona, Spain
T. 0034 935 952 283
T. 0034 932 654 883
info@hoaki.com
www.hoaki.com
hoakibooks

How Ideas Are Born. Illustrators on creative processes

ISBN: 978-84-19220-19-6

Publication © 2023, Hoaki Books, S.L.
Text © Miguel Ángel Pérez Arteaga
Personal images and texts © their authors

Author: Miguel Ángel Pérez Arteaga
Art director: Miguel Ángel Pérez Arteaga
Cover illustration: Raúl Guridi
Layout: Batidora de Ideas
Publishing coordinator: Anna Tetas

All rights reserved. The reproduction
of this book in whole or in part, its transmission
in any form or by any means or process,
whether electronic or mechanical,
including photocopying, recording, or incorporation into
a computerized storage and
retrieval system, and the distribution
of copies thereof by rental or public
lending are not permitted without the
prior authorization of the publisher.

DL: B 1243-2023
Printed in China

HOW IDEAS ARE BORN

ILLUSTRATORS ON CREATIVE PROCESSES

MIGUEL ÁNGEL P. ARTEAGA

Acknowledgments

I would like to thank all the illustrators who appear in this book for their generosity and effort, as well as for their enthusiasm and involvement in the project. It is not easy to talk about one's self or to explain something as ethereal and intangible as creativity and the processes that lead to the emergence of ideas.

	6 | 9
Elisa Arguilé	10 | 19
Pablo Auladell	20 | 31
Gary Baseman	32 | 45
Katie Benn	46 | 53
Ana Biscaia	54 | 61
Serge Bloch	62 | 73
Pep Carrió	74 | 85
Carolina Celas	86 | 97
Jesús Cisneros	98 | 109
Lisa Congdon	110 | 121
Fanny Dreyer	122 | 131
Delphine Durand	132 | 143
Isidro Ferrer	144 | 155
Guridi	156 | 163
Yoshiko Hada	164 | 175
Elizabeth Haidle	176 | 183
Chris Haughton	184 | 191
Isol	192 | 201
Martin Jarrie	202 | 213
Anita Kunz	214 | 225
Manuel Marsol	226 | 237
Flavio Morais	238 | 247
Pérez Arteaga	248 | 259
Simone Rea	260 | 271
Tom Schamp	272 | 281
Hervé Tullet	282 | 289
Valerio Vidali	290 | 301
	302 | 303

To illustrate has the same origin in Latin as the word *to shine* or *to polish*. My grandmother, whose name was Iluminada, always told me that I should be a person who shines. She was referring to my shoes being *polished* and clean, but I imagine deep down she was talking about the importance of presenting the best image of oneself to others.

I have always believed that an illustrator's function is this: to embellish, to enhance the image of a book, a product or an advertising message. In other words, an illustrator's task is to create a more attractive, more livable and more intelligent world.

According to the dictionary, *to illustrate* means *to grant understanding, to make clear through images, to teach, to enlighten, to shed light*. There is nothing more important for society than the professions devoted to this, to enlightening and teaching. These include the doctors who assist in our being born as well as the teachers responsible for educating us in our early years.

We could say that being an illustrator entails both things simultaneously. Another meaning of the word included in the dictionary and of particular interest to me is: *Said of God, to illuminate creatures with supernatural light from within*.

For me, to illustrate is precisely this. Because those of us involved in one way or another in the world of illustration are like little gods. We create universes and we invent the creatures that inhabit them and how they interact with each other. And we do it out of nothing, from a blank sheet of paper, with a dose of suffering but also a childlike madness. It touches on magic and mystery, which is why it is so attractive to people who do not have this gift.

Surprise, emotion and fascination

We have a strange relationship with books. When we are just a few months old, our parents already want to share these mysterious objects with us. At first, they are made of thick cardboard with rounded edges; if you are lucky, they are cloth. And the content is not important. It is merely a hint of what is to come.

When confronted with a book, each child has his or her own strategy: some try eating them, some struggle to test their durability, others try to step inside them. It is as if at this moment we are already making decisions about how we want to engage with the world. Some will decide to let themselves be carried away by the stories, others will want to make them their own, to create them and transform them.

Later, words arrive and with them, the daily ritual of whispering in the ear, in the darkness of night, as if we were basking in the glow of a magic flame. Words as mantra, the same gestures and intonations every night providing us with the sense of security we need before falling asleep and entering the unknown world of dreams.

Over time, we are initiated into the world of images, and with them comes surprise, emotion and fascination. And little by little, the pleasure of searching for details, for what is hidden, or what is imagined. For this reason, the images that we discover as children become fixed in our mind and stay with us for the rest of our lives.

Whenever we enter an old bookstore; when we see piles of books at a flea market; when we step into a library or visit a modern bookstore filled with art and design books, in a way we regress to our childhood. This is why billboards, magazine covers and product packagings come out to greet us, urging us to set out on the road to the source of everything. Chocolates, perfumes, wine and mineral waters are filled with illustrations to connect them to this period of happiness. Because at heart we all want to keep on being children, a kind of eternal Peter Pan.

A treasure chest

The book you are holding in your hands is like a treasure chest of images in the form of found objects. The images are compiled, selected and collected, but so are all the emotions contained within them.

Some are wildly childish. Others are emotional, suggestive and amusing. And others are brimming with virtuosity. They are the discoveries, the secrets that every child would like to show her and his new friends.

When we attend a magic show, or when we go to the theater or the movies, we know that nothing is real but we let ourselves be swept up and enter the play of this parallel reality. Yet occasionally a somewhat impish spirit possesses us, compelling us to discover, with all strength we have, what the trick is.

The featured illustrators appear throughout this book in their role as illusionists. They show us their sketchbooks filled with drawings and ideas. They invite us into their studios. They show us their capes, top hats and magic wands, but they do not tell us how to use them.

It is an invitation to peer through a kaleidoscope of styles, techniques and languages. You can read this book as a connoisseur, taking notes on each artist's reflections and trying to identify the hints contained in their sketchbooks. Or you can read it as a child, opening the pages randomly, allowing yourself to be inspired and attempting to step inside them.

My treasure chest contains twenty-seven illustrators from twelve different countries, two hundred and seventy illustrations and one hundred and ten earlier sketches or pages from personal notebooks. You are invited to see for yourself.

Elisa Arguilé

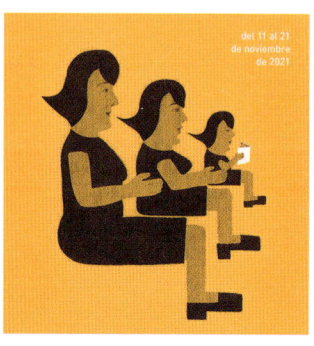

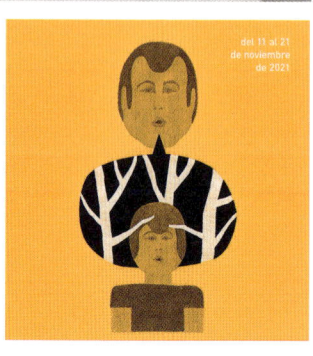

"I began illustrating books without really knowing what illustration was, simply by trying out a possibility, like some many others I'd tried, to earn a living doing a job related to drawing. At the time, I had a job that allowed me, in addition to putting food on the table and paying my bills, to buy materials and have enough time to devote to different search processes in which I would immerse myself temporarily.

I was searching for ideas, a poetics, a philosophy that could be expressed in a work of visual art. I was looking for a personal form of visual art, the kind that is supposed to define you after graduating from art school. I experimented with conceptual art. I devoted more time to thinking about the titles of paintings than painting itself. I started to make words and images collide to hear the sound they made. I searched for and ultimately found personality in my work. I accumulated large-format paintings and indefinable pieces that I didn't really know what to do with. I realized then that personality takes up a lot of space. I also realized that I don't like to keep mining an idea once I've already brought it to life. Maybe developing an idea is what gives personality to the work.

Anyway, my intention wasn't to fill space with illustrations. I just wanted a paycheck. I was buying time to think about my other work, the important work, the true work. I thought illustrating was going to be easy. Although I hadn't yet heard, as I later would in a movie, that a book isn't a salary but a great achievement, it didn't take long for me to realize this myself.

My first book for three-year-old readers was a tremendous accomplishment. It took me so many months to illustrate that I had to ask myself what new job I had to look for to be able to buy the time I needed to publish a book."

1

But what is it that makes things difficult?

"In reality, drawing is easy because it's natural, accessible, understandable, primitive. It hasn't changed since the caves. Drawing is easy because it's the best language for communicating our perceptions. Because we perceive through drawing. Outlining things with invisible lines. Drawing is easy when it's only a reminder. Hey, check this out. You're missing it. How can you not see it! Look at it! Don't worry. Here it is organized on a sheet of paper. Drawing is easy when it's simply a matter of capturing, of taming what's wild, of imposing order on chaos. Organizing in order to show.

In drawing, then, the act itself isn't what's hard. The challenging part is to search, through drawing, for something specific that we intuit but can't see yet. What's difficult is to capture in a drawing what the drawing was before it became a drawing. The idea. It's also difficult to recognize a drawing as the exact drawing. The one that represents the idea. How are we going to recognize something we've never seen if the idea is invisible? How do we know when a drawing is the exact drawing? And if there is more than one idea? How do we know which drawing embodies the unadulterated idea?

I don't know when a drawing is the exact one. But I know I can't stop until the pebbles in my shoes stop bothering me. Ideas are like pebbles in your shoes. Until you get them out, they're a nuisance. You only get pebbles in your shoes when you're walking. The more you walk, the more you have. I love walking. But at some point you have to get them all out, and some pebbles are reluctant to depart. They stay stuck between the nooks and stitches.

Since I made my first book, I haven't been able to stop illustrating. I didn't like it but the editor did, so he asked me to do another. I had no other choice but to accept the assignment. I had to fix some things. I started from scratch. A new aesthetic, a new style, a new identity. But I wasn't wholly satisfied with the second one either. So I had to try again. And here we are. I'm still drawing, that is, still immersing myself in search processes to find different ways to capture invisible ideas through drawing. Clashing words with images to hear the noise they make. Looking for the right drawing to represent the right idea. Trying not to use the same idea all the time. Taking up little space, just a few folders. Just trying to make it look better next time."

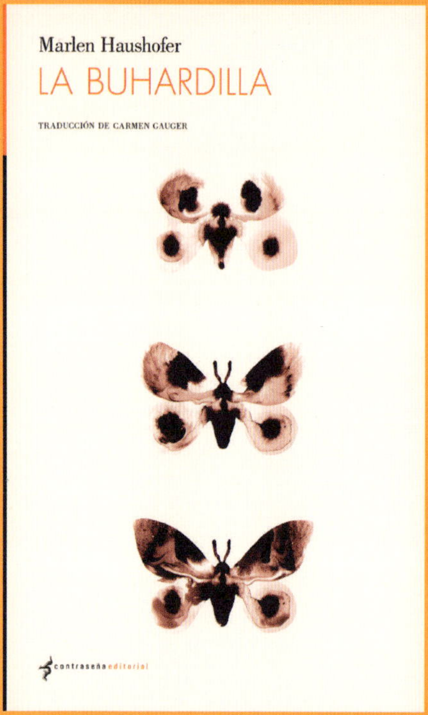

Marlen Haushofer **LA BUHARDILLA** TRADUCCIÓN DE CARMEN GAUGER	 **Patricia Esteban Erlés** **FONDO DE ARMARIO**
 **Cora Sandel** **ALBERTE Y JAKOB** TRADUCCIÓN DEL NORUEGO DE CRISTINA GÓMEZ-BAGGETHUN Y KIRSTI BAGGETHUN	 **Irene Vallejo** **EL SILBIDO DEL ARQUERO**

14 | 15

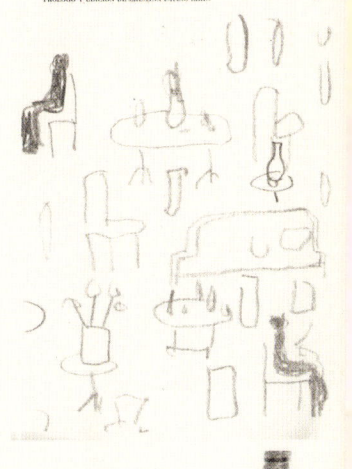

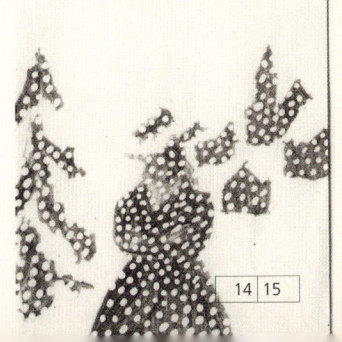

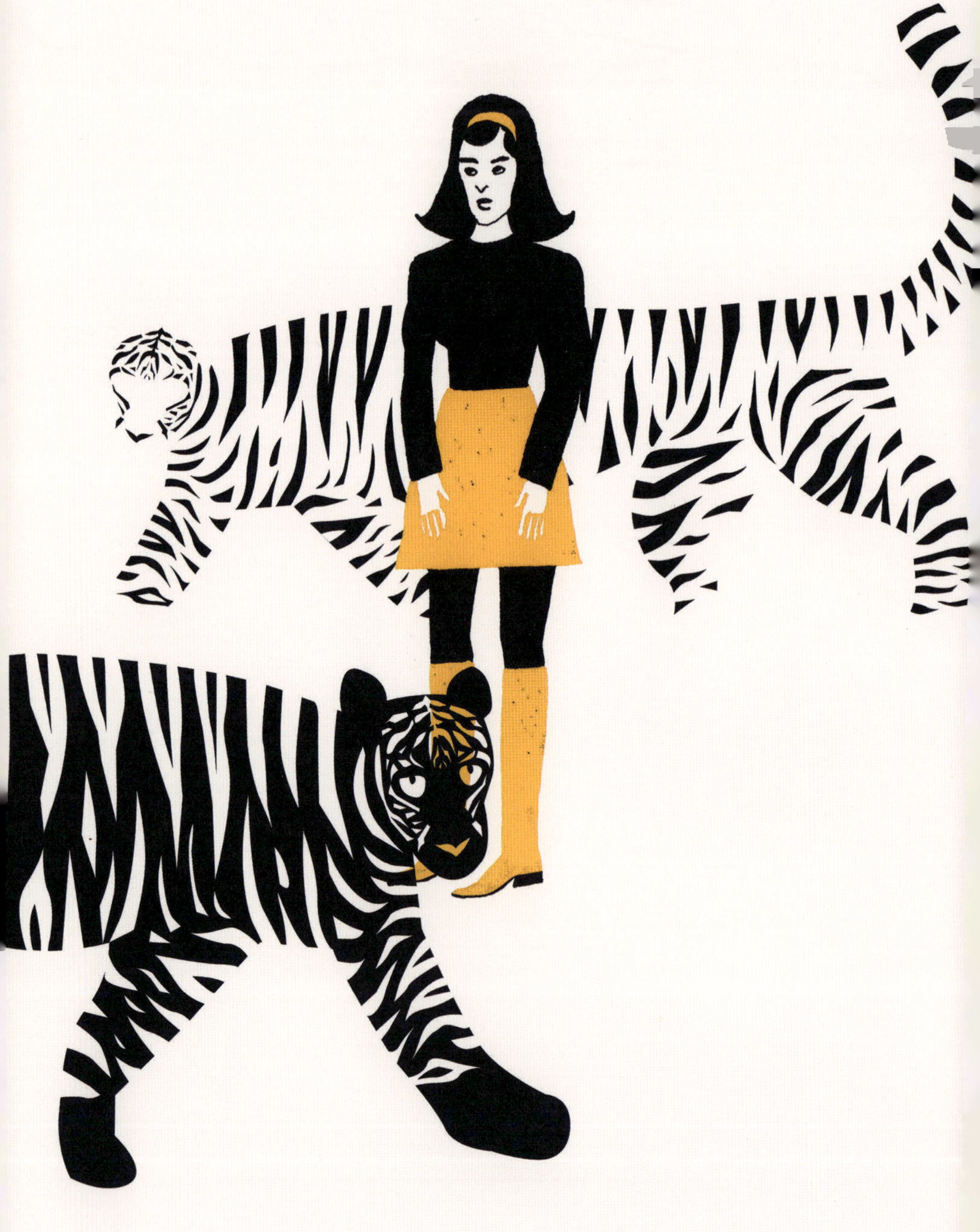

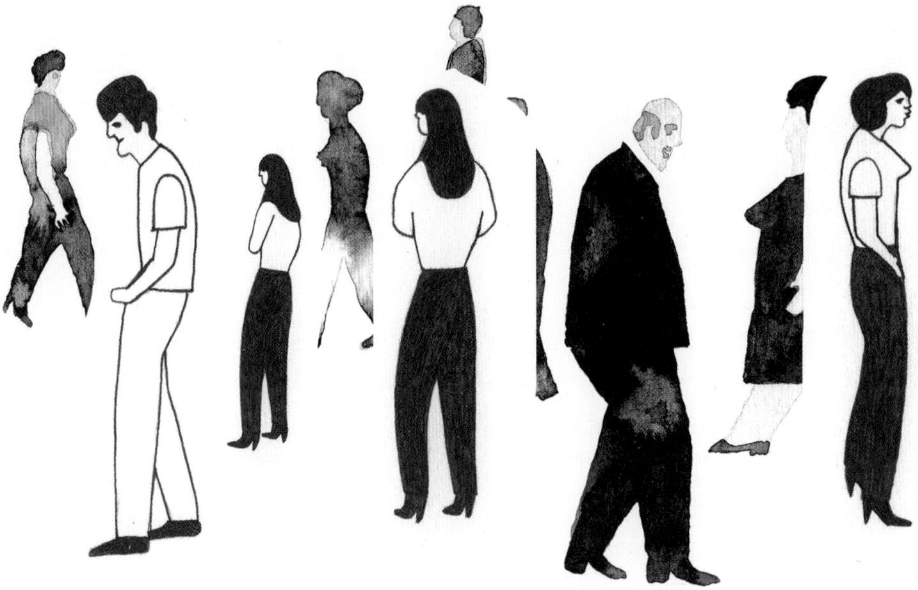

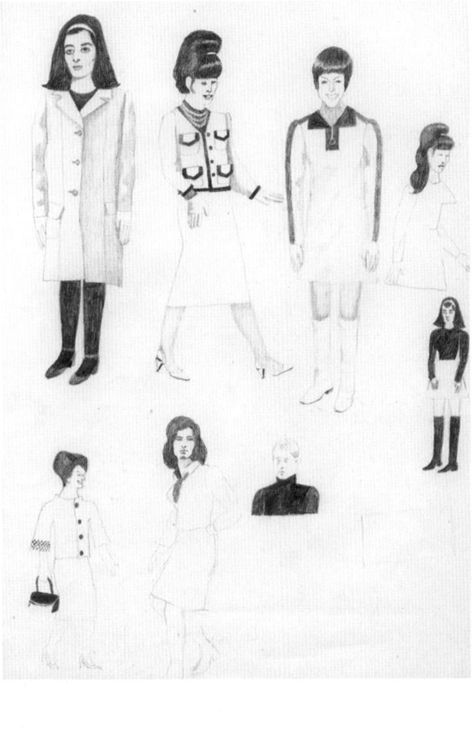

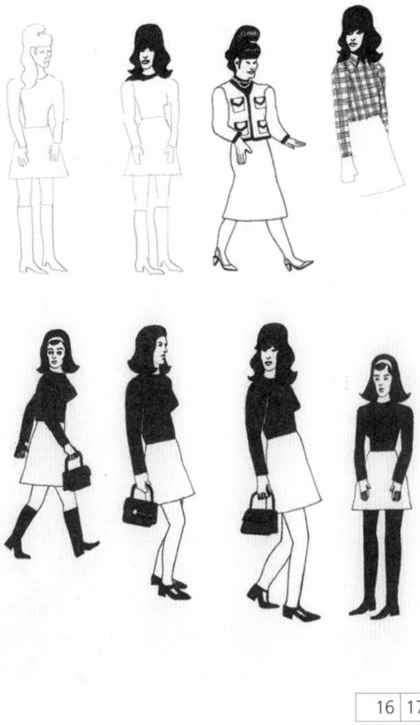

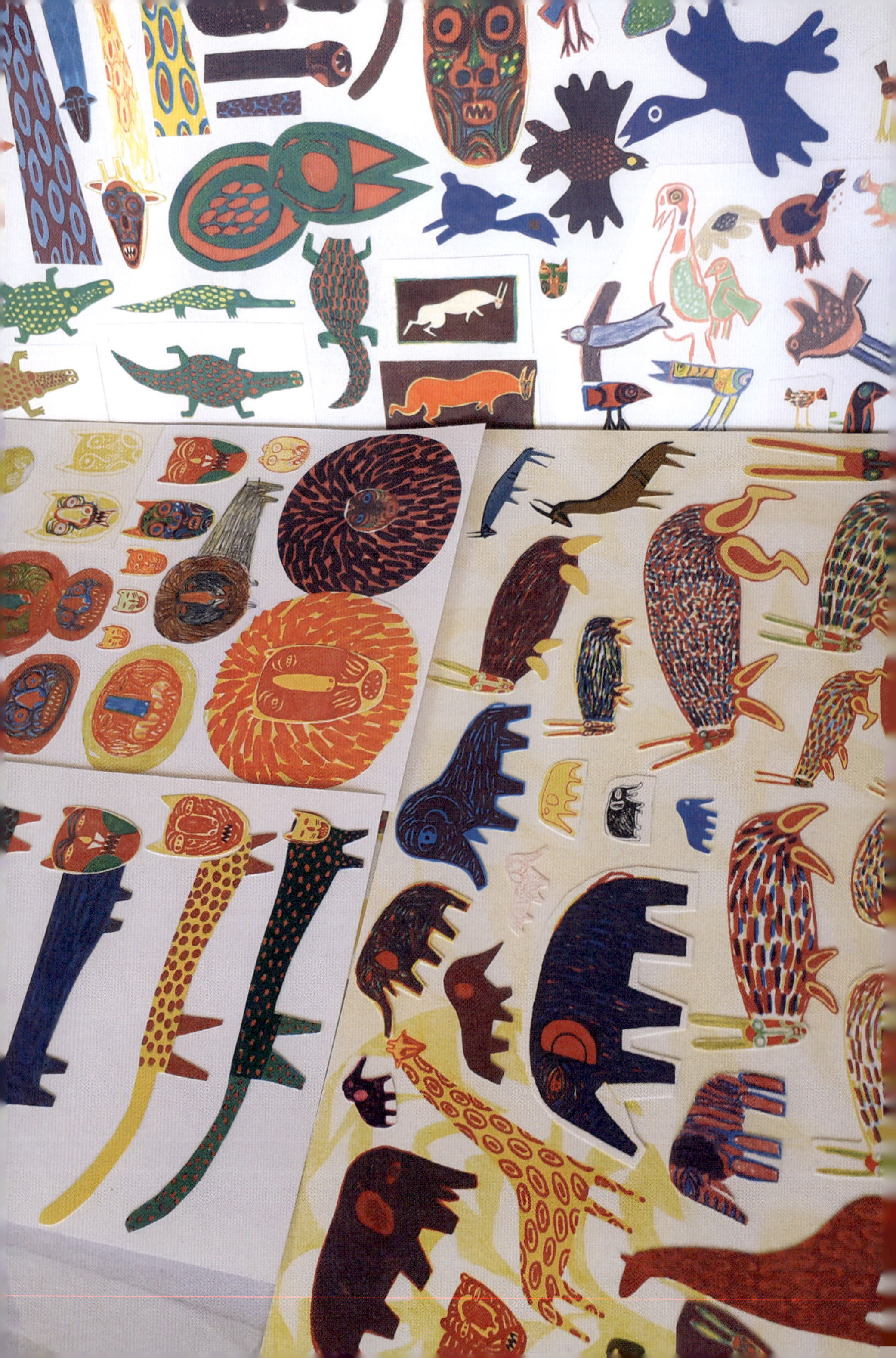

4

1. *My Family*, Anaya, 2006.
2. Covers for Contraseña publishing house, 2015-2021.
3. *Tracy's Tiger*, La Compañía Ilustrada, 2021.
4. *The Lion Kandinga*, Kalandraka, 2009.

18 | 19

Pablo Auladell

"The professional illustration landscape has changed dramatically in the twenty years since I set my innocent little plane down in it. A lot of these changes were brought on, of course, by the appearance in our lives of Narcissus's portable pool, which we all carry around in our pocket and in whose waters, a bit sinister despite their apparent purity, we constantly gaze at ourselves.

I am struck, more than anything, by how commonplace my profession has become, with legions of individuals showing up on the delirious playground of social networks. They peddle their wares at all hours. They label them as *'illustration'*, often without any justification, since what they do isn't so much illustration as drawings for decoration or portraits based on photographs of clothing or perfume models to which they digitally add a tattoo, or some flowers, or something emerging from the lips or hair. I also notice, with a combination of amusement and horror, the widespread and overwhelming self-complacency that can easily be seen just by glancing for a few seconds at this new bazaar."

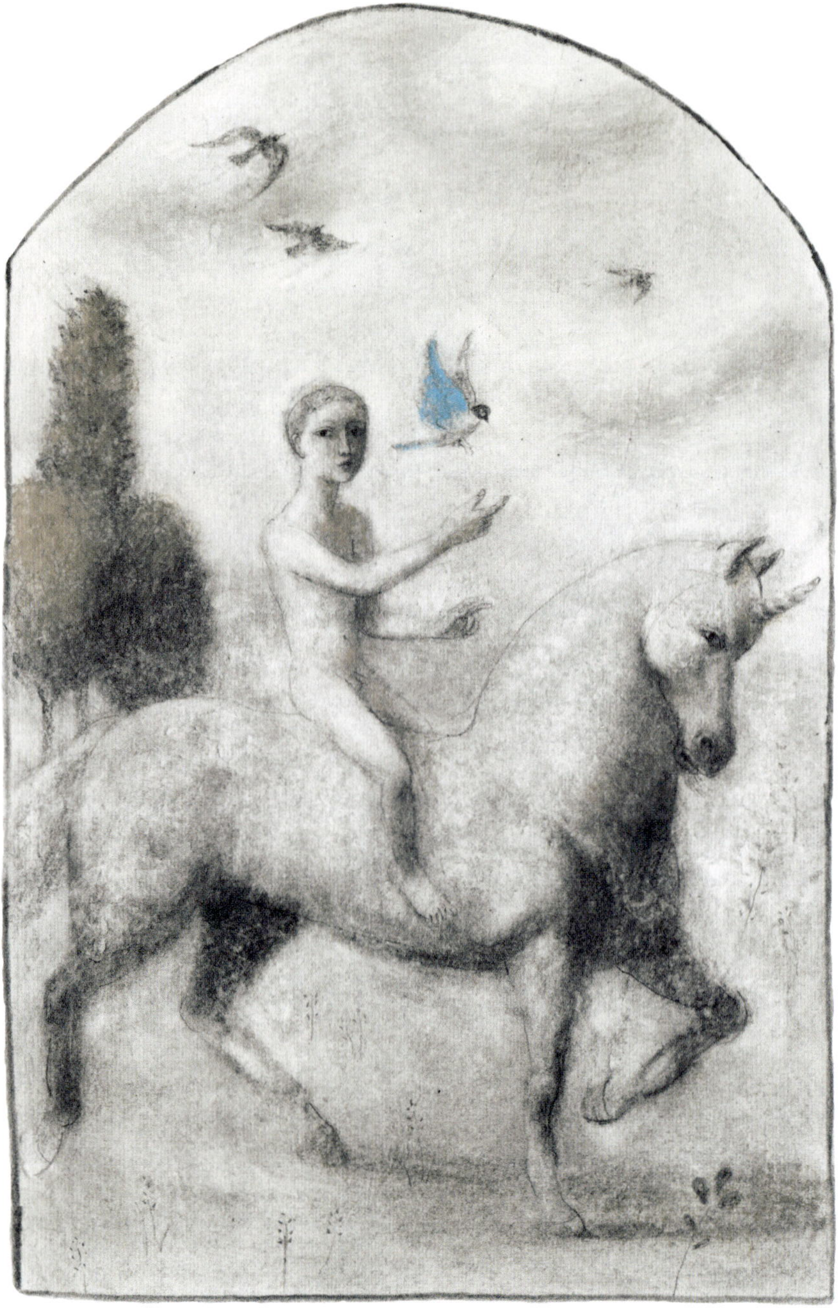

On fashions and classic style: the highway and the river

"As far as I can tell, there are two possible routes. The choice of one or the other isn't a question of better or worse. It isn't a moral difference. The decision is simply based on what you want to achieve in your artistic or professional endeavors.

You can go down the highway, filled with speed and noise, searching for the philosopher's stone or taking advantage of the one the market provides for you. You can position yourself in a certain way, develop one of the prevailing mannerisms, put on a show in full view of everyone and receive a lot of applause, attracting attention very quickly.

But since it seems to me that the voice that speaks about the present and about the time to come, about important matters that concern us now and that are going to be of concern to us later, needs to be a dual voice. It needs to be a voice that talks about the past as well as the present/future simultaneously, about a world in ruins and a new world. For this reason, I'm in the river, because on the highway you can only discover things about the present. Hence the river illustrator: sediment, slowness, silence. Drinking water from an ancient, remote spring, flowing from a source common to us all.

You plunge into this river, choosing a specific point along its length. It's a matter of placing yourself in the current of a tradition and over time, through work, becoming transparent enough that the water flows through you. The results aren't immediate. And there's no guarantee they're going to be better than the results obtained on the highway. There might not even be any results.

From time to time, you can see people in the river, there in the water sifting the sand from the bottom with a sieve. In reality, they've chosen the wrong path. They have the mentality of the highway and, all of a sudden, you see them rushing back to it, all worked up, carrying in the sieve a Polish avant-garde poster, an illustration by a forgotten press cartoonist from the beginning of the 20th century…

But you know it can't be that simple. You wait for the timeless light of the walls, the elegance and stability of your most admired dead, the mysterious happiness that has never been snuffed out in the stone or the silence with which all things speak. In short, the sacred silt swept along by the current gradually settles and accumulates within you."

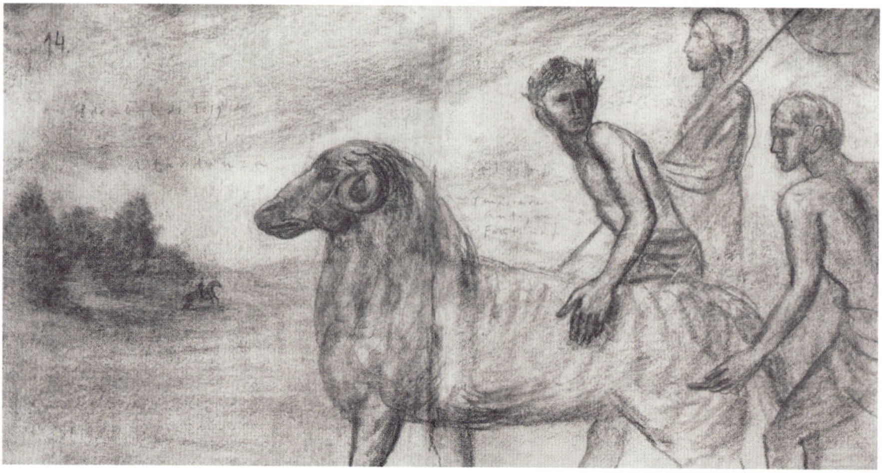
14.

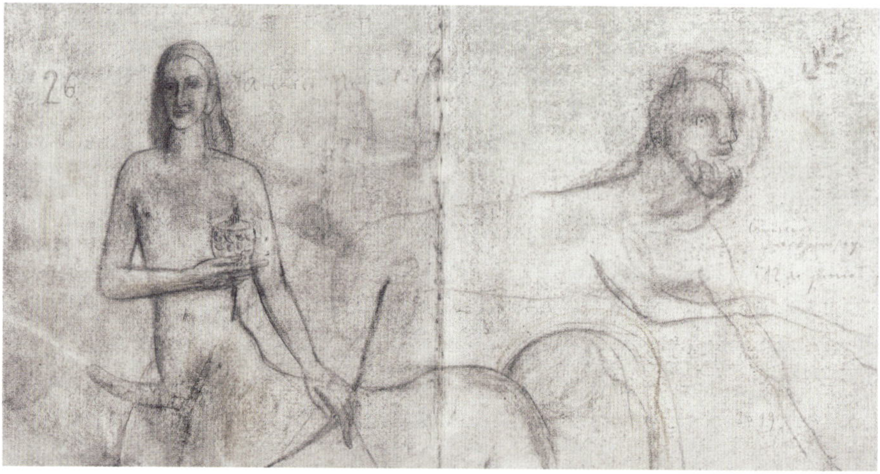
26.

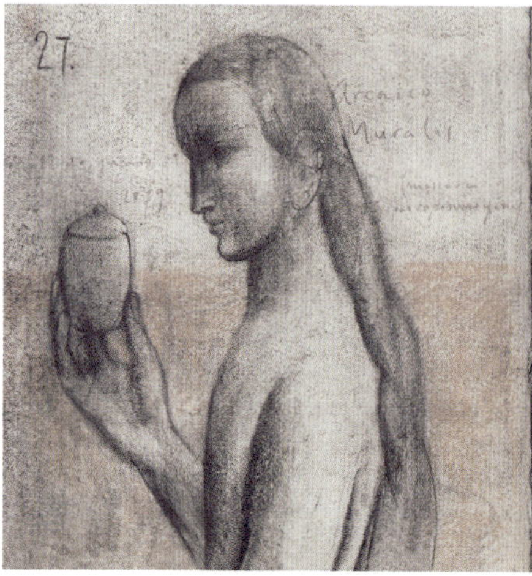
27.

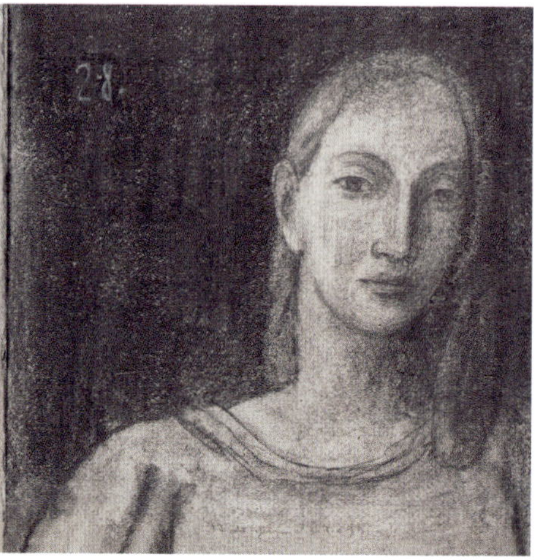
28.

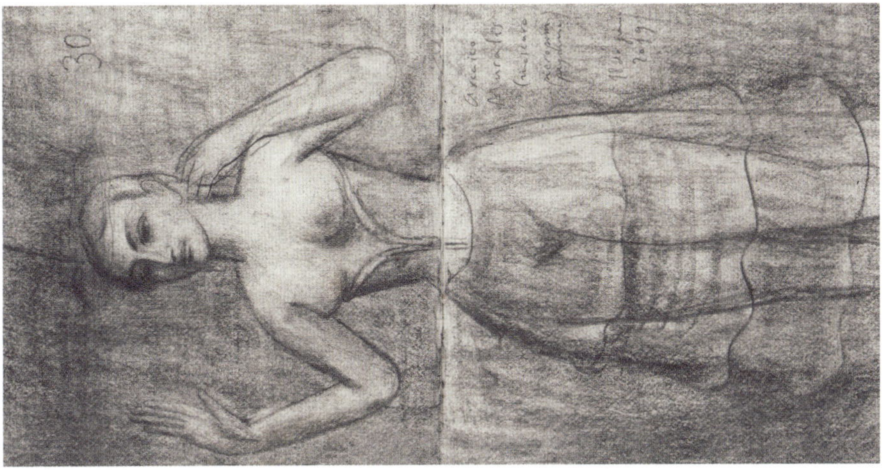
30.

37.
Arcaico
Muralis
(máscara
pierepompeya)
4 de septiembre
de 2019

58
antigua
Arcaico
Muralis
4 de marzo
de 2020

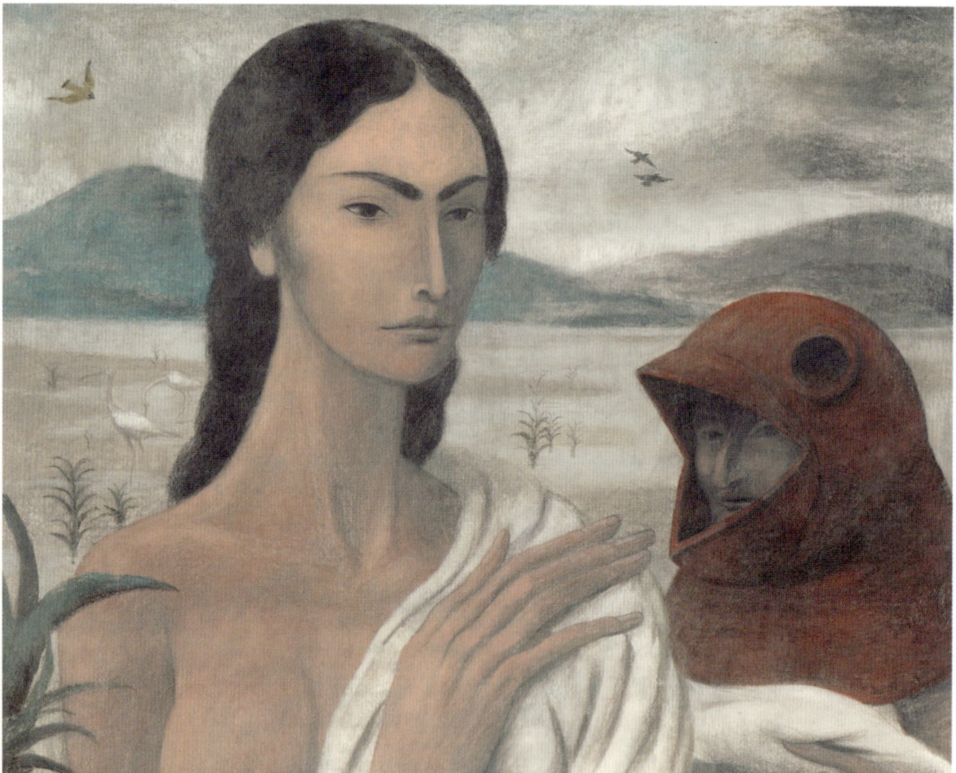

Vadè l'acrobat

"In 2010 I looked back and thought I needed to find a way to make fewer yet more powerful and influential books that would endure over time. I had to risk accepting fewer assignments, to be more selective in the projects I took on. I needed to find the right balance between the necessary concessions to the market that put food on the table and work in which I could at last develop an authorial voice, where I could polish this tool and refine it until I achieved the poetic tone that I thought was right for what I wanted to do.

One afternoon on my way to the doctor, to kill some time before my appointment, I took an unplanned stroll through an old garden, the Pantheon of Dr. Quijano, in the city where I live. This experience gave me the key to working in a different way. I realized that in that garden, in its fountains and hidden corners, there was everything I needed for my work: light, time, death, remote forgotten gods. And so I embarked on the construction of a system of laws for my work, a canon. The artists I admired most had one. It wasn't true that they improvised everything: their work concealed a system of laws that they followed to the letter. Since it was a matter of finding a balance, an acrobatics that would allow me, over time, to accomplish what I wanted to do and to meet a quota of commercial activity that would make it possible for me to survive, I called it *Vadè l'acrobat*.

I had never identified with the figures who my professional peers constantly referred to, mostly cinematographers or ones connected to the Anglo-Saxon world. I was basically a literary person. Graphically I was attracted to a body of work that Spanish illustrators tended to be utterly uninterested in. To endow my work with the poetic spirit and mystery I was aiming for, to speak with the dual voice that at once bears witness to and accounts for past, present and future, I needed to steal something from the sacred fires. I found the most appropriate model in the archaic mask. I confirmed that, learning how to use it well, I could better express the soul of things, the hidden, the invisible of the visible. I keep modifying and distorting this essential mask, depending on the specific project I'm working on. I combine it with different influences, depositing in it sediments from the river I mentioned before."

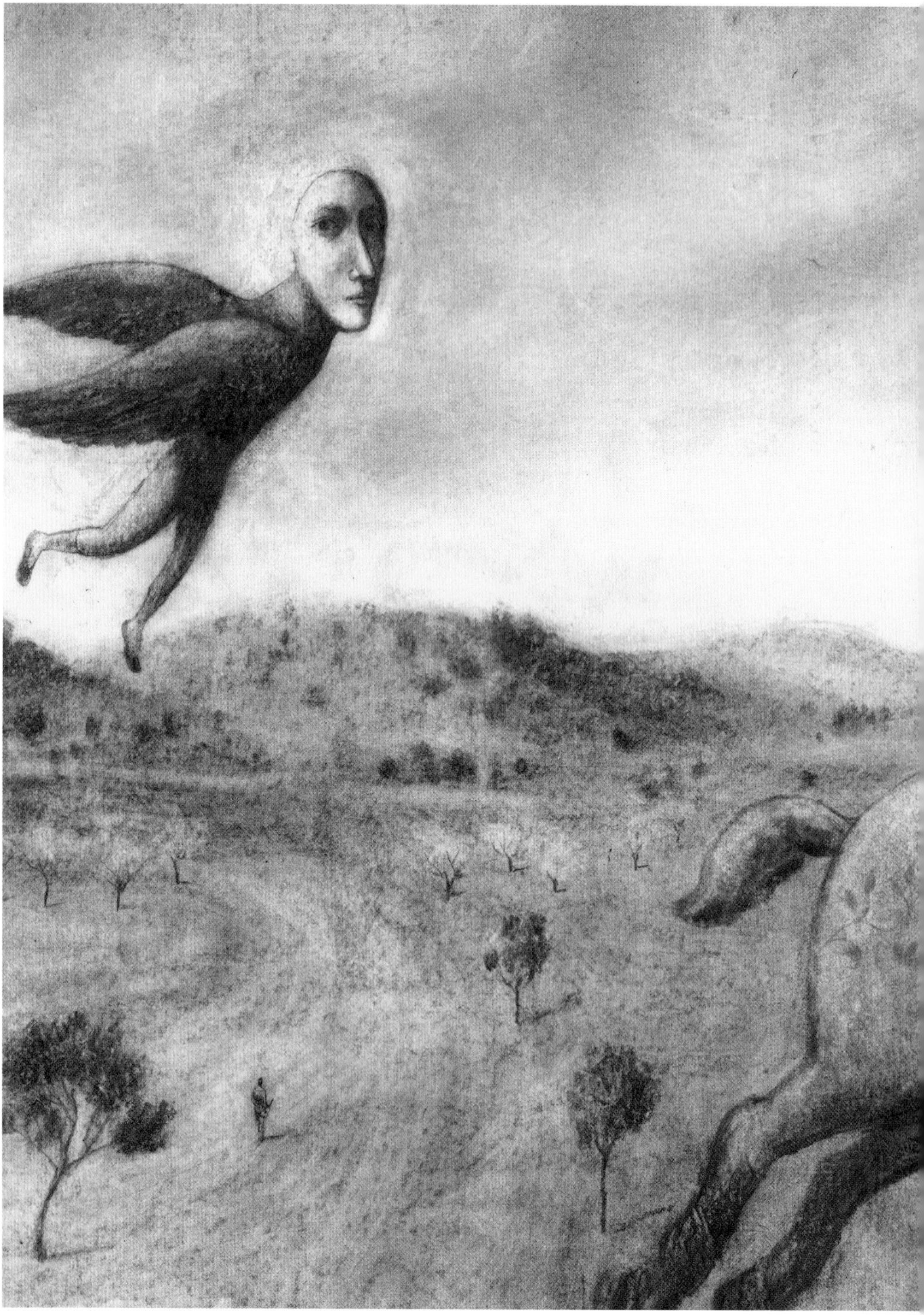

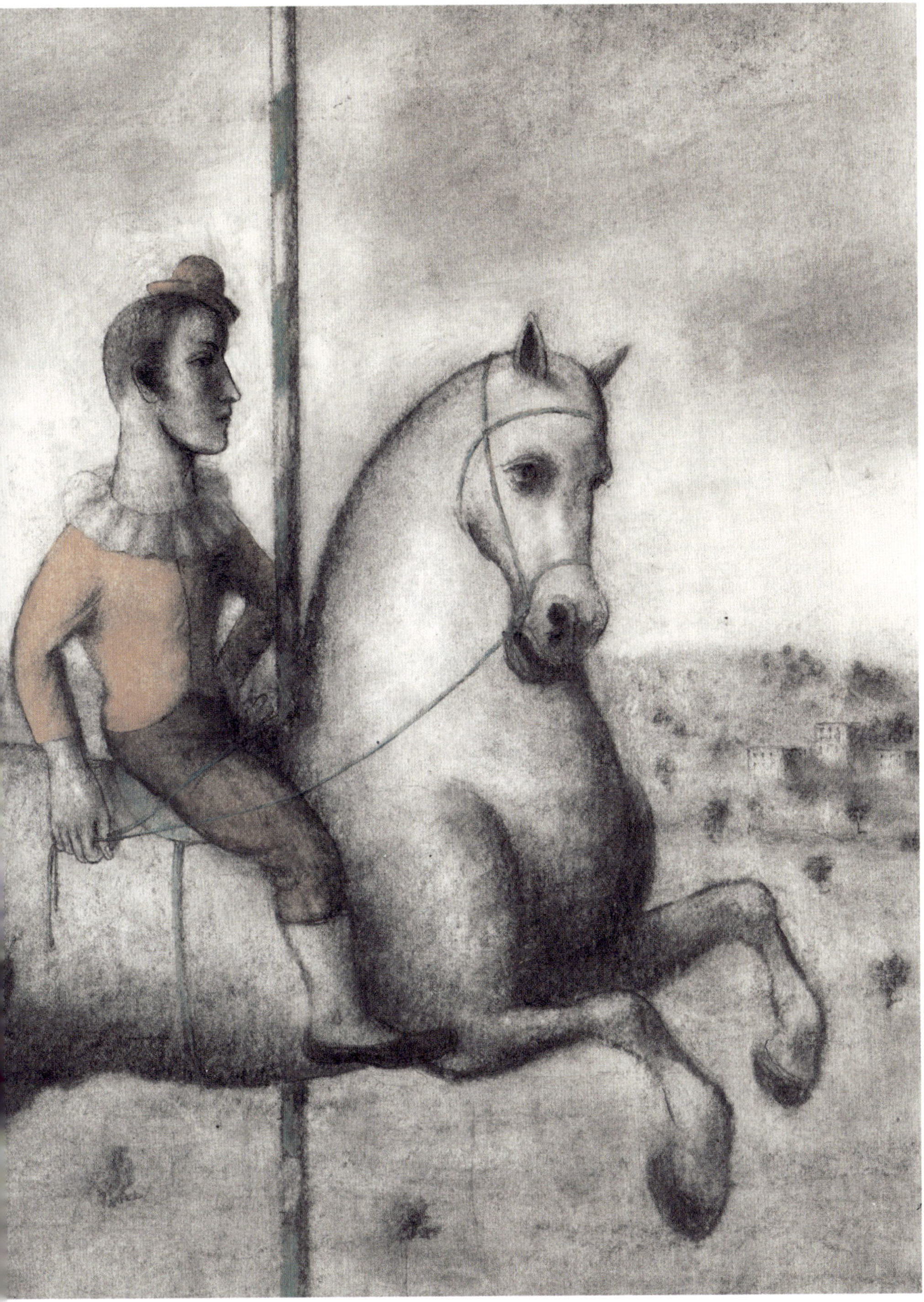

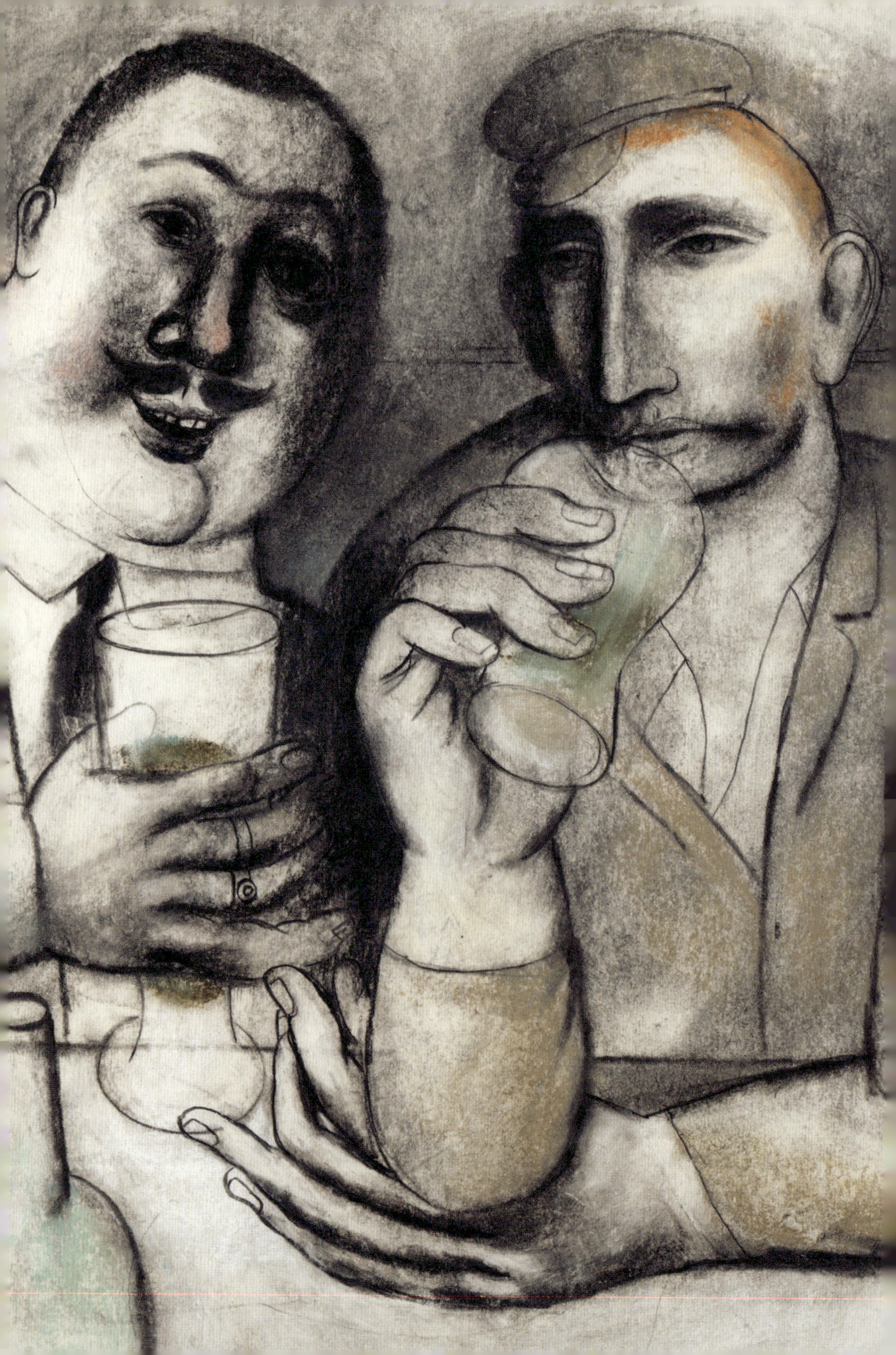

Texts and mirrors

"The ancient masters used mirrors and a camera oscura to filter and organize reality. However, when they painted over the reflected image, paradoxically the result wasn't a more faithful representation of reality, which they undoubtedly sought, but a window into the very heart of the mystery. Because it seems obvious to me that what we see in the mirror isn't exactly reality but a kind of other world.

In this sense, the text is a reflection of the world, a filter already shaped by the writer. The text is already that other world. So by working from a reflection, the illustrator actually creates the image of an image. For this reason, we have to find a way to cross over to the other side of the mirror, to submerge ourselves in its waters, to work not from reality but absolutely immersed in the text.

Illustrators must separate themselves from the current of life. We have to step over to the other side of the mirror, submerge ourself in the text/lake until the silence rings in our ears, the silence of the diver or the drowned. It is then when we can begin to experience the depths and see what slumbers within them. Eventually you have to come back to the surface, to life, with an image, with an impression of that other textual world. It's like diving deeper and deeper into a lake until you can start to make out the houses of the flooded town, the sunken ships. You salvage an image, bring it up to the surface. To come back from the lake or mirror with it and breathe life into it."

Gary Baseman

Photography: Carlos González

Photography: Mark Hanauer

Gary Baseman is an interdisciplinary artist who explores history, heritage and the human condition (in particular love, nostalgia and loss). Through unique iconography and imaginative visual narratives that celebrate "the beauty of life's bittersweetness," his work bridges the worlds of popular culture and fine art.

Baseman is the youngest of four brothers and the first to be born in the United States. His parents, Ben and Naomi Baseman, both Holocaust survivors originally from eastern Poland (now Ukraine), were strong believers in the American dream and instilled democratic ideals in their son. They encouraged him to show empathy and compassion for others, and to be true to himself.

From 1986 to 1996, Baseman lived and worked in New York, where he developed a wide range of advertising and publishing campaigns for international publications and corporate clients (*The New Yorker*, *TIME*, *Rolling Stone*, Nike, Gatorade, Levi's and Mercedes-Benz). Baseman expanded his artistic horizons in the late 1990s. He designed the visual identity for the best-selling board game CRANIUM and created the ABC/Disney animated series *Teacher's Pet*, which won several Emmy and BAFTA awards.

Baseman has been a recipient of Fulbright and Sundance New Frontier Lab grants. His most recent projects include collaborations with COACH, Dr. Martens and Lladró, along with a documentary about his family heritage entitled *Mythical Creatures*. *The Door is Always Open*, a retrospective of his work, was shown in Los Angeles, Taipei and Shanghai (2013-2015). Baseman's work has been exhibited in museums and galleries throughout the United States as well as in Germany, Brazil, Canada, China, Spain, the Philippines, France, Honk Kong, Israel, Italy, Mexico, New Zealand, the United Kingdom, Russia and Taiwan.

1

34 | 35

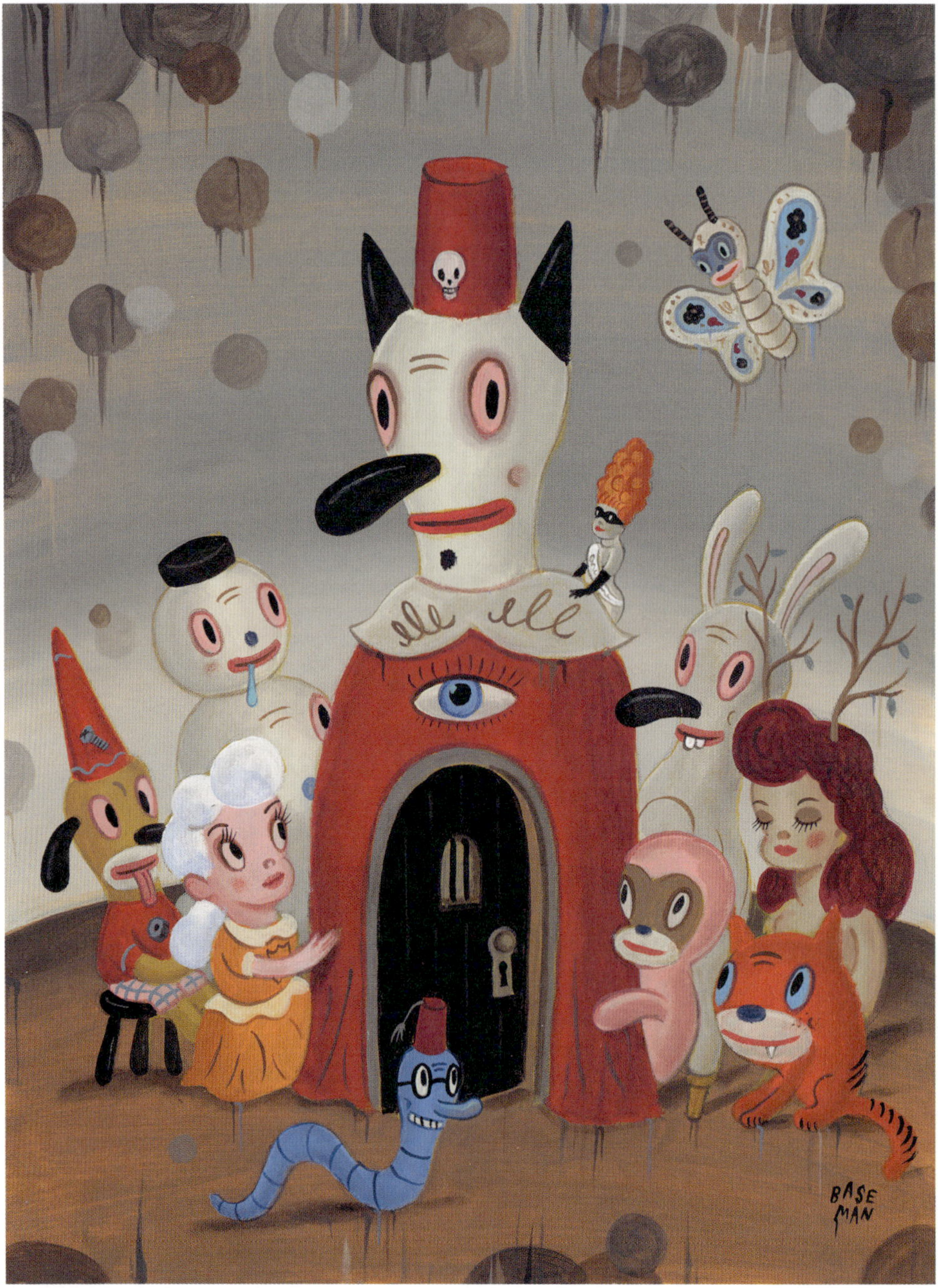
BASE
MAN

3

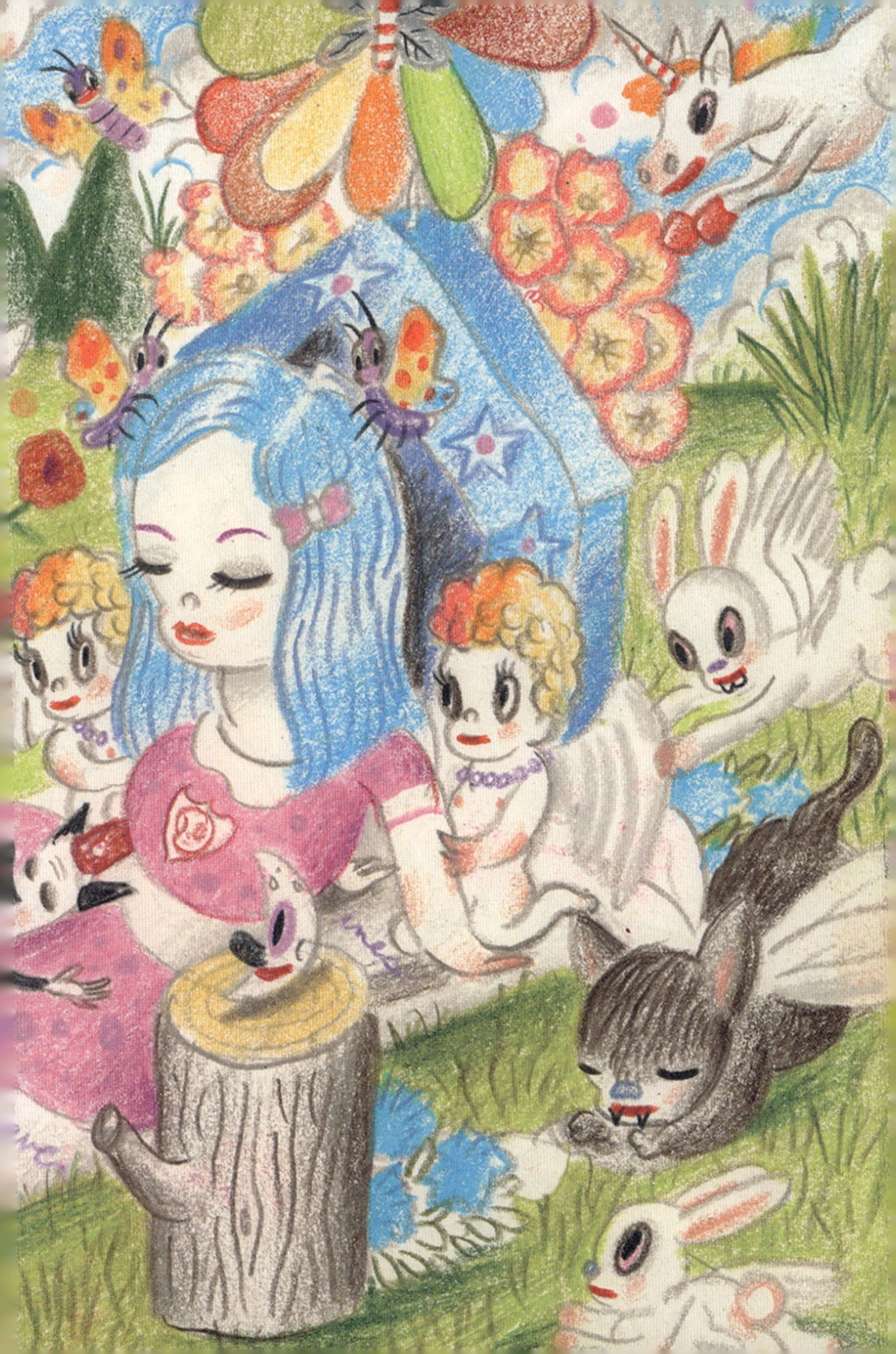

Tauranga New Zealand

April 2019 Bolton Street Cemetery

Photography: Carlos González

"The best ideas come when we're able to appropriate what we are and use it in our art. Being able to use your background, your interests and your desires is what makes you unique as an artist. It could be an observation or an exaggerated response to something that occurs in the world, or it could be a completely alternative universe. Finding your unique artistic voice is important. It comes from doodling, from creating images and from sharing ideas that can only come from you."

"I take a sketchbook wherever I go. It's like a diary in which I record my experiences. I draw from real life. But what ends up on the page isn't exactly what others see. It's my 'dreamed reality', an imagined existence and another world that I find more interesting than real life where an exaggerated and poetic narrative emerges. Most of life is dark and painful. For this reason, through art I try to embrace it and make something beautiful out of it. It's what I call celebrating life's bittersweetness.

Especially over the last two years, I've felt less connected to people and more in tune with spirits and animals. Humans seem to behave more like monsters these days. When I draw a scene in a room, I feel more comfortable drawing my own mythic creatures. Through my work, I use these creatures to explore in my own way such ideas as mortality and memory, history and heritage.

In many ways, I have a deeper connection with animals. Blackie the Cat was my best friend and taught me many essential virtues such as compassion and perseverance. I'm starting to learn many things from my new cat Bosko, especially how to play."

Red's Sandwich Shop

Here Lies the Body of Toby

Remember to Die

Yvonne's

Self-Righteous Denial

Woodman's of Essex

5

"When I travel, I love to immerse myself in the local culture. I always try to learn about the history, heritage and religion of the place. I try to spend at least one afternoon in a cemetery. One of my favorite places in London is a private club with trophies of taxidermied animals displayed on the wall and on pedestals. Each room is a work of art. Not only because of the animals but because of the way the floor, the wallpaper and the overall design envelop the visitor. These dissected animals are beautiful and disturbing. They're also the same animals that I saw wandering through sanctuaries in Africa and that are now endangered and protected species. While it's arresting to see so many, I can understand why people want to exhibit them.

I've been thinking about which ones still exist and which are already extinct. How do we think about death? What are memories? And who, if anyone, remembers them?"

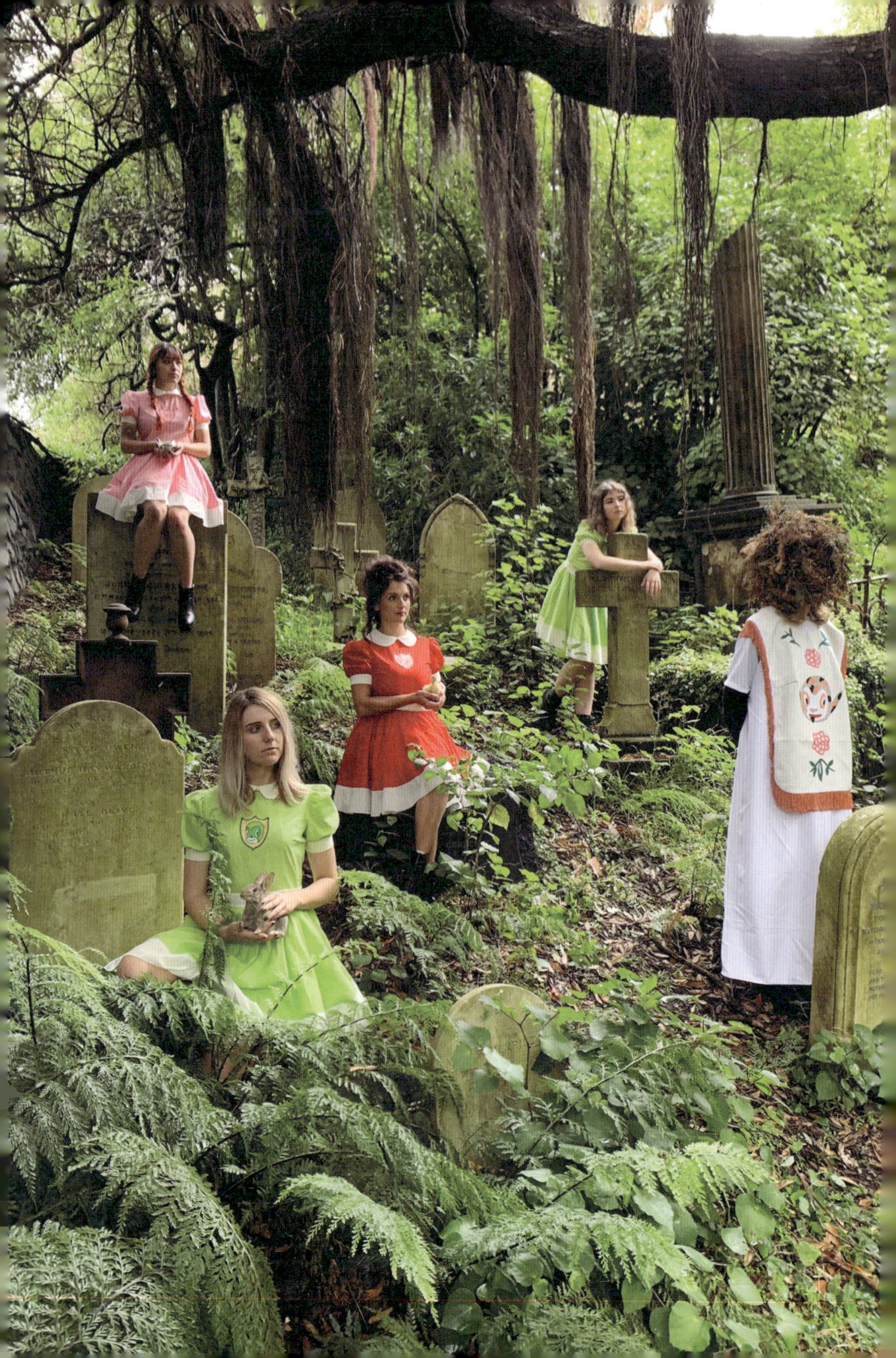

7

1. *The Birth of the Domesticated*, 2012.
2. *The Door is Always Open*, 2012.
3. *The Ascension of Blackie the Cat*, 2020.
4. Memorial for Blackie the Cat, 2021.
5. Toby's Travels (The King's Head, London), 2019.
6. WildGirls Series (Bolton Street Cemetery, New Zealand), 2019.
7. Toby's Travels (Swellendam Cemetery, South Africa), 2019.

Katie Benn

"My work is playful, colorful, childish at times, but also emotional, honest, slightly serious, fun, grouchy and dreamlike. I like to explore the human condition. In doing so, I expose myself as the disorganized and emotional person that I am while simultaneously using humor to hold up a mirror for others.

My main priority in my work is to be faithful to myself. As a result, the tools I use often change. I feel like many facets of myself appear when I draw, paint and design. I don't want to stifle these parts just to seem more versatile on social media or in my *portfolio*. I have a lot interests and ways of expressing myself. I believe allowing these parts of myself to be alive in my work, this exploration of self, is the most exciting and interesting path for me as an artist.

I've always looked for variety in life and self-expression. I see illustration as only one facet of my creative life, the same as murals, paintings, writing, product design, etc. I don't just like to work in the medium that brings me more joy at the moment. Instead I like to use the materials that I believe help me find myself where I am, allowing me to be as genuine as possible."

R 18
Vin de France

BILL GRAHAM PRESENTS IN SAN FRANCISCO
BEACH BUNNY
MILOE
THE FILLMORE
TUESDAY, DECEMBER 7, 2021
1805 GEARY AT FILLMORE

COURTNEY BARNETT
DECEMBER 2, 2021
THE DEPOT SALT LAKE CITY, UT

ALVVAYS
AUGUST HALL
OCTOBER 31 2021
SAN FRANCISCO

"A while back, for a year I got to illustrate Marissa Ross's wine column in *Bon Appétit*. Every month, I would get a preview of Marissa's articles and create print and online work based on her tasting notes. I really enjoyed it. I admire Marissa. Her writing style is so honest and funny. I learned more about wine than I ever knew before. I loved being able to translate her writing into images every month. At the time, I was illustrating mostly digitally. All of my work for the column was created on the computer or on an Ipad.

Ever since, I've asked myself several times what I would have created if I were to do it all again. Because in the last few years, I've become more of a pastel painter in my personal work. Lately, whenever I can, I try to do more analog illustration for my publishing clients. For example, for the past two months I've published work in one of Germany's largest newspapers, the *Süddeutsche Zeitung*. All the pieces submitted for printing were scans of pastel drawings. I continue to work digitally often for clients and for myself when I feel the idea or project demands it. Still, drawing on paper, right now, feels more genuine and enjoyable to me.

For a couple of years, I've been creating posters for musical performances, which has been a dream. They've all been primarily digital, with a few exceptions where I included oil illustrations and textures that I've hand-drawn and scanned and then added in Photoshop. Since music is one of my main sources of serotonin, I feel like I owe my life to it. So being able to do work for musical artists has made me feel in a way like I'm giving something back. Even if I'm asked to create a piece of work for a musician or a band I don't know at all, I cherish the whole experience of familiarizing myself with their catalog. I listen to their albums, look through their artwork and past album posters and then work on coming up with something new but that still fits with who they are and, hopefully, resonates with them and their fans, if only at first glance."

KATIE
BENN

"I think creativity is one of the greatest byproducts of being this strange, complex human creature that for some reason lives on this planet, for some reason in this universe. Of course, you have to be curious, otherwise you'd never get started. But artists have this desire to know more about who we are and why we are and why things are the way they are, even unconsciously. And those who have creatively tapped into the experience of being alive, I think, have found a way to get closer to life, noticing more of it, feeling more of it. If the answers to life's most important questions are faint strains of music heard from another room, I listen with my ear to the wall and try to decipher them.

Ideas appear as we do: from everywhere and nowhere. These days, my bad ideas come from a noisy place of over thinking. My more genuine or favorite ideas, however, come from a quieter, more instinctive place. Sometimes ideas just appear in my mind's eye fully formed. It's like when, if you're a dreamer like me, you have a long dream at night that plays out like a full theatrical movie and you wake up and think: 'How did my brain come up with that?'

My artistic style is partly inspired by certain color palettes found in old mid-century paperbacks. I have a large collection of pulp novels, romances and reference books from this period that are a major source of inspiration. I also find the product and toy packaging of that time very interesting; they contain extremely funny, humorous and quite elegant illustrations and typographical work. I guess it's a bit of a compulsion, but I love to surround myself with old things and weird objects. They energize me.

My house is packed with purchased and used items that I've found and that have an energy that resonates with me in one way or another. I'm definitely a maximalist type, though I often think I come across as a bit of a minimalist in my work. I frequently wish life were simpler and smoother. I guess I create works like these not just to reassure myself but to introduce more simple things into the world."

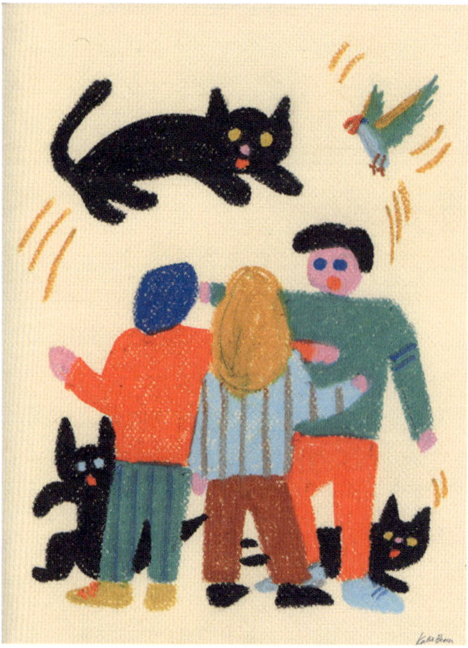

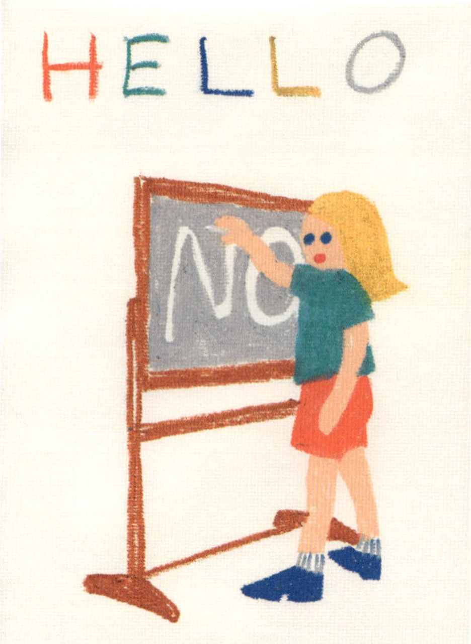
HELLO
NO

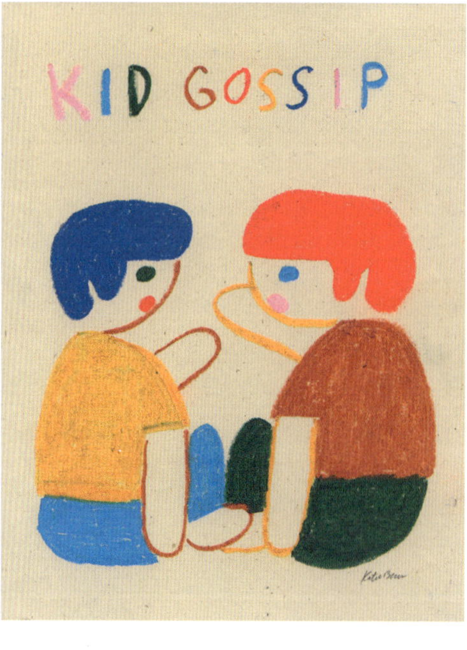
KID GOSSIP

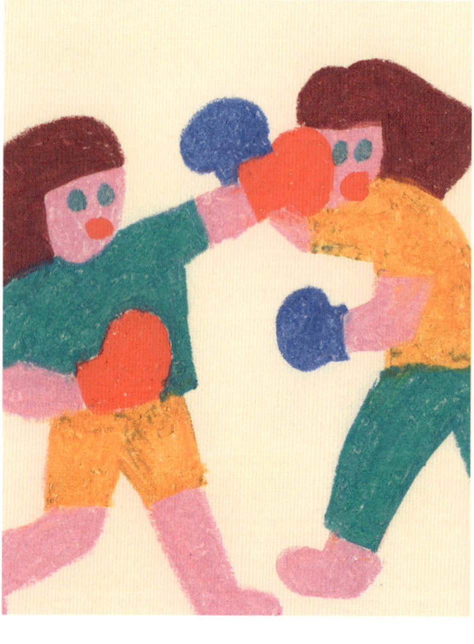

OH
OK

Ana Biscaia

"My work is my way of life and it gives me space for freedom. A path that is blazed every day. I've been an illustrator and graphic designer, and also an editor, since 2014. Sometimes I teach classes. And I learn. With students, with people I meet along the way. When I teach, I like to systematize and find space to write. My work is a combination of several things, but when I think about it I'm reminded of the books that I've already created and illustrated. One of the best things about being an illustrator is being in the same boat with people I know, admire and respect. I like the word 'illustration' very much, and I know this work entails a great deal of responsibility. My work can be very intuitive at times and for this reason it isn't predictable. The work always contains emotions.

I like to draw, because drawing teaches me that I don't always know how to understand. Only later do I learn these lessons, when I realize what's happened. I like to read books and try to play with what's been drawn with words. Lending the text a hand is key. Illuminating it from within. It isn't easy. In fact, at times, it can be really difficult.

I like the sea and small cities. I have the river vice. I know how to be silent, because I'm an only child. Is that why? Or is it because I grew up in a small town? I like to think that time is an essential tool in artistic work. Like the time of a tree or a flower.

When I think about my work, it makes me proud that in 2014, I created Xerefé, a small publishing company that allows me to publish books and create them at my own pace and according to my own tastes (with friends, people I admire and love). In 2013, I won the Portuguese National Illustration Award for the book *The Chair That Wanted To Be A Sofa,* by Clovis Levi. Next came the Theater. It's a space for camaraderie and collective creation where illustration emerges from the texts of great children's authors and the permanent and unceasing interaction with the actors, director, set designer, light technician and sound technician. This was some of the most rewarding work I've done in my life."

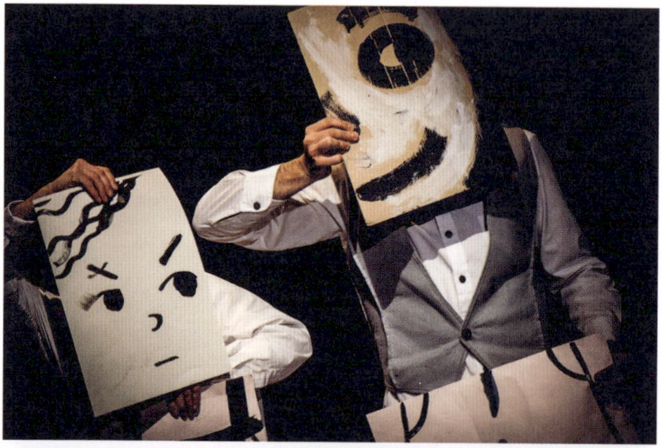

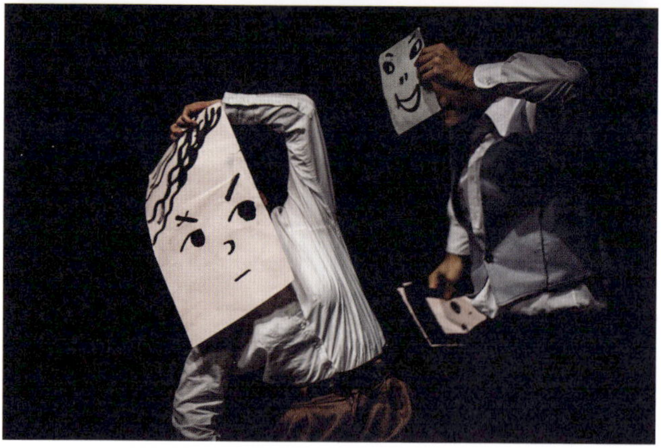

QVIS VIDIT
HVK SIMIL

Sou uma cadeira antiga. De porte nobre. Formas clássicas. Bonita. Imponente. Elegante.
E não consigo mesmo perceber porque me chamam de "aquela coisa antiga dos tempos da bisavó".
Não imaginam como eu fui lindíssima, elogiadíssima, como vivi cercada de galanteadores. Quantas cadeiras de espaldar alto – aquelas do Diretor da Escola – quantas e quantas já me cortejaram.

"I really like to use graphite and absorb the malleability of the pencil. I like drawing marks. I like drawing as a gesture. A communication signal (like the stories we tell each other)."

"I like to think of creativity as a space for freedom. Creativity as a space for experimenting without defined objectives. Ideas can come from anything. But I think ideas often arise from the cultivation of memory. And, of course, from everything that is new and learned. Ideas can come from anywhere. It can be a word, a sound, a new book. It can be a very big tree. It's important to play, to search for things inside of us and inside of life. The creative process isn't rational, although I know it can be planned. Sometimes I'm inspired by coincidences or simply feelings of tenderness, meaningful stories.

When I have a creative block – and what exactly is a creative block? Is it laziness? – it's best to do something else, to gather forces, eat well and rest. Or drink a good red wine. From there to play is a mere step. Play is crucial.

I always tend to include in my work things I experience and that happen to me. I like to mix reality and fiction and construct images out of small provocations (things that I think and that I experience and that can appear in the illustrations).

Mistakes, like play, play a key role. It isn't necessary to clean the drawing – to erase what's dirty – because these are the drawing marks. If I make a mistake, I fix it, re-cut, glue; I always make use of what isn't good, without limitations, shame or modesty. I like the idea of not being afraid when I make a mistake.

A good illustrator has to know what she wants to say when asked for an illustration. Because what one says is really important. The secret for this to happen, in the first place, is to know how to read the text we're working with well or understand the challenge we're asked to meet. Reading a text always produces a surprise, and the illustrator should know what to do with it. It's mostly a matter of confidence, of knowing what to say. The creation of a visual discourse is a highly important human skill. To flourish, the body, the heart and the head must be nourished. You need to know how to create metaphors, relate knowledge, put one thing in place of another. You need to know the work that came before us. And to learn from your peers."

Pensei: «Kalil!» Mas alguns livros tinham sobrevivido. Comecei a apanhá-los do chão, dos buracos entre as pedras. E, enquanto lhes sacudia o pó, dizia para mim: «Kalil, Kalil, que luz estarias a ler?»

Quando a guerra terminar, levarei estes livros para a nova escola. Sobra-me tempo para descobrir o que Kalil andava a ler. A seguir vou ler esse livro. Será, certamente, o que irradiar mais luz das suas páginas brancas.

Ontem caiu outra bomba, desta vez na nossa
escola. Alguém gritou o meu nome: «Aysha! Aysha!»
Abri os olhos, como quem acorda de um pesadelo
e sacudi a poeira da roupa e do cabelo. Estava viva.
«Levaram os corpos de Kalil e de outros meninos», disse a minha mãe a chorar.
Hoje à tarde corri para a escola. Agora chamam-lhe escombros.
Havia manchas de sangue e os meus olhos encheram-se de lágrimas.

Serge Bloch

"Drawing is writing. I like to rely on all the nuances of the word 'to tell'. As with Chinese or Japanese calligraphy, to write a poem is also to draw it. The line sets the tone; that's what matters. Illustrators like Klee and Steinberg know it."

"What interests me about *collage* is the contrast, the interaction between the line and the object that I'm gluing or the graphic element that I'm introducing. It's also the relationship between the moment of collection and the moment of drawing. For me, *collage* is the humor, the poetry in these associations, the collusion of these two moments.

"A graphic clown, a languid gaze, five marabous, the gender of the angels, elegant collages, a skeleton, a few quirks, two medallions, a dirty drawing, twins and an added brightness. The titles of my drawings tend to be humorous. Bits of poetry, words as automatic writing. Again, it's the story of the encounter of two materials that inspires me, the words and the line. A drawing sometimes reveals itself through its title."

Archipel
6 — 14 novembre
2021
textes de
Italo Calvino
un spectacle de
Nicolas Musin
avec
8 rideurs
(skateurs /
BMX / rollers),
3 traceurs,
3 comédiens
THÉÂTRE
TNP
NATIONAL POPULAIRE
Pour découvrir l'illustration
animée de la saison,
il suffit de scanner !
direction Jean Bellorini
tnp-villeurbanne.com

Entre
chien
et loup
20 novembre —
4 décembre 2021
mise en scène
Christiane Jatahy
THÉÂTRE
TNP
NATIONAL POPULAIRE
Pour découvrir l'illustration
animée de la saison,
il suffit de scanner !
direction Jean Bellorini
tnp-villeurbanne.com

Le Jeu
des Ombres
13 — 30 janvier 2022
de
Valère Novarina
mise en scène
Jean Bellorini
THÉÂTRE
TNP
NATIONAL POPULAIRE
Pour découvrir l'illustration
animée de la saison,
il suffit de scanner !
direction Jean Bellorini
tnp-villeurbanne.com

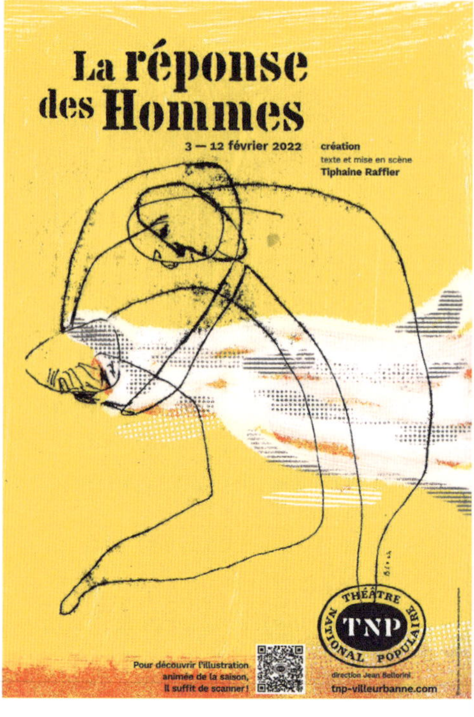
La réponse
des Hommes
3 — 12 février 2022
création
texte et mise en scène
Tiphaine Raffier
THÉÂTRE
TNP
NATIONAL POPULAIRE
Pour découvrir l'illustration
animée de la saison,
il suffit de scanner !
direction Jean Bellorini
tnp-villeurbanne.com

La Troupe éphémère
C'est tout.
création
2 — 4 mai 2022
mise en scène
Thierry Thieû Niang
et Marie Vialle
avec
20 amateurs
de 9 à 18 ans
Bloch
Pour découvrir l'illustration
animée de la saison,
il suffit de scanner !
THÉÂTRE NATIONAL POPULAIRE
TNP
direction Jean Bellorini
tnp-villeurbanne.com

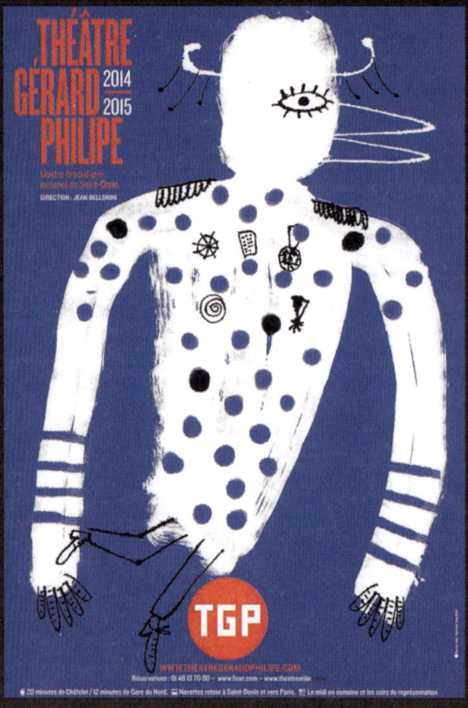
THÉÂTRE
GÉRARD PHILIPE
2014
2015
DIRECTION : JEAN BELLORINI
TGP
WWW.THEATREGERARDPHILIPE.COM
Réservations : 01 48 13 70 00 – www.fnac.com – www.theatreonlin

IMPASSE DES ANGES
CRÉATION
DU 7 AU 23 JANVIER 2016
TEXTE ET MISE EN SCÈNE
Alain Gautré
Jérémie Bédrune, Julien Cigana, Karyll Elgrichi, Florent Fichot, Blanche Leleu, Teddy Melis, Aurélie Messié avec la participation d'Agnès Pontier
Les décors on été réalisés par les ateliers de construction du théâtre de l'Union à Limoges.
Réservations : 01 48 13 70 00 – www.theatregerardphilipe.com
Théâtre Gérard Philipe
Centre dramatique national de Saint-Denis
Direction : Jean Bellorini
TGP

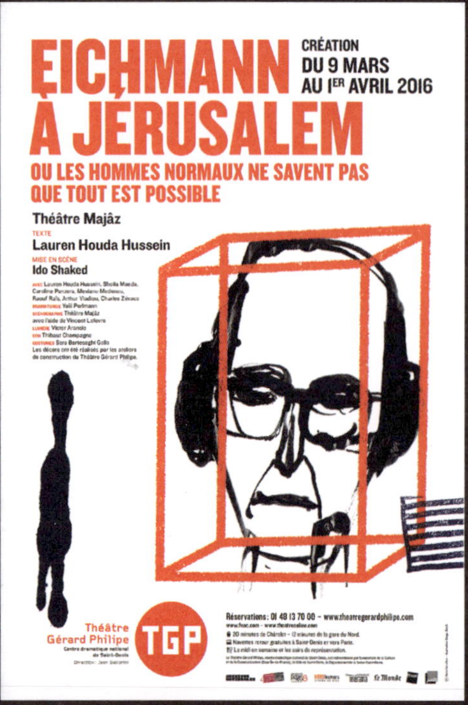
EICHMANN À JÉRUSALEM
CRÉATION
DU 9 MARS AU 1ER AVRIL 2016
OU LES HOMMES NORMAUX NE SAVENT PAS QUE TOUT EST POSSIBLE
Théâtre Majâz
TEXTE
Lauren Houda Hussein
MISE EN SCÈNE
Ido Shaked
Les décors ont été réalisés par les ateliers de construction du Théâtre Gérard Philipe.
Réservations : 01 48 13 70 00 – www.theatregerardphilipe.com
Théâtre Gérard Philipe
Centre dramatique national de Saint-Denis
TGP

TRISSOTIN
OU LES FEMMES SAVANTES
CRÉATION
DU 11 AU 29 NOVEMBRE 2015
DE
Molière
MISE EN SCÈNE, DÉCOR ET COSTUMES
Macha Makeïeff
Réservations : 01 48 13 70 00 – www.theatregerardphilipe.com
Théâtre Gérard Philipe
Centre dramatique national de Saint-Denis
Direction : Jean Bellorini
TGP

THÉÂTRE GÉRARD PHILIPE

2016 2017

Centre dramatique national de Saint-Denis
DIRECTION : JEAN BELLORINI

TGP

WWW.THEATREGERARDPHILIPE.COM
Réservations : 01 48 13 70 00 — www.fnac.com — www.theatreonline.com

20 minutes de Châtelet / 12 minutes de la gare du Nord. Navettes retour à Saint-Denis et vers Paris. Le midi en semaine et les soirs de représentation.

Le Théâtre Gérard Philipe, centre dramatique national de Saint-Denis, est subventionné par le ministère de la Culture et de la Communication (Drac Île-de-France), la Ville de Saint-Denis, le Département de la Seine-Saint-Denis.

TEMPÊTE SOUS UN CRÂNE

DU 11 MARS AU 10 AVRIL 2016

D'APRÈS *LES MISÉRABLES* DE
Victor Hugo

ADAPTATION
Jean Bellorini et Camille de La Guillonnière

MISE EN SCÈNE
Jean Bellorini

AVEC Mathieu Coblentz,
Karyll Elgrichi,
Camille de La Guillonnière,
Clara Mayer,
Céline Ottria,
Marc Plas,
Hugo Sablic

Théâtre Gérard Philipe
Centre dramatique national de Saint-Denis
Direction : Jean Bellorini

TGP

Réservations : 01 48 13 70 00 — www.theatregerardphilipe.com
www.fnac.com — www.theatreonline.com
🚇 20 minutes de Châtelet – 12 minutes de la gare du Nord.
🚌 Navettes retour gratuites à Saint-Denis et vers Paris.
🍽 Le midi en semaine et les soirs de représentation.

Le Théâtre Gérard Philipe, centre dramatique national de Saint-Denis, est subventionné par le ministère de la Culture et de la Communication (Drac Île-de-France), la Ville de Saint-Denis, le Département de la Seine-Saint-Denis.

telerama · Le Monde · fnac · inter

TNP posters

When Jean Bellorini was named director of the Théâtre National Populaire, he asked me to follow him. Needless to say, I didn't hesitate even for a second. The TNP has a history of creation, a powerful identity. Jean Vilar, of course, and Jacno have left their mark on the place. Jacno created the TNP logo and posters and this character, the Chaillot, which is still being used and has shaped the TNP's history and identity...
So what do you do when you have to fill such big shoes?
Well, you keep doing what you know how to do. With the TNP team and Dans les Villes, a communication agency and graphic studio with which I've always worked, we sought to bring color to life.

TGP posters

Jean Bellorini had seen my drawings in an issue of *UBU* and thought it would be interesting to introduce these images into the world of the Théâtre Gérard Philipe, where he had just taken over as director.
We understood each other right away, or at least I think we did...
With Philippe Delangle and François Rieg (Dans les Villes agency) we developed the communication for the TGP. For six seasons, I designed the posters for the programs. It's been a beautiful story. Creating a poster means putting an image on the street, in the subway, in people's lives. It's opening a window to the city, bringing emotion, lightness or seriousness to the public space. It's a collective creation; each image is drawn spontaneously. We discuss it. Sometimes it's fast, sometimes it takes longer, but it's always freedom, surprise and poetry that we strive for – to create a poetic and narrative universe but also a strong and consistent identity.

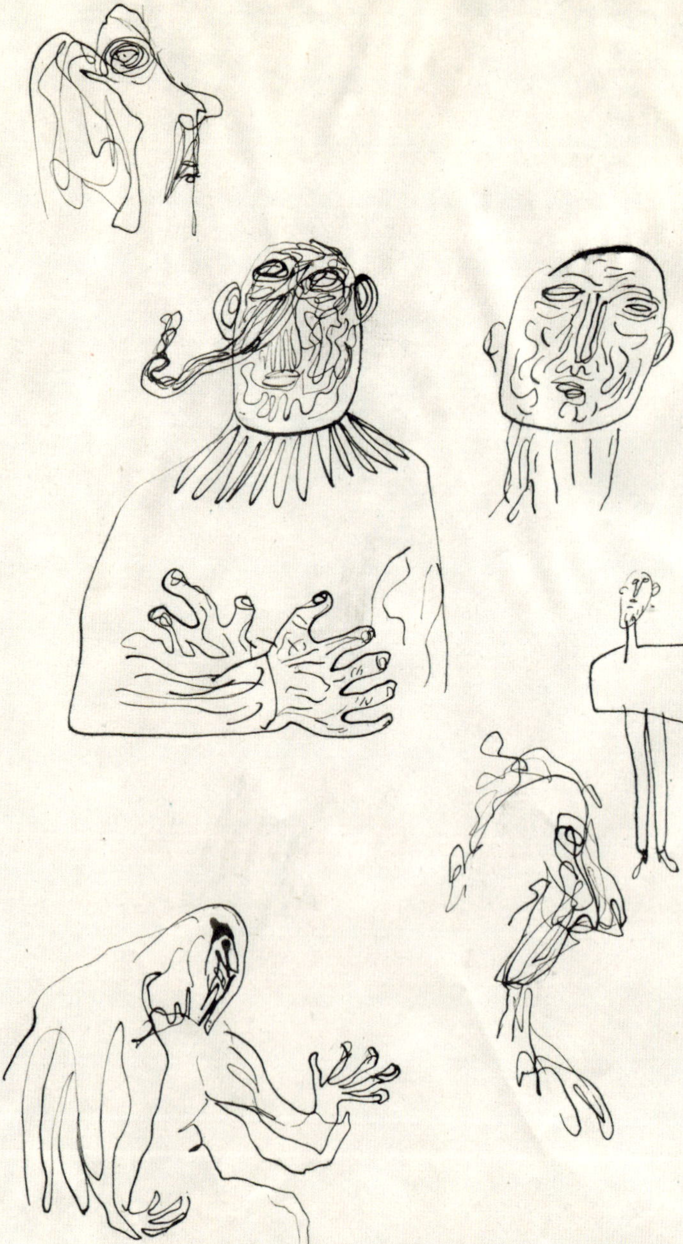

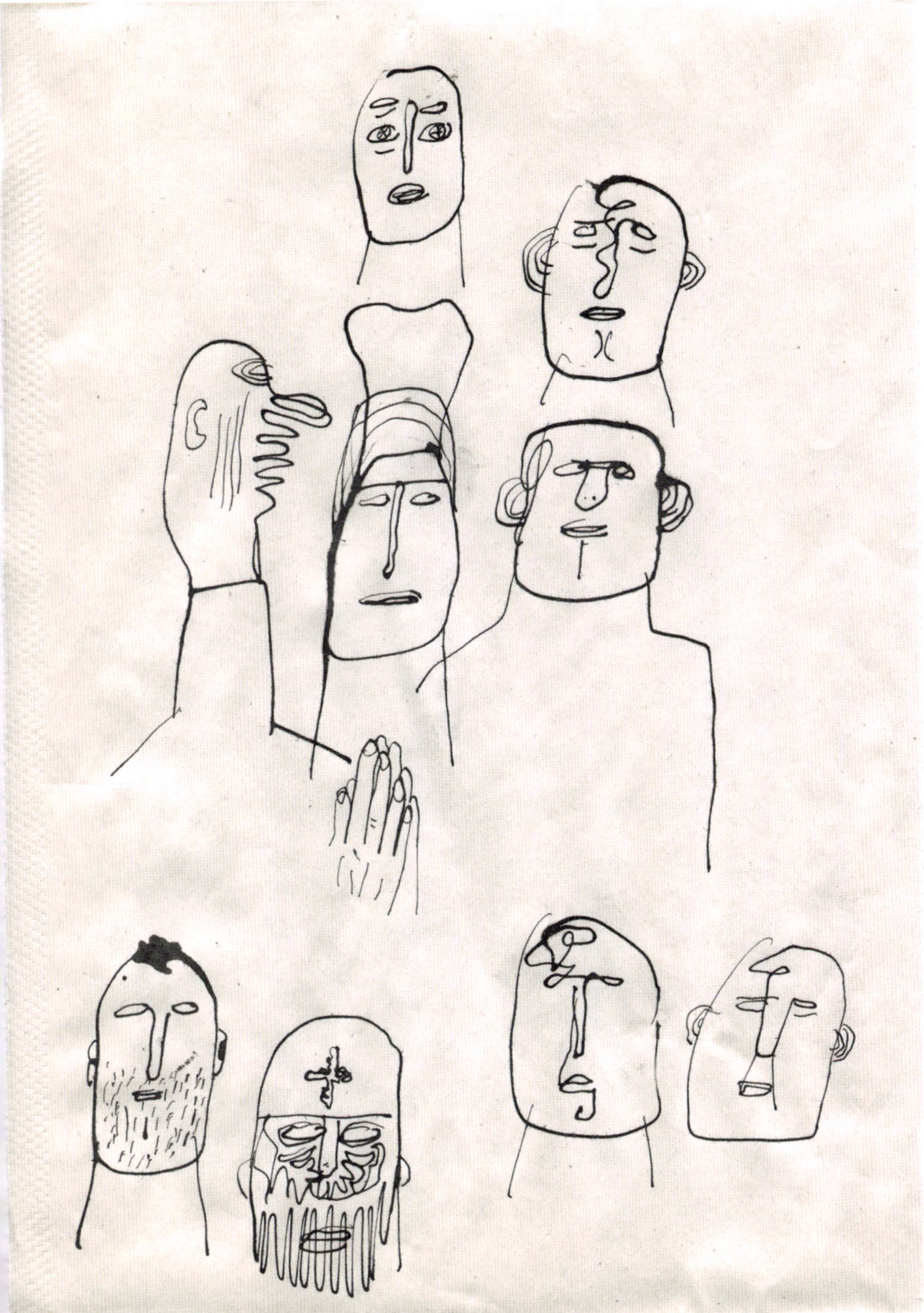

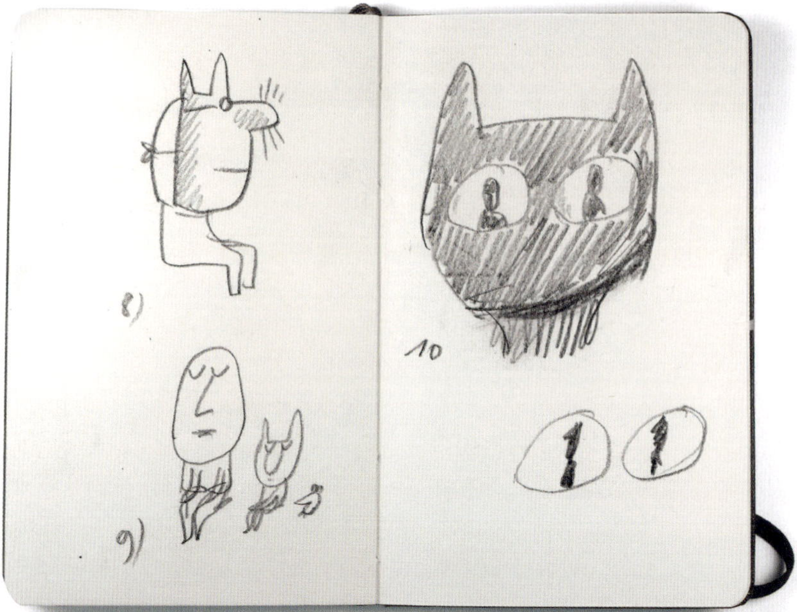
8)
9)
10

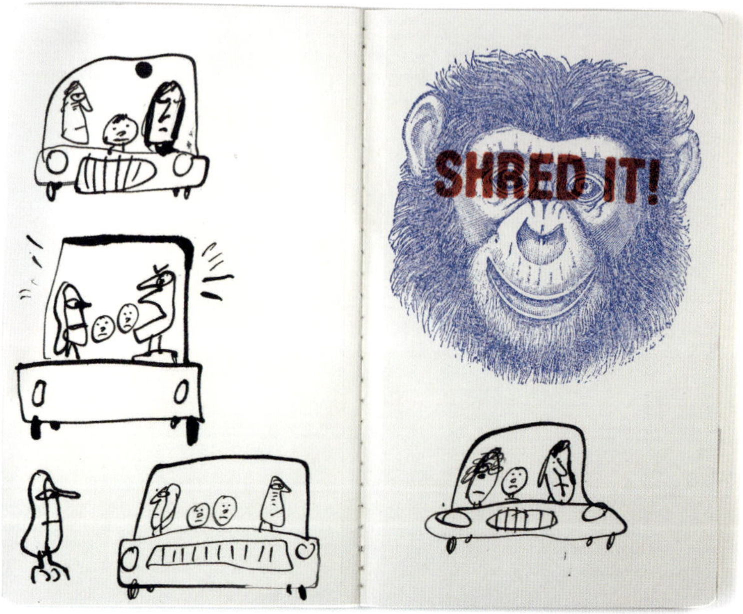
SHRED IT!

72 | 73

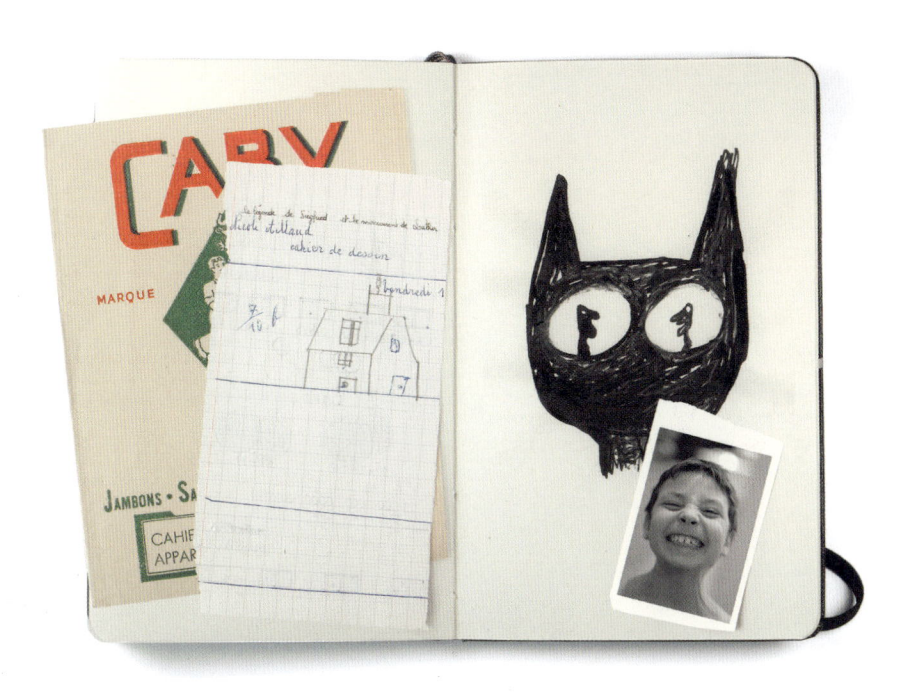

Pep Carrió

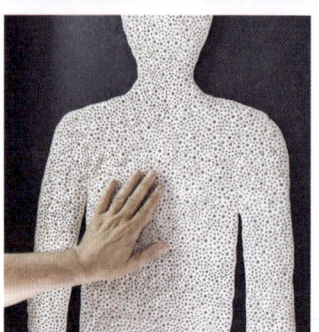

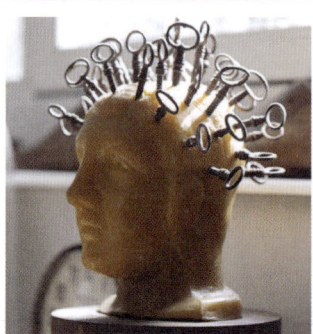

Photography: Laura M. Lombardía

The polyhedral gaze

Illustrator, graphic designer, editor, draughtsman, photographer, carpenter, sculptor, artist. Pep Carrió is an author in the original Latin sense of the word: someone who makes something grow, sprout, emerge. To get an idea of this activity and differentiate it from other occupations, from other names, we need to dispense with certain semiological concepts that we are accustomed to using like a Swiss Army Knife. Focus, method, language, style, discourse, signs of identity, etc.

If we do not go any further than that, we would end up saying what has already been said about others, even what has already been said about him. Nor does it seem appropriate to detail the catalog of rhetorical procedures. Rhetorical devices (metaphor, metonymy, ellipsis, repetition) are clear cut and must necessarily coincide with those of other authors. When considering Pep Carrió's work, the best recommendation is to understand it as a way of life.

A way of life is always unique. Pep Carrió has a rare and unusual way of life: he is fueled by what is material, by what already is and often already was. It progresses from an indefatigable search that leads to discovery: it is not enough just to be; it has to appear, to be there. It is based on the principle of relationship: what was and is always leads to another reality that also was and is, and this to another, and this to yet another. And in the end, it bestows meaning by recognizing the possibility of metamorphosis: what was and is, sooner or later, will be something else.

Text: Grassa Toro

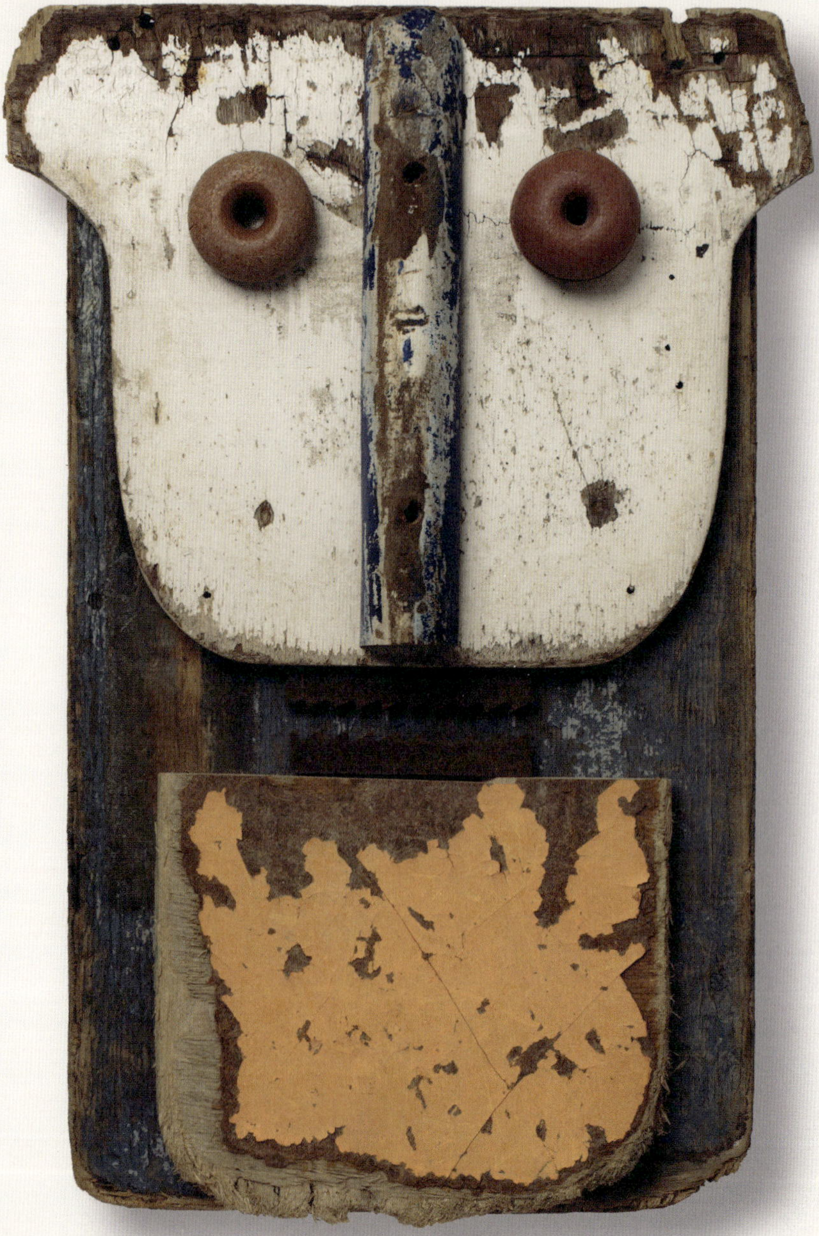

1

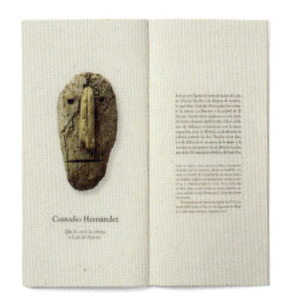

"Perhaps what best defines my creative process are the spaces it occupies, physical spaces but essentially mental ones.

I share my design studio with my partners. We develop projects for different commissions in the cultural and publishing fields. Covers, identities, catalogs and a long etcetera. We strive to find the best communication solutions for each one. The workshop, the game room, an intimate space where I create my most personal work, a laboratory for experimenting with self-imposed assignments where the only objective is to be carried away by intuition.

The notebook: a portable laboratory. A place that is always with me. This is where I've created a visual diary that has grown day by day over the years. A space to record immediate impressions, to experiment, make mistakes, return to and gain perspective.

A book is a container of finished projects, a space for collaboration with other authors, a place to leave a concrete memory."

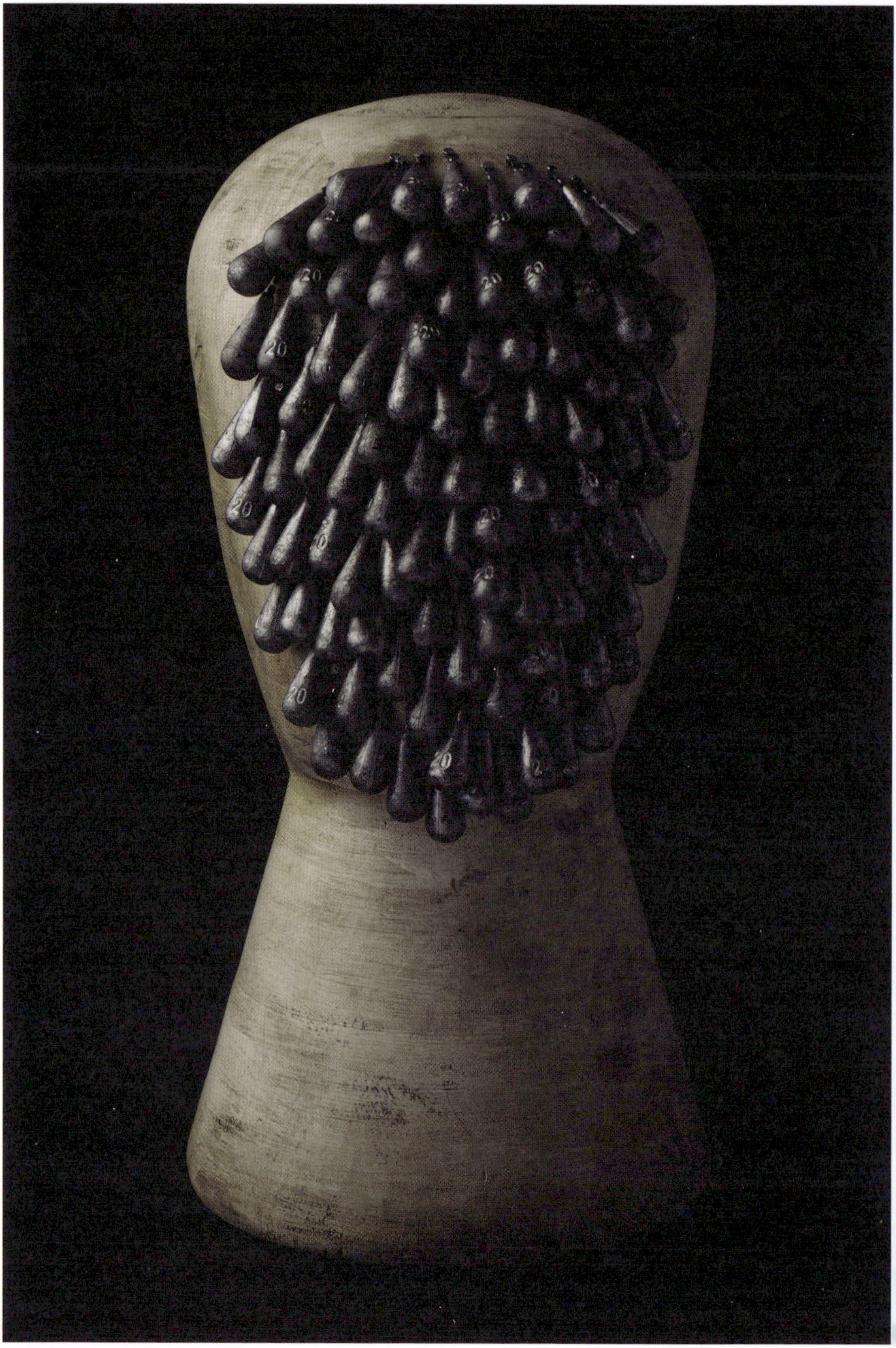

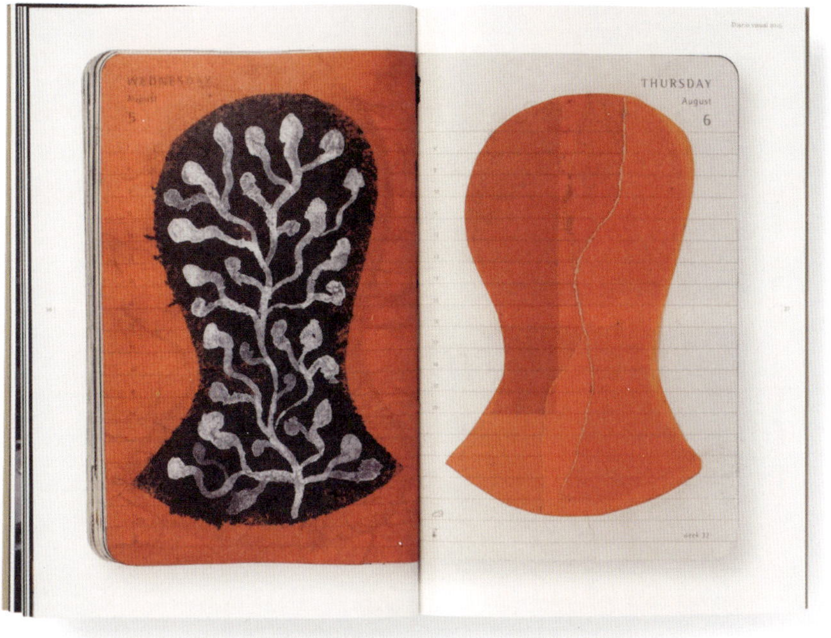
THURSDAY
August
6

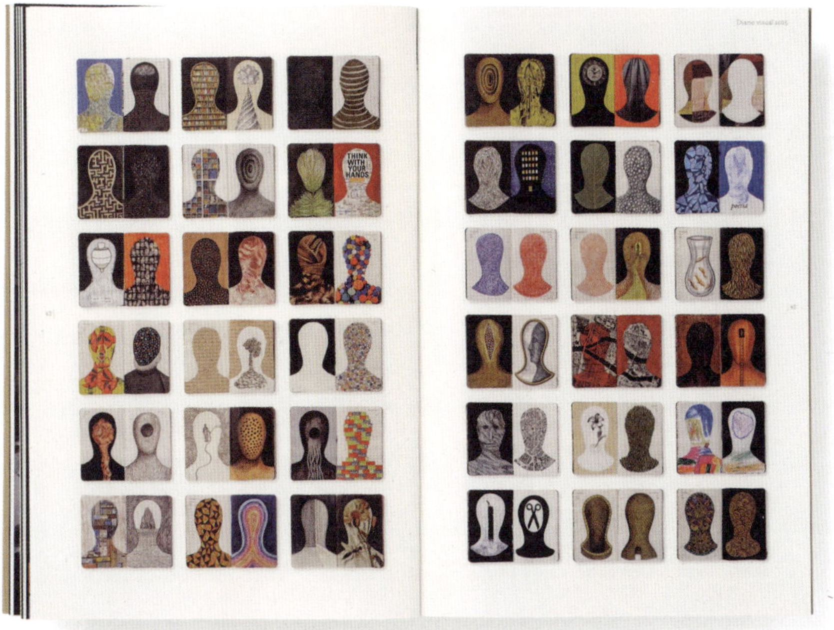
THINK WITH YOUR HANDS

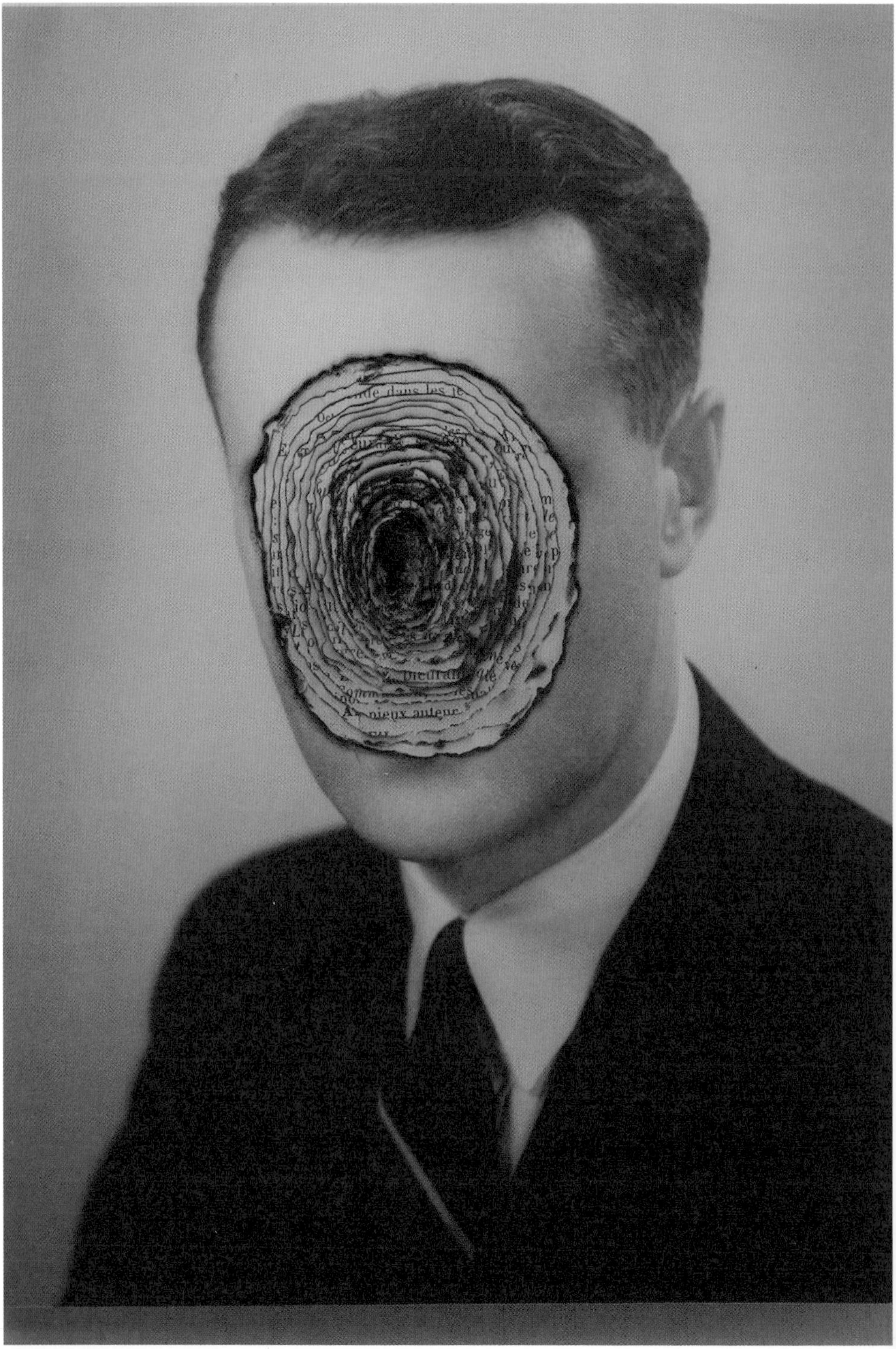

3

80|81

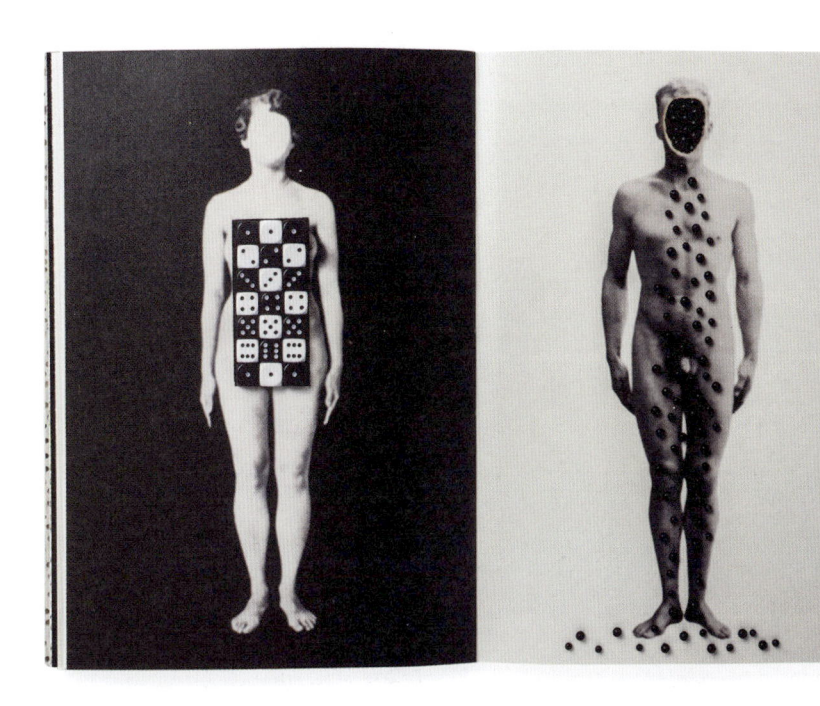

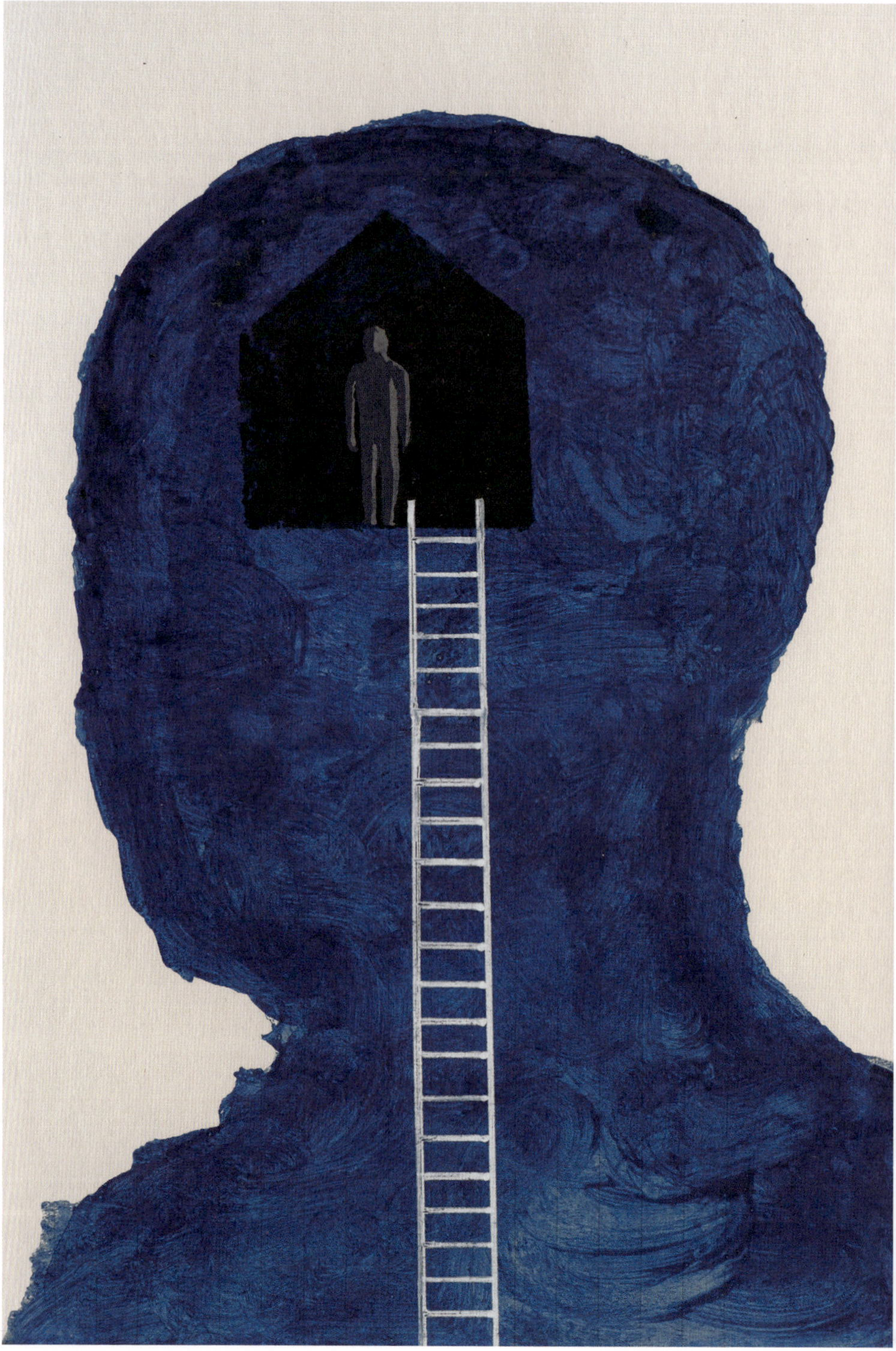

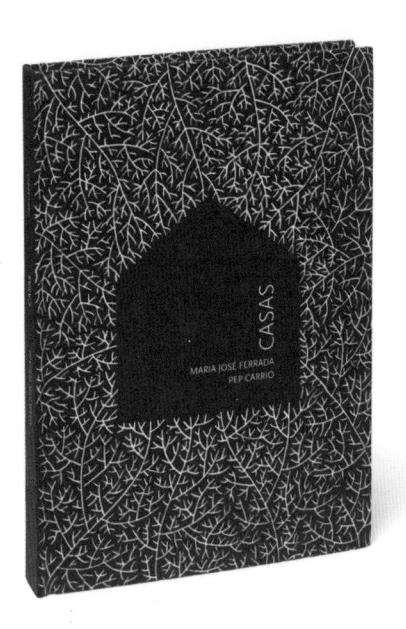

"I view the creative process as a river along which I flow, exploring its different tributaries, which cross and intermingle. For me change is imperative. I don't want to be bound to a single visual language. I think of my creative work as a garden in which I can grow different species. Monoculture bores me."

"Certain things recur in my work: discovery, chance, memory, time as an element that shapes processes. My materials are remains, driftwood, a loss object, a forgotten photo, boxes as pages, a pocket notebook, endless heads, series and repetitions. Though the materials are different, in the end you realize there's a common process, different paths that inevitably lead to a way of doing and thinking."

1. Book *Conquistadores en el Nuevo Mundo,* Grassa Toro - Pep Carrió, Tragaluz Editores, 2013.
2. Book *El fabricante de cabezas,* {in pectore}, 2016.
3. Catalog *There is nothing deeper than the skin,* {in pectore}, 2018.
4. Book *Casas,* María José Ferrada - Pep Carrió, Alboroto Ediciones, 2021.

NOEL COCTEAU

Noel Cocteau vive en la cima de una burbuja poliédrica generada –de modo dinámico y constante– por la respiración de una esponja marina. Cuando un periodista de La Provence le preguntó qué pasaría con su casa si un día la esponja dejaba de respirar, Noel Cocteau le respondió: "desaparecerá".

Y después de un silencio, que le alcanzó para volver a llenar su pipa con tabaco, continuó: "las casas de aire corren la misma suerte que las de cemento o madera ¿lo ha notado?"

JOAO ALMEIDA

Joao Almeida, poeta, vive en Coímbra. Durante sus últimos cinco años ha trabajado en la construcción de un barrio –casas de bordes blancos– para sus 128 heterónimos.

En el muro de la casa 7, escrito en letras también blancas, utilizando una lupa leemos: "Cada uno de nosotros es varios, es una prolijidad de sí mismos".

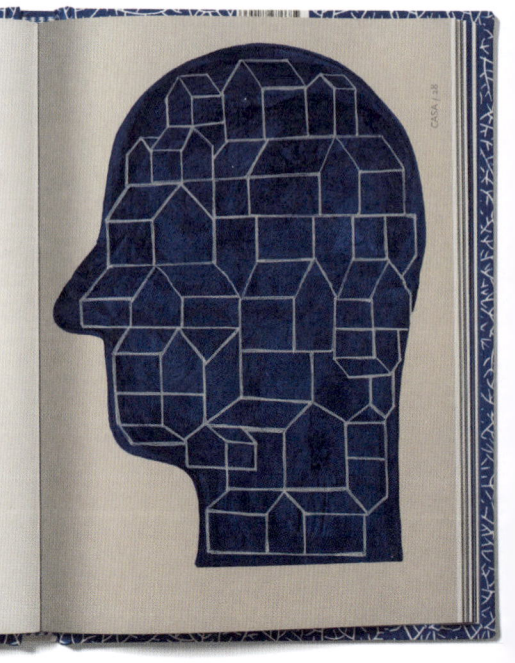

84 | 85

Carolina Celas

Carolina Celas lives and works in Lisbon. She graduated with a degree in Design from the University of Aveiro and later pursued a postgraduate degree in Illustration at Eina, in Barcelona. In 2015, she completed a visual communication course at the Royal College of Art in London and established herself as an illustrator.

The poetry and harmony in her work inspire children and adults to experience limitless spaces. Carolina encourages a look beyond the physical gaze that enables viewers to become lost in her illustrations, immersing themselves in them. Her main focus is on book illustration, although she works in different media. Her illustrations create mini-stories somewhere between fiction and reality, exploring detail, humor and surrealist effects through natural and spatial elements.

She is the author of the book *Horizon*, published by Orfeu Negro, which has been translated into twelve languages. She has taken part in several national and international exhibitions such as: Bologna Fair in 2016 and 2019; Golden Pinwheel Shanghai 2018; Nami Island International Picture Book 2019 and 2021. She received an honorable mention at Illusalon 2018, a special mention at Ilustrarte 2018 and a revelation award at BIG Guimarães 2017.

1

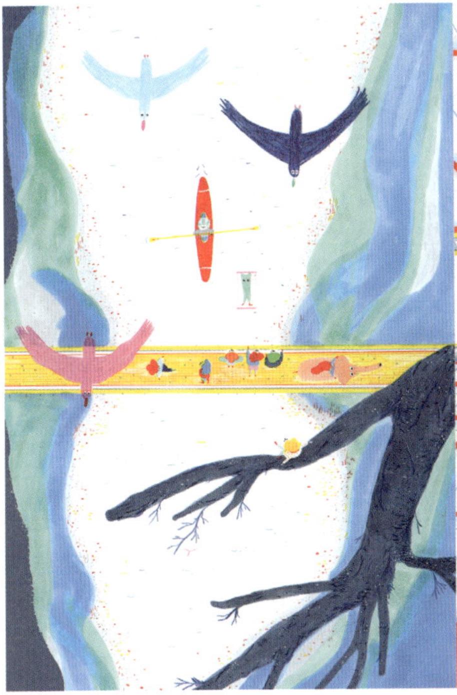

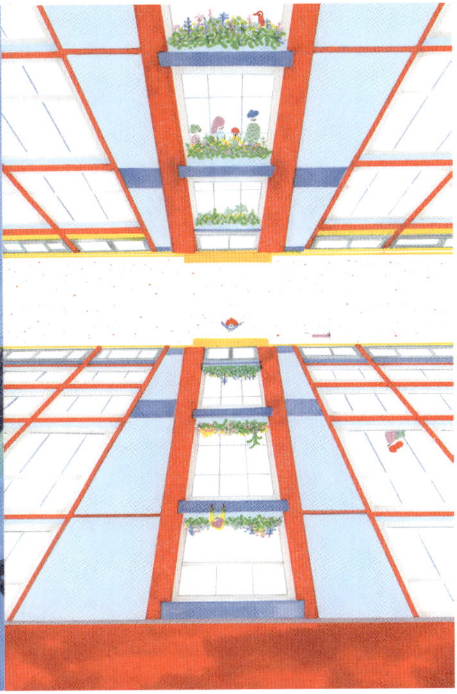

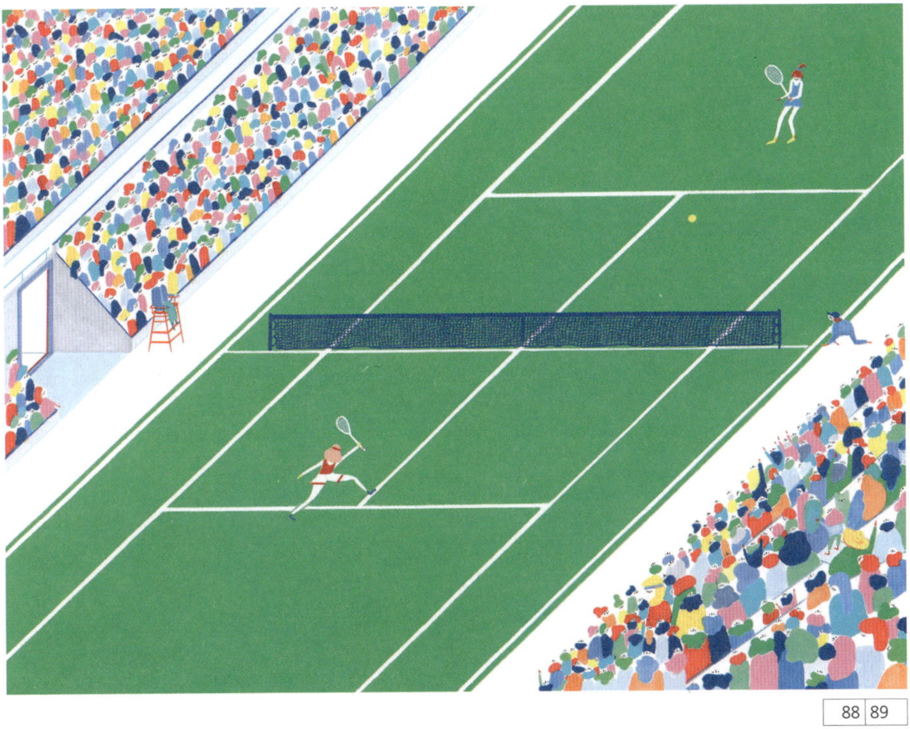

1

"I don't think there's anything that differentiates me that much from other illustrators. Though I do believe we look at the same thing from different perspectives. The environment, the culture, the surroundings in which we grow up, what we see, who we come across and what we experience make us think differently and do things differently. Still, in the end we all have a similar objective: to convey a message and communicate through images. In my case, I believe this communication is achieved poetically and emotionally in an attempt to get closer to the reader who is watching, and by leaving a door open for them to follow the story through their imagination. For me, this freedom of interpretation is very important.

What fascinates me about creating picture book narratives is their universal scope and capacity. I enjoy the challenge of eliciting something different in everyone at the same time, both in children and adults. They are books that require some kind of predisposition to reading and are meant to be read and reread. Sometimes they aren't so immediate and take you on parallel narrative journeys. In my drawings, this game is heavily based on immersive spaces, micro-narratives and layered colored compositions.

While at times the images might be simple, they arise from the observation of detail and the reader's ability to make the leap through their curiosity and imagination. They create a trigger to something else that isn't there. I love creation and the mental game of how it can be perceived by another person. The interesting thing is that you're always surprised by the diversity of interpretations and responses generated around the same book. That's why the reader plays such an important role in my work.

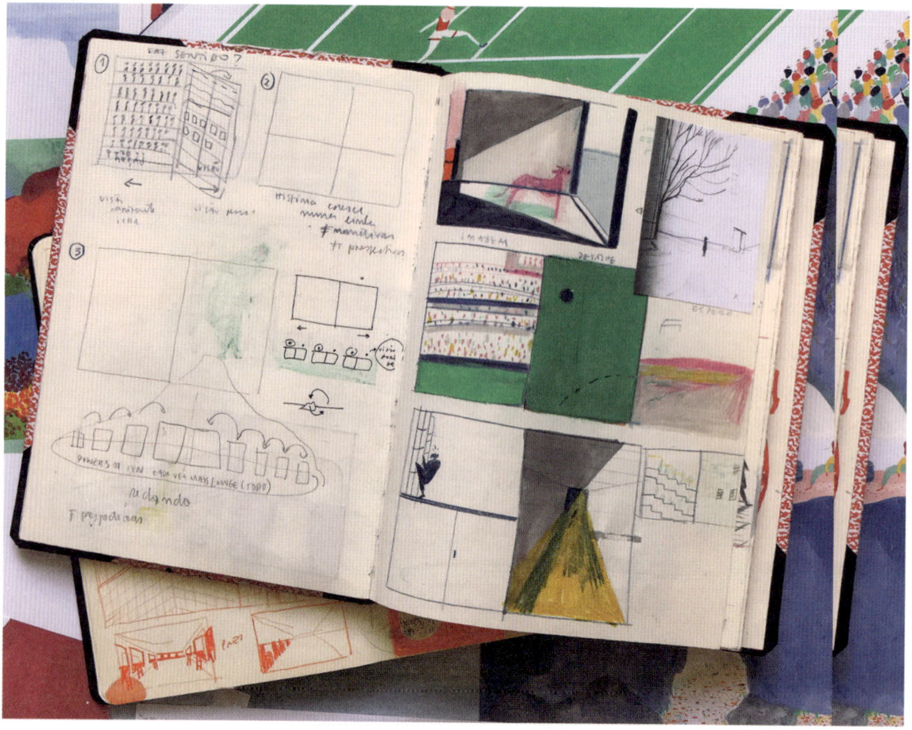
FAZ SENTIDO?
redondo

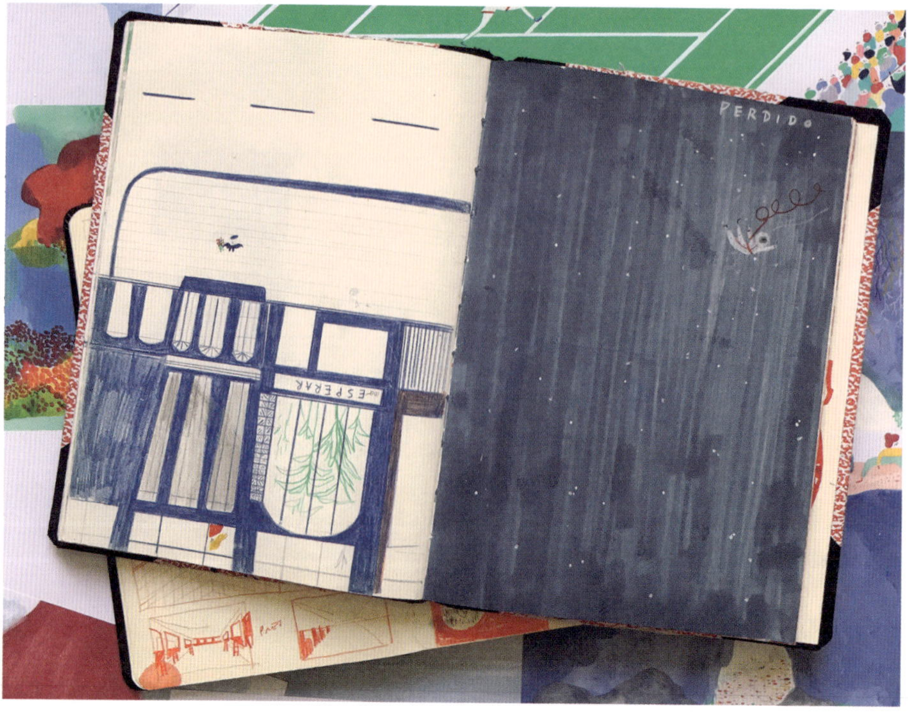
ESPERAR
PERDIDO

EDUARDO GALEANO

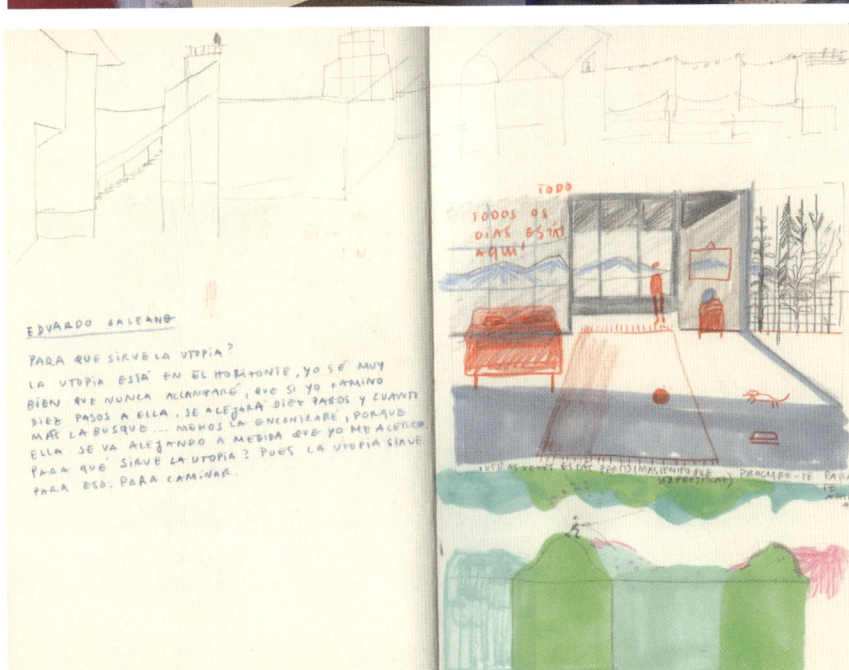

PARA QUE SIRVE LA UTOPIA?

LA UTOPIA ESTA EN EL HORIZONTE, YO SÉ MUY
BIEN QUE NUNCA ALCANZARÉ, QUE SI YO CAMINO
DIEZ PASOS A ELLA, SE ALEJARÁ DIEZ PASOS Y CUANTO
MÁS LA BUSQUE... MENOS LA ENCONTRARÉ, PORQUE
ELLA SE VA ALEJANDO A MEDIDA QUE YO ME ACERCO
PARA QUÉ SIRVE LA UTOPIA? PUES LA UTOPIA SIRVE
PARA ESO, PARA CAMINAR.

2

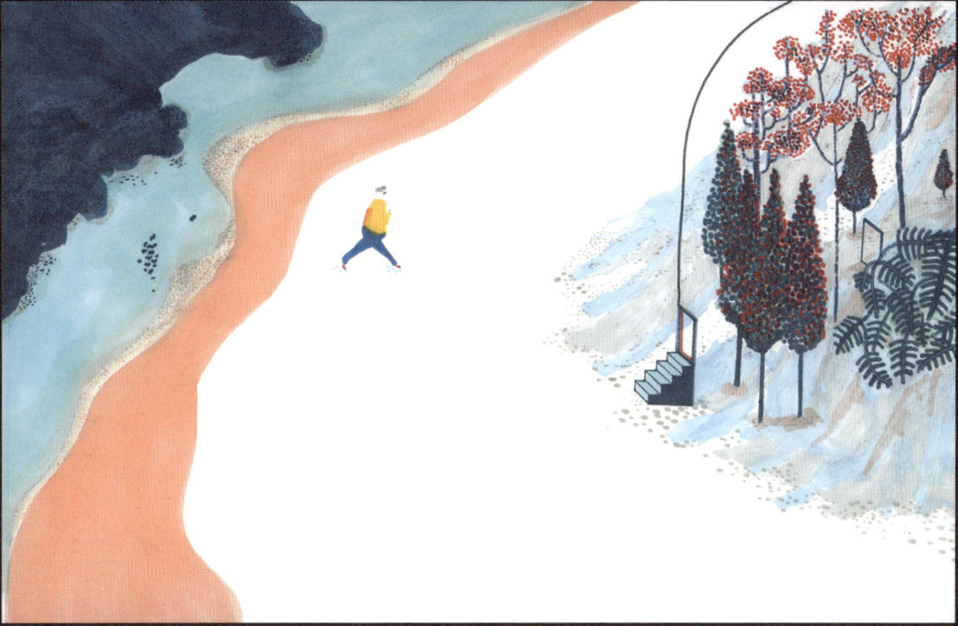

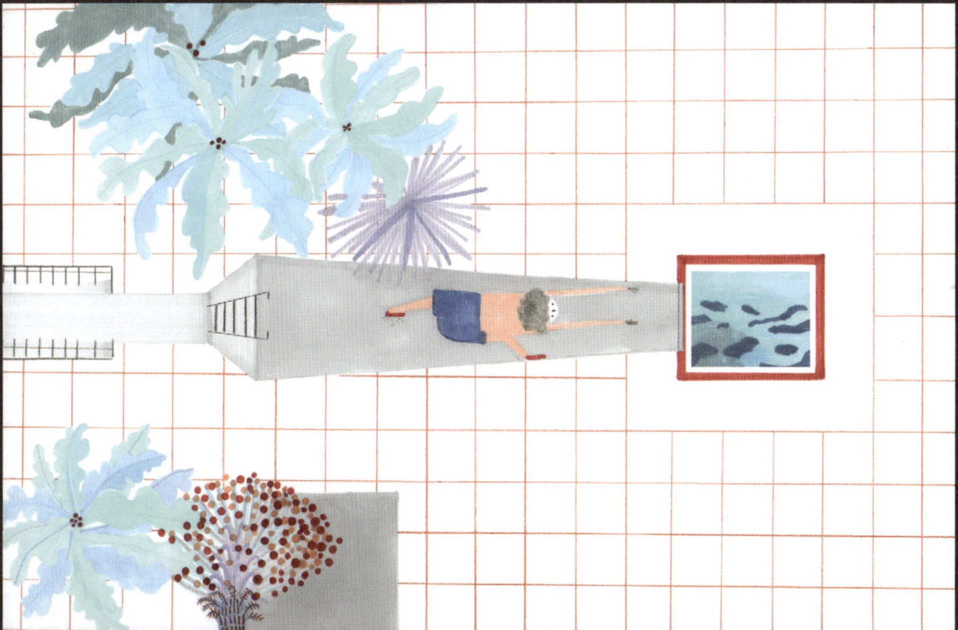

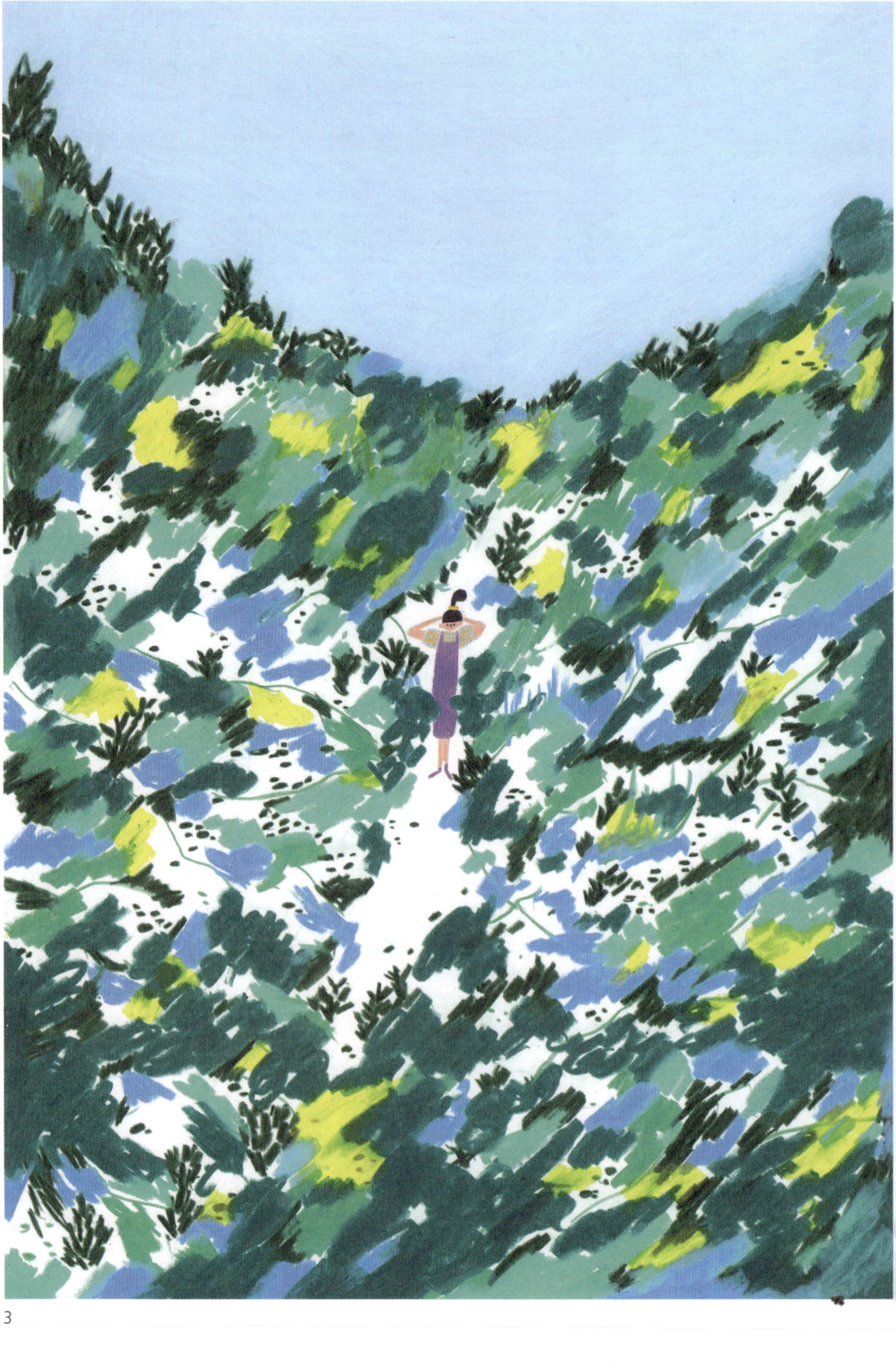

"Every project is different, and I tailor my way of working to it. I don't have a method or a specific process. However, I do make a distinction between commissions and personal projects. The process involved in a personal project is much richer and more interesting because it relies much more on experimenting with new techniques and narrative forms.

Reinventing ourselves within our own illustration style is not always easy and we often fall short. But the simple fact of trying new things is what keeps me engaged. For this reason, I believe that personal projects are useful to search for new paths, to make mistakes and at the same time to surprise ourselves.

I believe ideas are born from observation, from daily life, from our experiences, from whom we meet, from reading and staying curious. Sometimes I collect small drawings, photos, sentences, objects, textures or little things that inspire me. Then at some point I end up incorporating them into a drawing that calls for it. Observation triggers my imagination. Often decontextualizing or deconstructing an idea helps me in the process of generating ideas.

Play is very important in my work. I like to play with viewers' perception, immersed in the illustrations, and simultaneously make them an important part of the book. The reader completes the reading cycle with their own interpretation, giving wings to their creativity."

"There are no secrets to being a good illustrator. You just have to have a strong desire to do what you love. What works for me doesn't necessarily work for everyone else. For me, maybe it's the love-hate relationship with illustration. Sometimes I hate the process of illustrating. But it challenges me to try and experiment more, to look for answers the harder the journey becomes. Maybe you can call this passion, in a very poetic sense."

1. *Horizon*, Orfeu Negro, 2018.
2. *Private Landscapes*, Self-published, 2021.
3. *Joana. Another random day*, Ó! Gallery, Exhibition.

Jesús Cisneros

Studio photography: Karto Gimeno

"I work in three areas: drawing, illustration and teaching. As an illustrator, I create my work mainly in sketchbooks. I've used them for many years. Now they're a reflection of my daily experiences with drawing and illustration. One page leads to another. And almost without realizing it, day by day, you learn new things. So I think having a sketchbook is the best way to keep the experience of drawing alive and fresh. For me, more than anything else, it's a source of learning.

There are three concepts that I believe play an important role in the creative process and that motivate me as an illustrator: play, memory and imagination. I'm also interested in the drawing process, how an idea evolves and transforms on paper until the final product emerges. The technique we use to express an idea is crucial to the final result.

In recent years, I've had exhibitions in Mexico, France, Spain, Portugal and South Korea. This has given me the opportunity to try new formats and apply the freedom and experimentation of my sketchbooks to exhibition spaces."

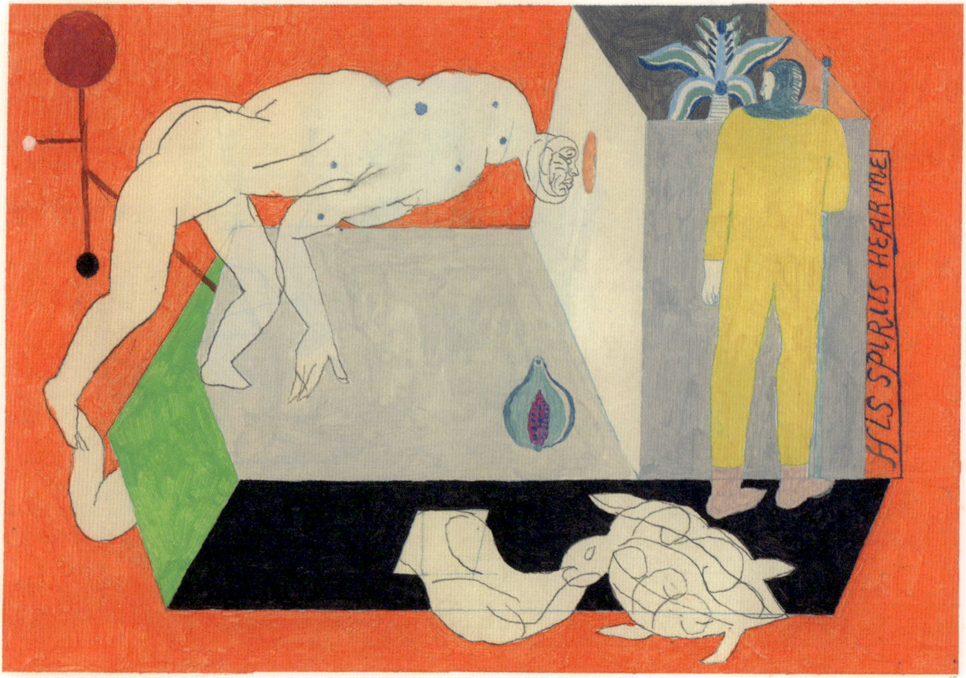

35

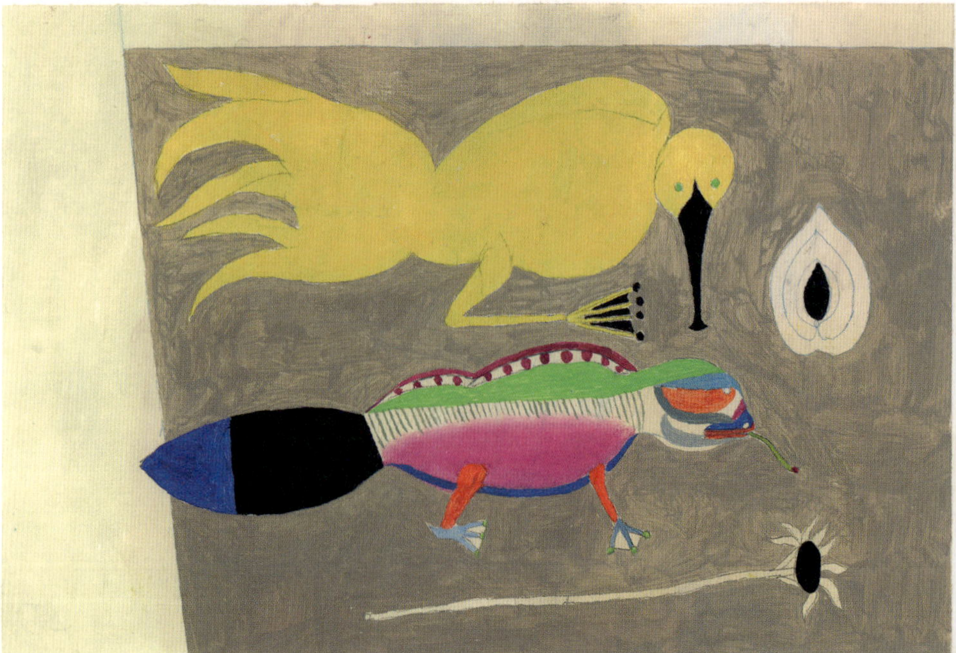

16

"Although I'm a professional illustrator, my core work is drawing. I think that drawing as such is one of those activities that don't have a practical use but are essential. Like music and singing, poetry, etc.

My illustration work has been mainly in the form of illustrated books, some thirty to date. I've also made posters, illustrations for magazines and print media and done graphic work. Books have always attracted me as a reader. Their form and design fascinate me. I started working on illustrated books at a very young age.

I'm very interested in the relationship between word and image. I believe this is the key to the illustrator's work, especially illustration associated with literature. I've illustrated classic texts by Euripides, Quevedo, Cervantes, Shakespeare, Bécquer and Kafka. I've also illustrated books of poetry and children's books.

Another highly important aspect of my professional life is teaching. For seven years, I've taught at different schools and offered workshops in different countries: Mexico, Italy, Spain, Russia, France, Germany, South Korea and Thailand. These international workshops are very interesting because they occasionally bring together students from different countries. Although they speak different languages, they communicate in an idiom that knows no borders: drawing.

In my classes and workshops, I always try to transmit the pleasure of drawing and creating images that tell stories and contain meanings. We also analyze the tools that make visual communication possible: graphic language, construction of images, form and color, composition."

LANDSCAPES AND BODIES: MAPS OF THE EXPLORING ILUSTRATOR

Literatura de viaje: Conferencia de Eduardo Martinez de Pisón.
a) Geografías imaginarias.
b) Viajes fantásticos e imposibles.
XVIII. Los viajes de Gulliver (1726) / El viaje de Ulises / Utopía de Tomás Moro
Finlandia / Atlántida / Libro de las Maravillas del mundo, Juan de Mandeville
XIX. Contemporáneo: Finnegans y Moriartor / Alegorías (Mapa del país de la ternura, 1658)
Dino Buzzati / Lugares transformados por la escritura: Eternal Virgilio / Vuelo sobrenatural
Aleteo (Mary Shelley) / Lugares para una ficción: Julio Verne (La isla misteriosa)
Stevenson (La isla del tesoro) / A. Gordon Pym / Insómbola / San Juan de la Cruz
Subida al Monte Carmelo / San Brandán.

23

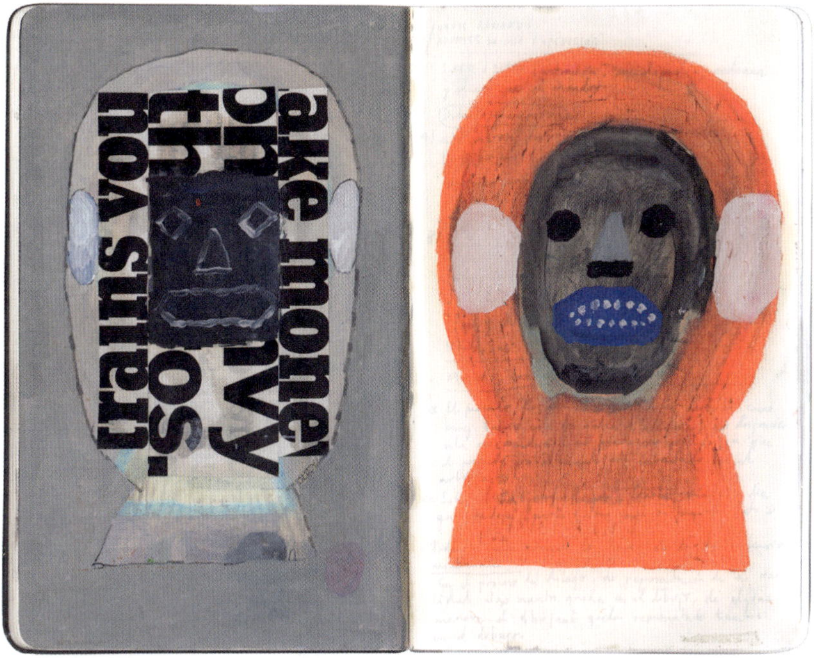

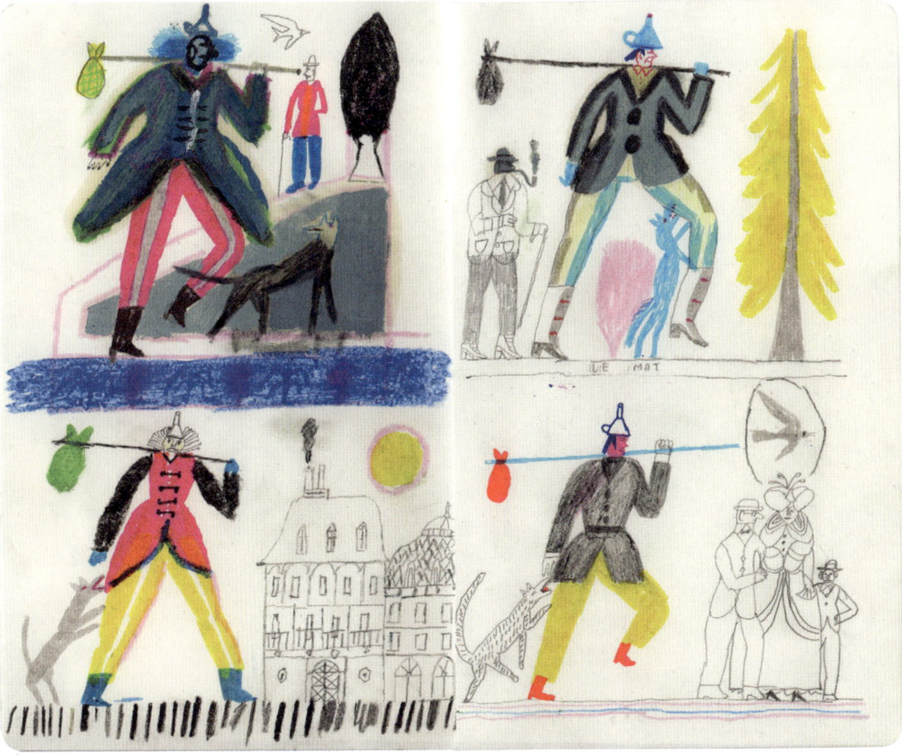
LE MAT

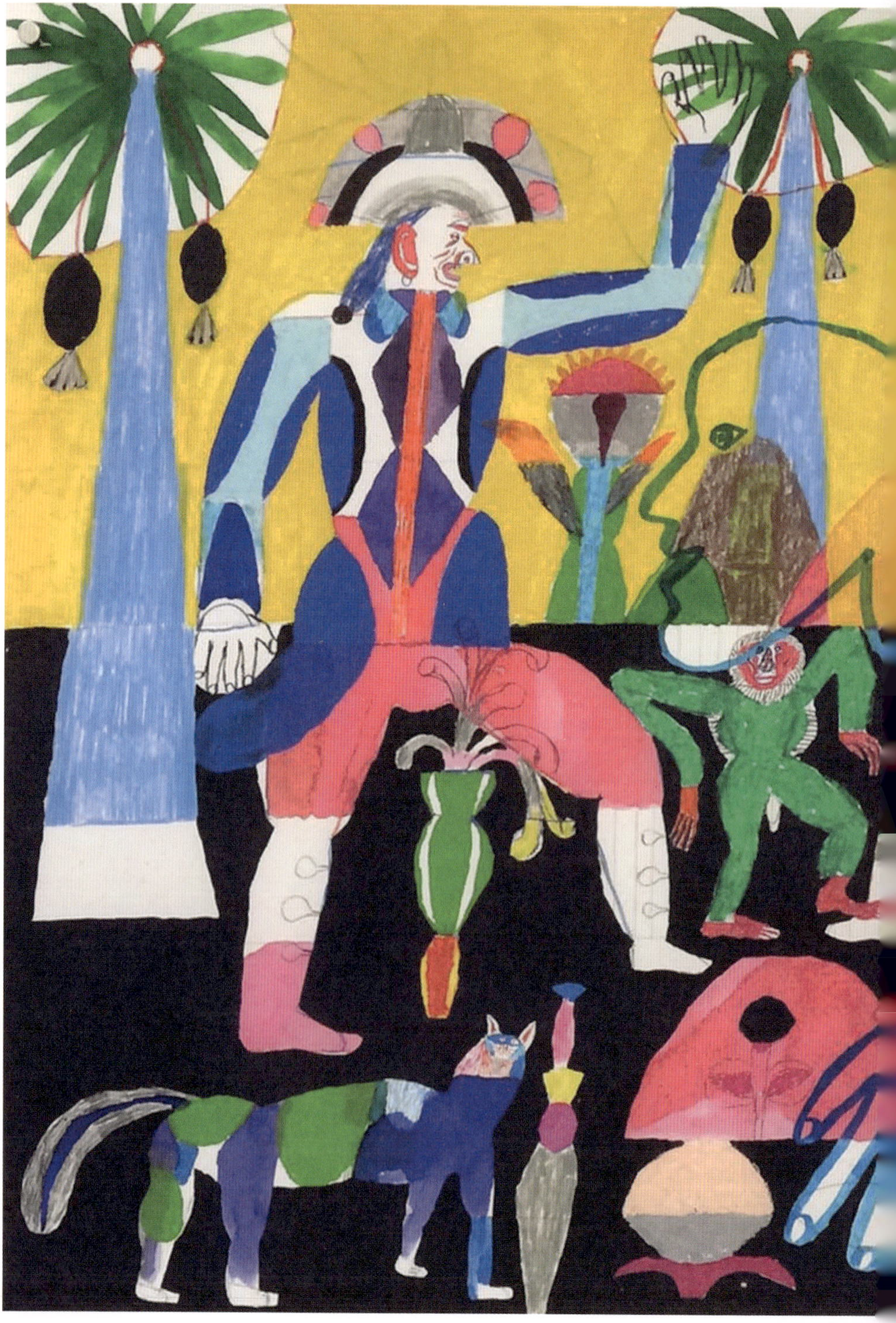

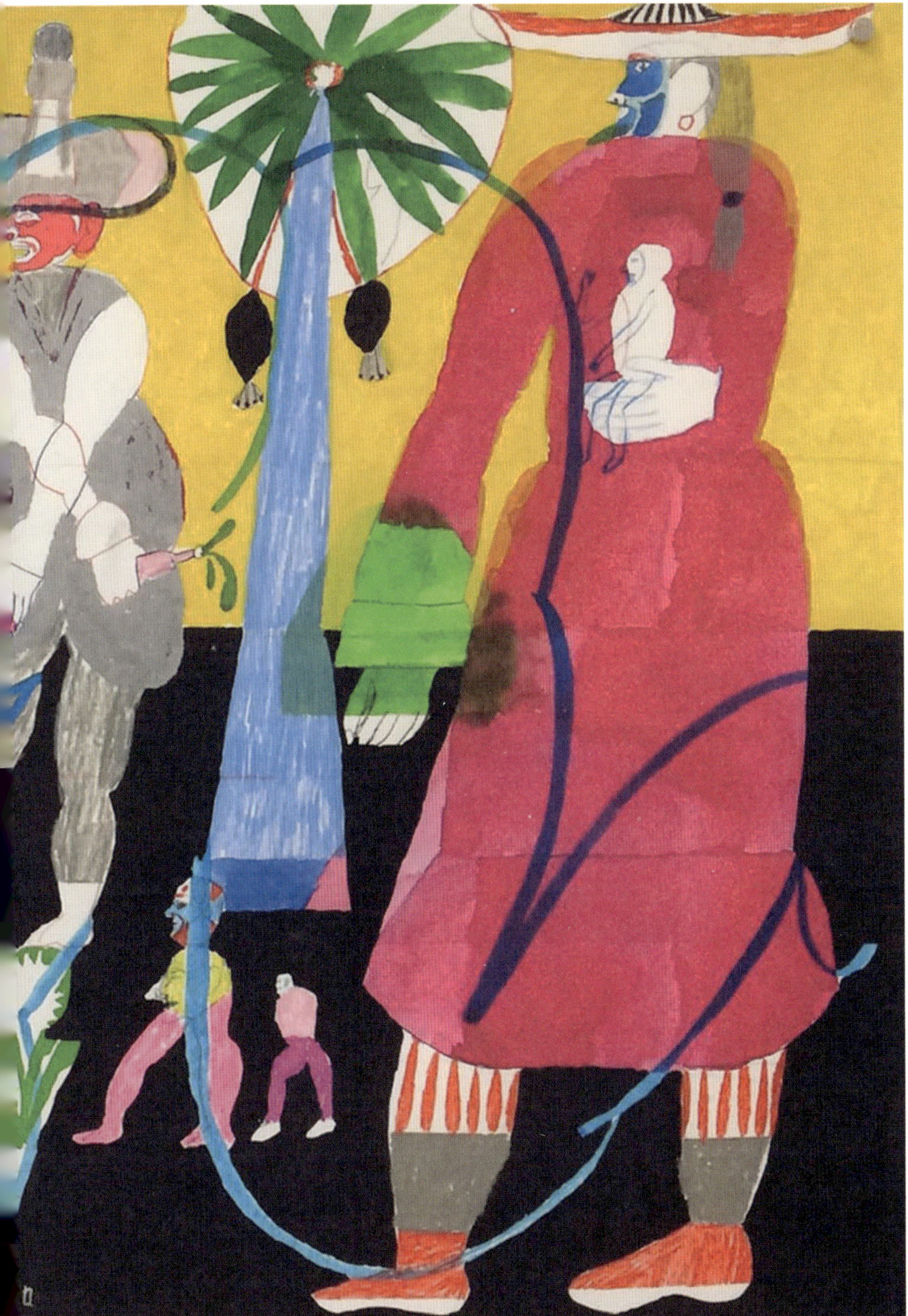

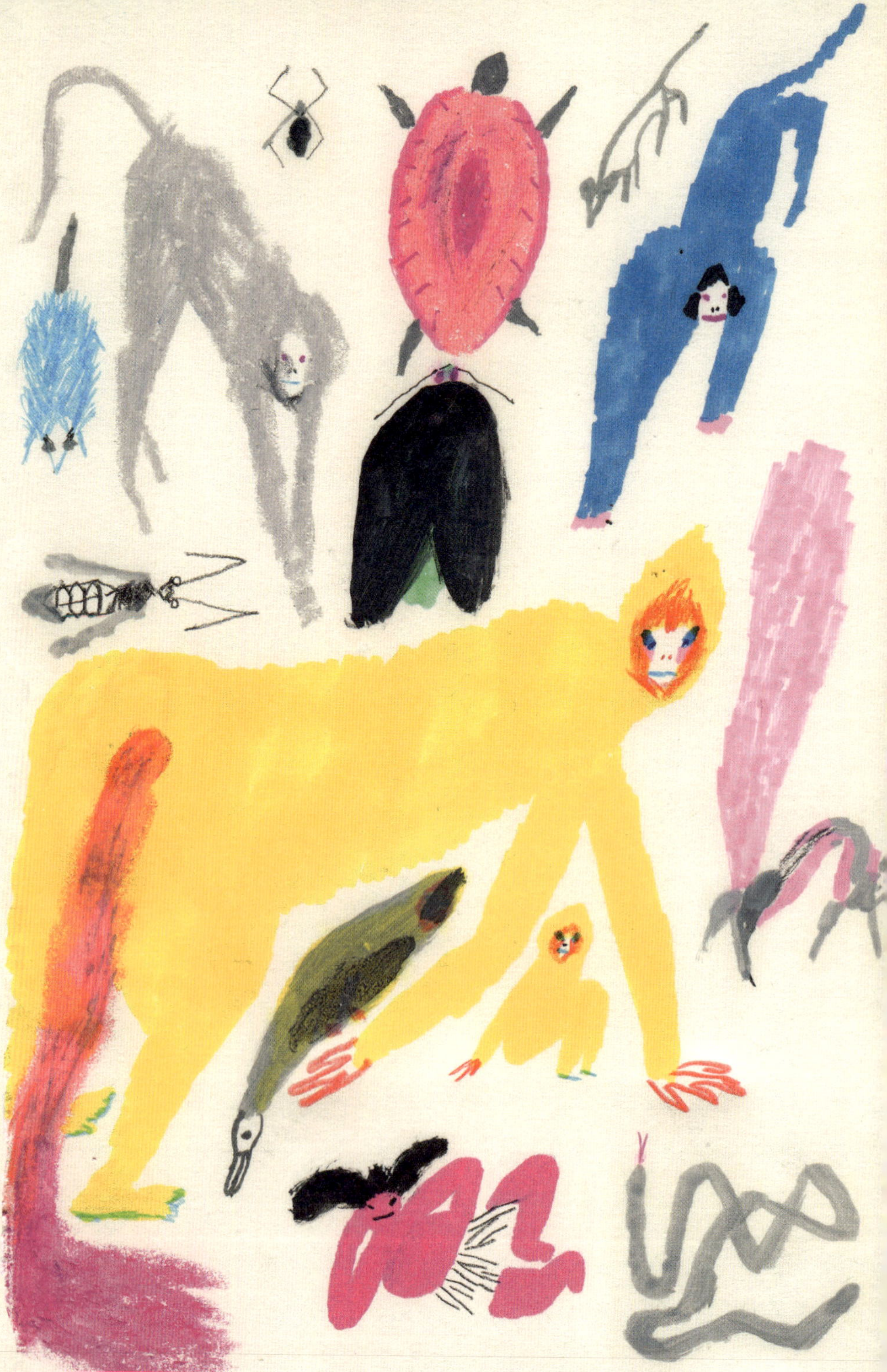

"I think the important thing is the combination of dedication and determination. In my experience as a teacher, I've been able to witness the importance of education. I believe proper teaching is essential. Not only focusing on skill and imitation but also analyzing the fundamentals of graphic language and visual communication, stimulating curiosity and continuous learning; in other words, something that gives students the tools they need to develop their work."

"I try to make the process of illustrating surprising and new to me every time. I believe that if I find the work I do in a book stimulating, these feelings will be transferred to the reader. As a result, every project is different. Usually it's a slow process. I need to explore a lot to finally discover the right path.

Currently, I'm illustrating a children's book of poems by Argentine author Jorge Luján. Each poem will be accompanied by an image. These are highly visual poems. This is interesting and difficult because I need to establish a special connection between two images: the image the text suggests in the reader's mind and my drawing. It's exciting when the drawing expands the meaning of the poem without changing its essential meaning. On the other hand, I like to explore new materials and techniques. In this book I've experimented with water-based charcoal pencil for lines and intense liquid watercolors for the areas inside the lines. The liquid watercolor produces very bright colors and the water expands the charcoal. I like this effect, imperfect and fresh.

I believe that continuous learning is extremely important. I try to be open to as many art forms as possible: literature, music, painting, cinema. Folk art always amazes me: masks, textiles, ceramics... I love the wisdom contained in the way folk art uses form and color, and this also influences me. I'm also drawn to the natural world, to plants and animals. These natural elements fill my sketchbooks, though transformed by my imagination. A simple step can be very inspiring.

I think of drawing as a way to keep my curiosity about the world alive. And a lot of things inspire me: a face, a building, a leaf, a story..."

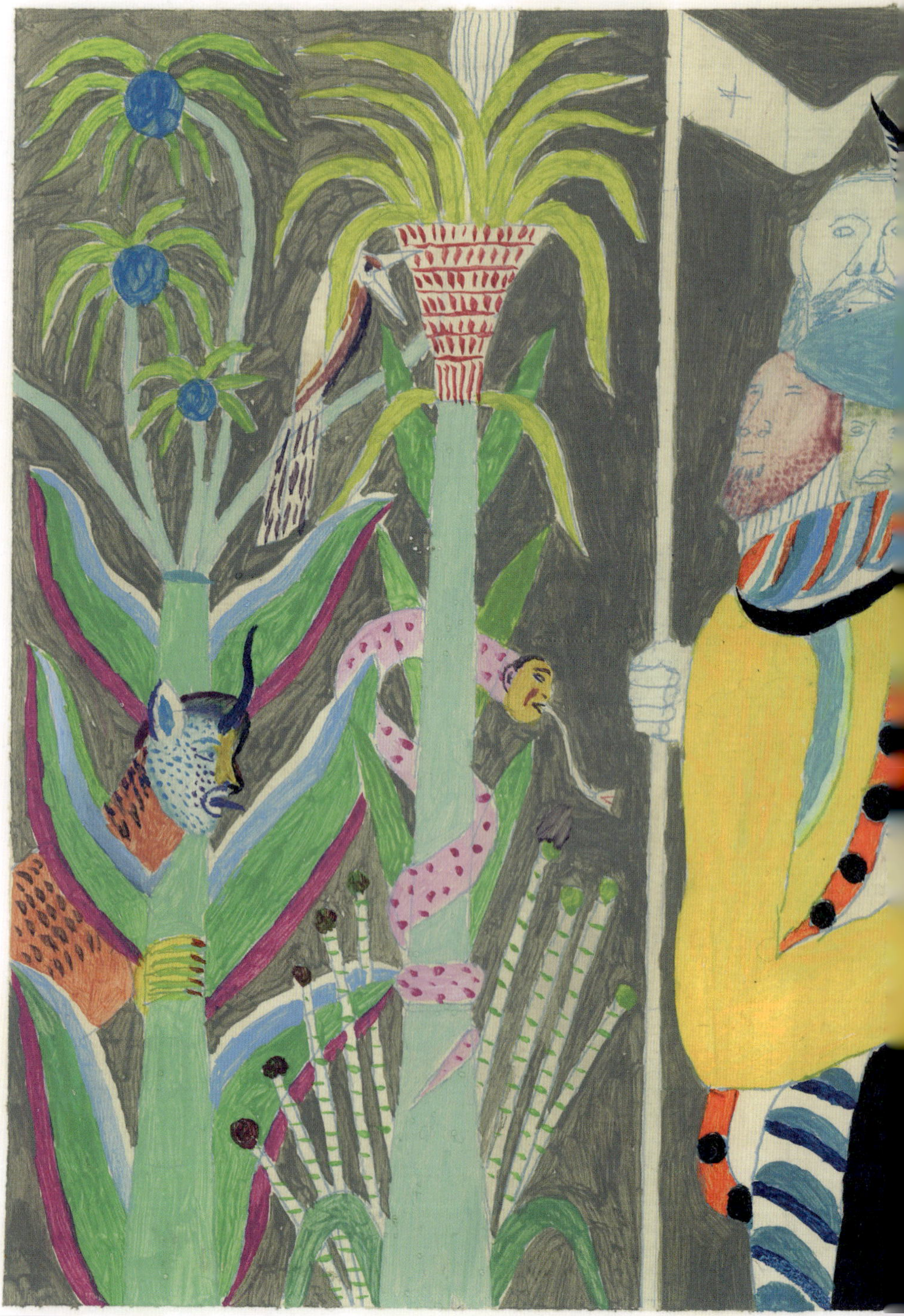

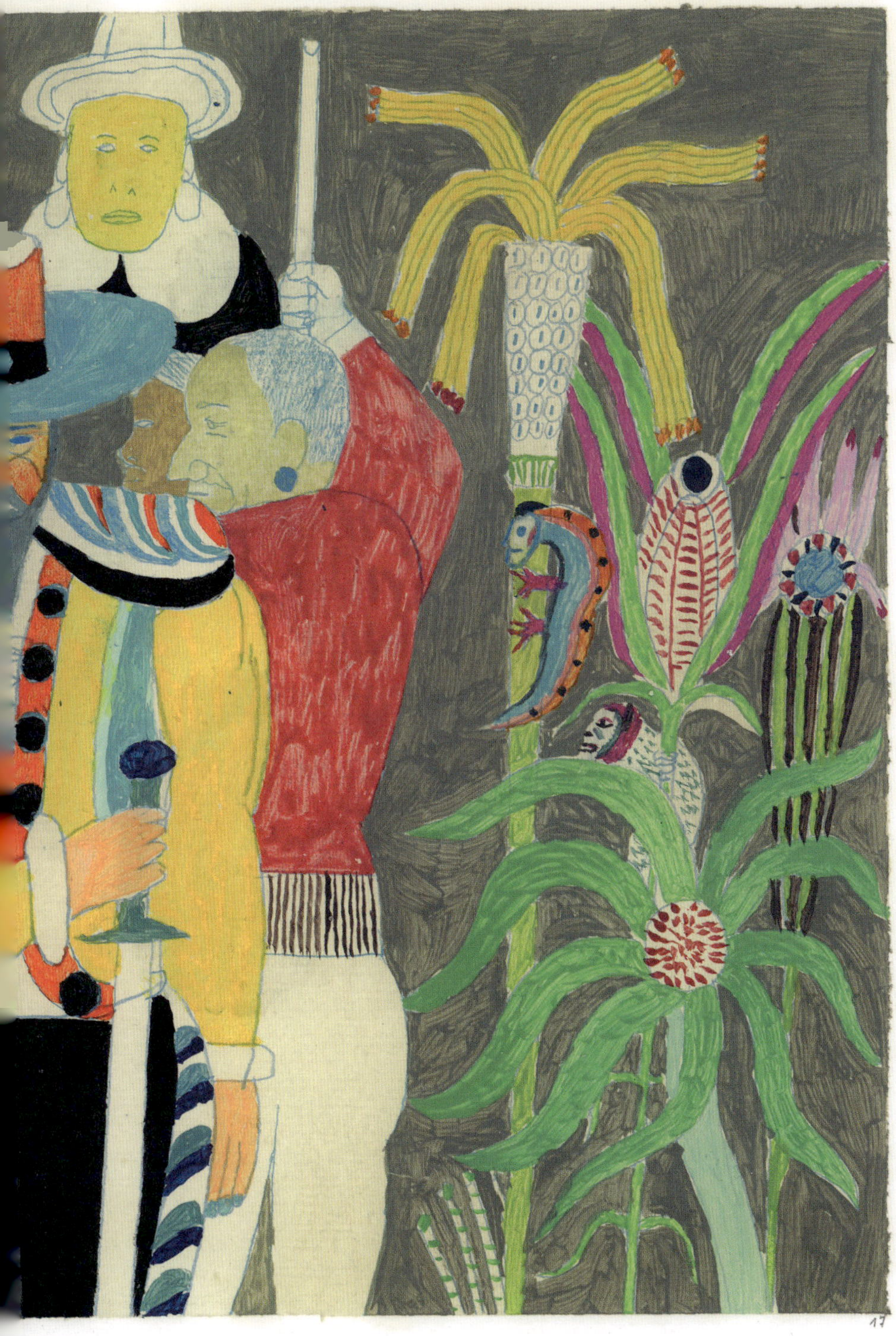
17

Lisa Congdon

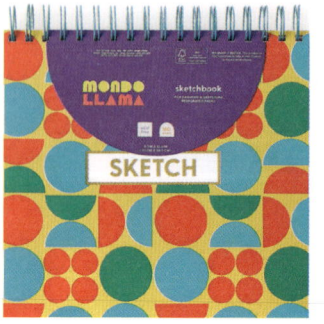

"I define myself first and foremost as an illustrator. I combine narrative and abstract work. I work both with paint, ink and cut paper and digitally with an iPad. I work on all kinds of projects, from publishing to mural design, brand collaborations, packaging design, posters and everything in between.

I'm known for my use of a bold and limited color palette and my distinctive hand lettering styles. I'm also known for arranging things in an imaginary grid and for the use of objects, flora, fauna and symbols. I use my work to convey messages about mental health and wellness, vulnerability, joy, risk-taking, social justice and the realities of living a creative life.

I produce art for clients all over the world, including Method, Amazon, Google, Warby Parker, Brooks Running, Comme des Garçons and Target, among others. I'm the author of ten books, including *Art Inc: The Essential Guide to Building Your Career as an Artist* and *Find your Artistic Voice: The Essential Guide to Working Your Creative Magic*.

I'm the host of the podcast *The Lisa Congdon Sessions* and I teach Creative Entrepreneurship at Pacific Northwest College of Art.

I've gained recognition not only as an artist but as a leader in the industry for my work in fund raising, knowledge sharing, mentoring and teaching. In March 2021, I was named one of the 50 most inspirational people and companies according to industry creative directors published in *AdWeek*. In addition to illustrating, I create textile art in the form of quilts and ceramics. I also collect antique art, office and school supplies and ephemera, and I make compositions of things that are similar in color and photograph them."

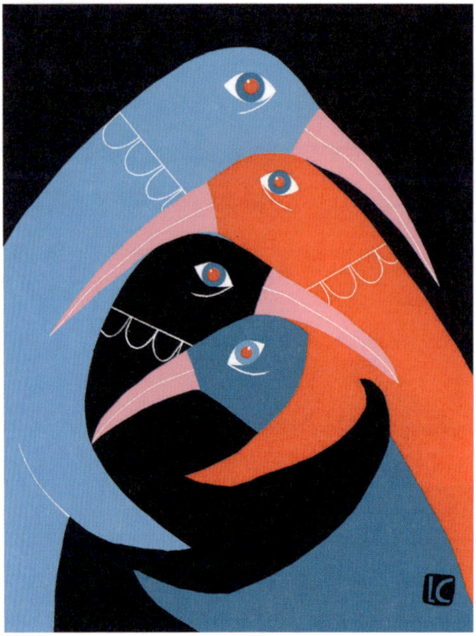

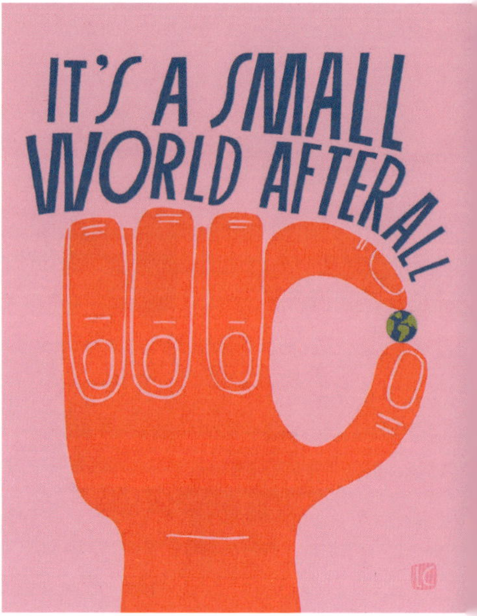
IT'S A SMALL
WORLD AFTER ALL

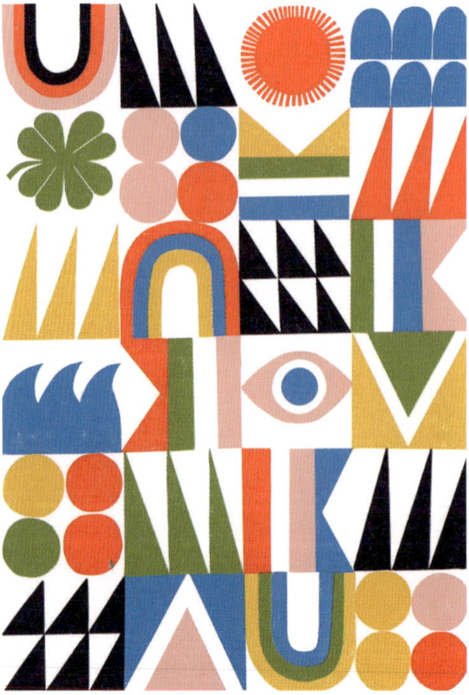

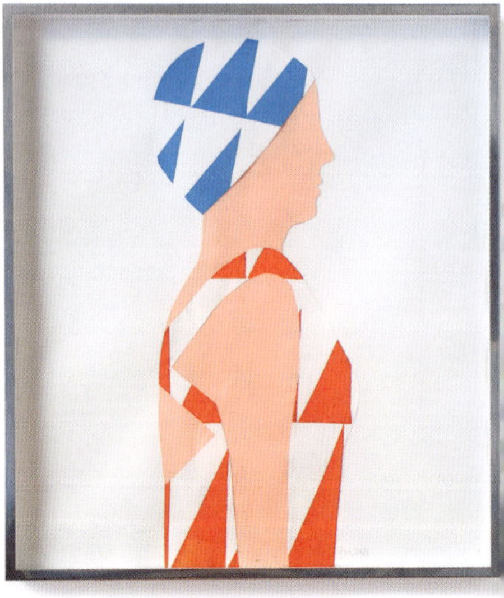

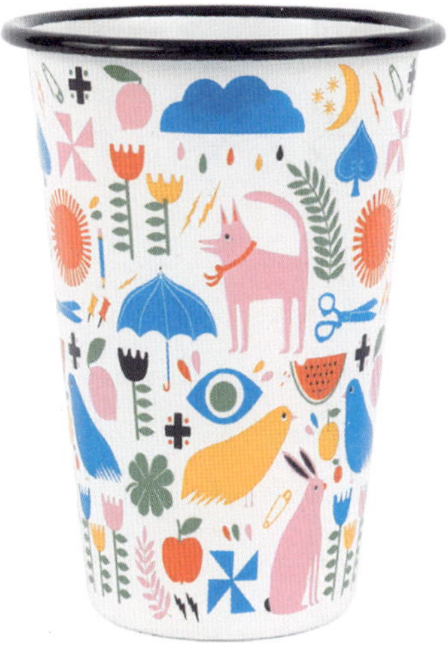

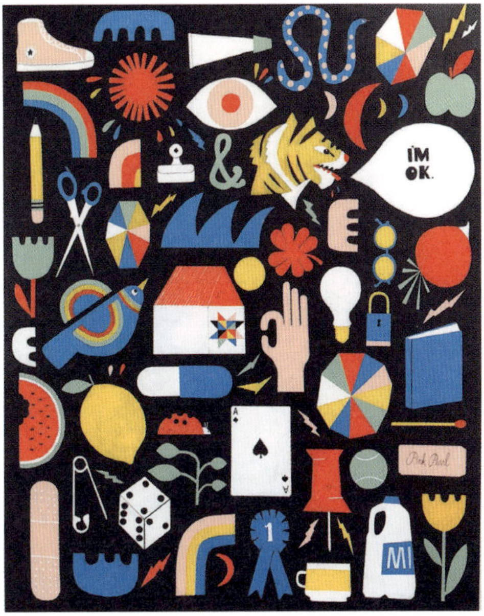
I'M OK.
MI

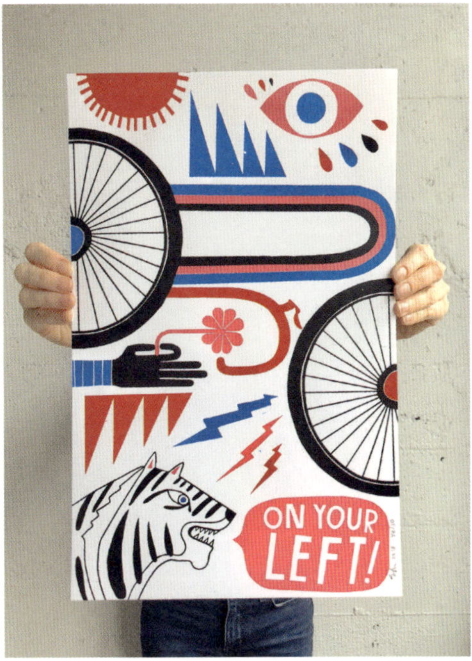
ON YOUR LEFT!

ROCKEFELLER CENTER

ROCKEFELLER CENTER

@ROCKEFELLERCENTER
@ARTPRODUCTIONFUND
@LISACONGDON

"My ideas are the result of curiosity and observation. I always look for the interesting angle of a building, the unusual color of a flower, or the strange typeface of an old poster. Starting from there, I develop my visual vocabulary, which always expands, transforms and changes according to new things that inspire me."

"I believe we're all born with unlimited creative potential. Creativity is based on our ability to be open to new ideas, to find new patterns, to establish connections between the literal and the figurative, to see potential and to come up with solutions to problems. Creativity requires thought and imagination, but it also requires doing: bringing ideas to life. Creating requires action: writing, composing, drawing, sculpting, programing, etc.

My favorite artist of all time is Alexander Girard. I love the way he included traditional folklore motifs with modern colors and daring geometric patterns. I'm heavily influenced by mid-twentieth century design and illustration, Scandinavian design (particularly Marimekko and Josef Frank) and traditional folk symbols and patterns. I love to draw icons and distill objects, animals and flora into their most basic forms.

I love to travel. Traveling the world is my favorite hobby. When I visit a different country, I look for flea markets where I can buy as many old small things as I can for my collections. And I love to go to bookstores, design stores, record shops and antique shops, to see architecture and visit museums. Every time I travel, I get new ideas and inspiration from everything around me."

EVERY MISTAKE IS PROGRESS

"I take a notebook with me everywhere. I write down ideas whenever they occur to me. If I don't have my notebook with me, I write down my ideas on my phone. Sometimes I use a technique called 'mental map'. I start with a word or an idea and then build on it with other ideas that arise from it. It's a useful technique to explore an idea in depth. I also make lists of things that interest me and keep a visual 'bulletin board' of color palettes, vintage images and new subjects.

When I have a creative block, I'm usually tired and exhausted. I try, as much as possible, to step away from what I'm working on for as long as I can. That helps me a lot. I think when you try to force ideas, the effect is usually the opposite, that is, you get more irritated and stressed. On the other hand, when I let myself relax, or go for a long bike ride or simply stop working or drawing, I get my best ideas. Creativity requires a certain amount of space, time and fun. I always try to remember this.

Lately, I promised myself I would play more. Play is very important. Not only when I'm traveling but also in my daily work. Sometimes this means I devote an hour to playing in my sketchbook with thick colored pencils. Sometimes I listen to my favorite music while working with a client. Sometimes I stop working early and go to the library to look at books. In the United States, we're bound to our work ethic and the idea of productivity, and we've lost contact with the notion of play. I can see the damage this has done to me. And I work ceaselessly to ensure my work place is more playful for my employees and me. I want to have fun. Without joy, what's the point?

I'm known to say that 'every mistake is a step forward'. This is because I think that every time you put your foot in your mouth in your life or in your work you grow. Mistakes are gifts. They teach us things such as 'don't do that again', and emotional things such as to be nicer, more gentle and tender and present in the future. All human beings make mistakes. When you forgive yourself and you use the experience to learn and grow instead of staying bogged down in self-loathing and negativity, you're much less likely to make the same mistake twice."

110
U.S.A.
INK
Union
PENCIL
EBERHARD FABER
SAND & PENCIL ERASER
ink
pencil
Pedigree®
by EMPIRE
MADE IN U.S.A.
310
INK
Union
PENCIL
5¢
EBERHARD FABER-USA
"EFFACINE" Nº280
TUKZAR®
TZ-09
110
U.S.A.
INK
Union
PENCIL
EBERHARD FABER
SAND & PENCIL ERASER
ink
pencil
TUKZAR®
TZ-08
LiveLine®
FOR PENCIL INK
BALL PEN
Doppel Läufer
UNIVERSAL-440

SENNELIER
SENNELIER
Artist's Paintstik
SENNELIER
SENNELIER

HEAD
ABOVE
WATER

GO FOR IT.

"To be a good illustrator, you have to find your point of view and your individual style, and create a lot of work that reflects your perspective and style. I also think it's important to love solving problems. To be a professional illustrator, you need to make conceptual connections between the product or the story you're illustrating and the intended audience. Also, it's important to want to collaborate. Illustration is not an individual endeavor. It's really important to collaborate with clients and art directors and to accept their suggestions. Of course, you have to have a deep sense of style, but you also have to be able to leave your ego at the door. You need to be open to suggestions, to changes in direction and to taking the time to do the best job possible.

And finally you need to stay connected to the joy of creating art. Make your work fun and entertaining. If you don't enjoy it, it's going to be a miserable experience."

Fanny Dreyer

Photography: Claire Vandamme

"My images exist somewhere between realism and innocence. I work with mixed media ranging from ink markers to pencils, acrylics or diluted ink and, occasionally, risographic printing. I don't have a single graphic style. Instead I offer a multi-faceted universe where landscapes, folklore and children are uniquely important.

My universe is far removed from digital and commercial drawing. It's the world of traditional drawing on paper with my preferred tools. Narrative is very important. I like to feel the sensation of the tools on the medium, the spreading ink, accidents and the clumsiness of my hands.

I work digitally if the print method requires it (silk screen, risograph, direct ink), but I always start with a drawing on paper which is later reworked using Photoshop, to separate the colors, for example.

When I draw, I don't think about my audience very much. I draw for myself. I try to come as close as possible to what I want to say. If it seems coherent and important to me, I tell myself that other people might like it. If I created images thinking about what might attract others, I'd have few readers who think I know what they like. I try to be true to myself, as much as possible.

Recently, I published a very personal children's book, *La colonie de vacances (Summer Camp)*, with Albin Michel Jeunesse. The book tells the story of a week at summer camp through the eyes of five children of different ages and dispositions. From the preparations to the anxiety of the bus trip; from the first encounters to the joys of communal life, the book explores the road to autonomy and personal fulfillment, as well as children's ability to recreate a balance outside of the family structure.

I've also worked for the web series *Mon petit Oeil,* of the Centre Pompidou and Mille formes Clermont Ferrand, drawing and animating three short videos for children between the ages of three and five, *Les petites suites..* Each video depicts a little world about the four seasons, the four elements and the five senses.

Recently, I had the opportunity to illustrate a Christmas scene at the top of the Parisian department stores BHV. My illustrations, which depict winter in the mountains, appeared on the buildings, bags and their gift wrapping paper. It was a very gratifying assignment.

In addition to my published work, I like to experiment with other media, transplanting my images onto wood to make small sculptures, sewing my shapes to make blankets and embroidering my images on fabric. I like to step away from the book form and explore a wider universe related to my craft."

1

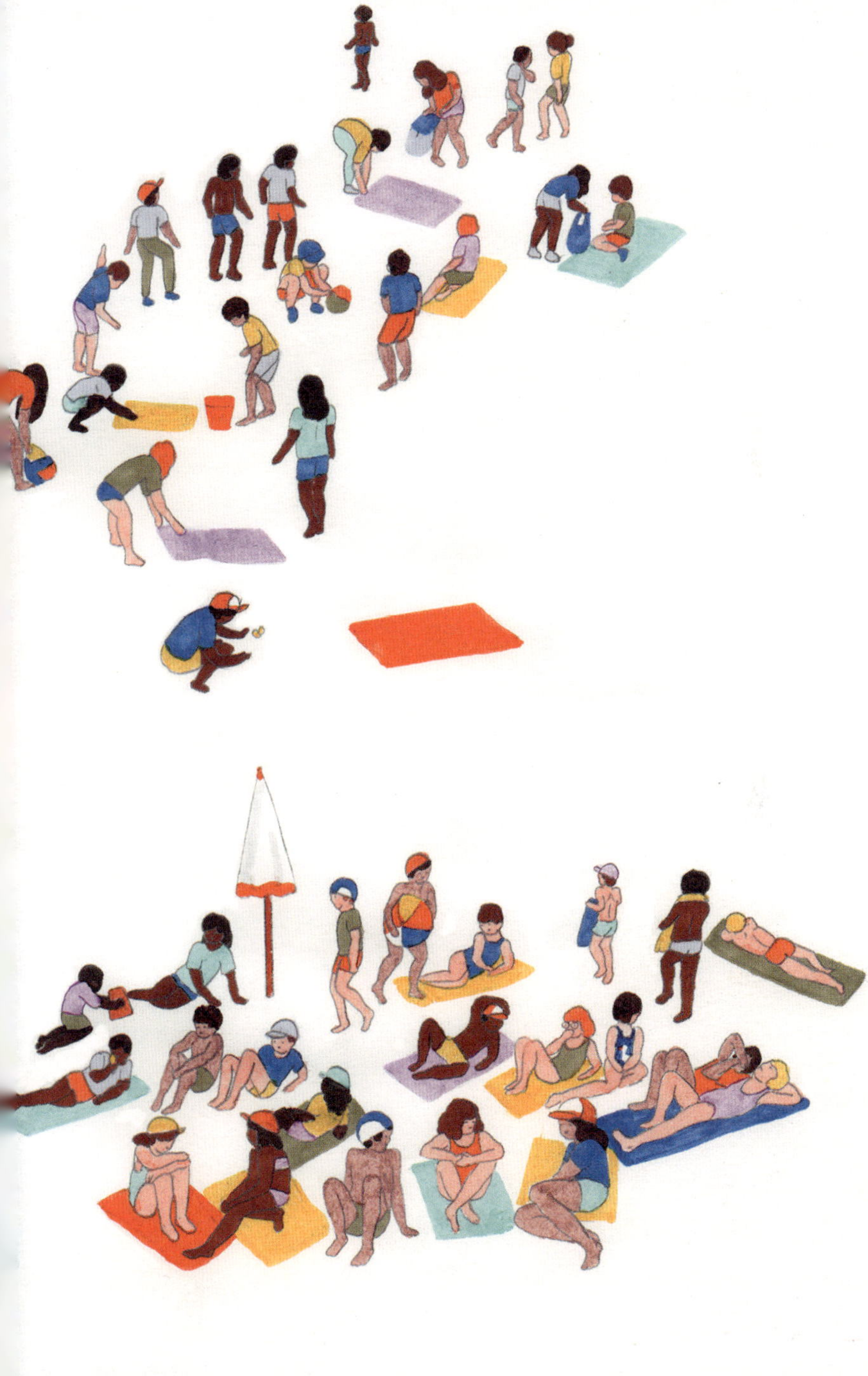

1

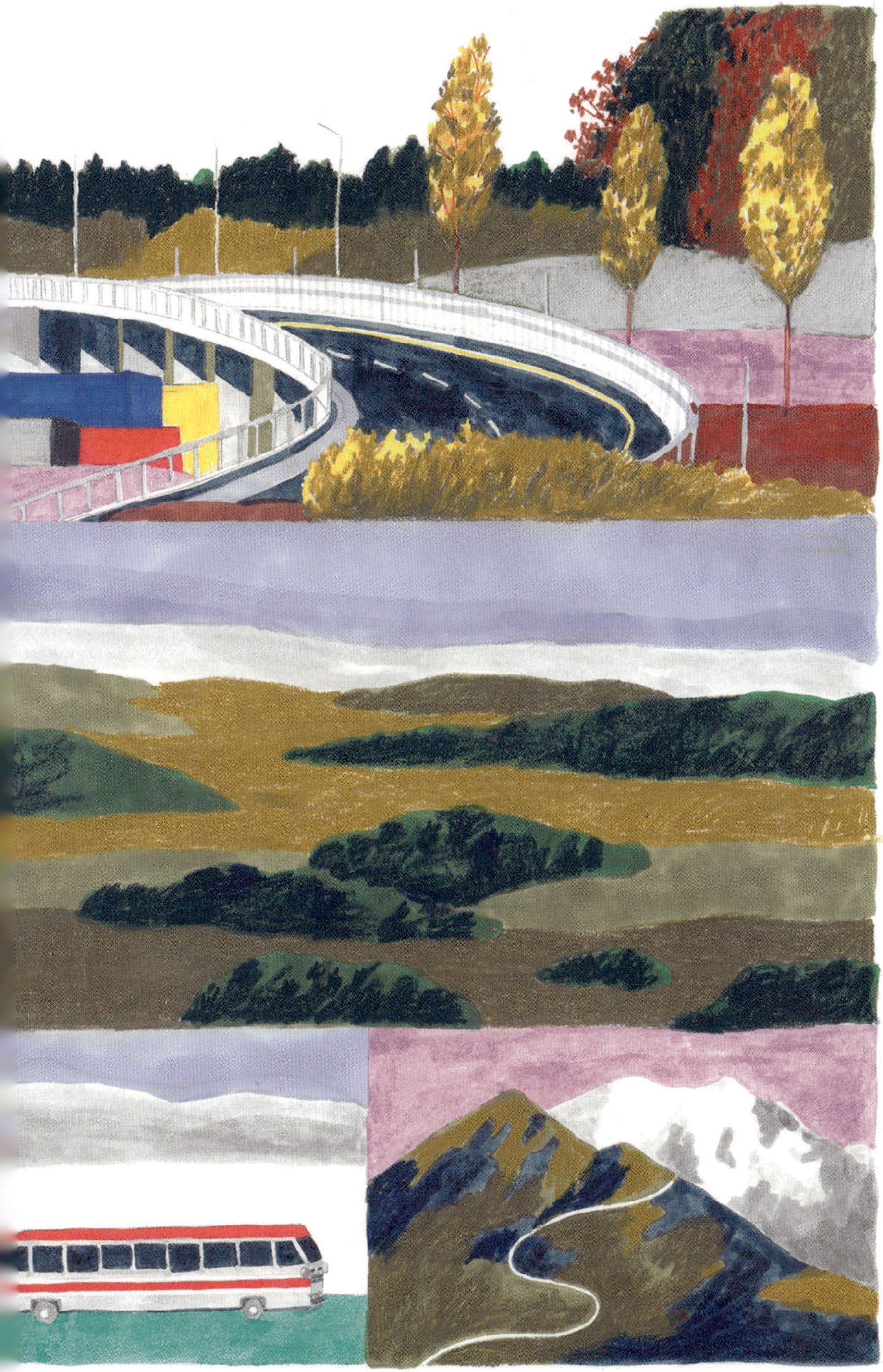

1. *La Colonie de vacances (Summer Camp)*, Édition Albin Michel.

"What is the secret to being a good illustrator? I've never asked myself that question. In my case it's a matter of being very curious, of being a sponge that soaks up the world, and of making connections between what I see and feel, digesting them and then transposing them in the form of images and stories."

"The landscapes of my childhood are a great source of inspiration. Nature in general, folklore, children, dance, textile arts, ceramics. It's difficult to list them all.

I have in mind or write down things that interest me. I keep collections of images, photos, pictures and books that inspire me. I allow ideas to jell. Often I have creative obsessions that translate into the desire to draw something specific. If this desire doesn't wane over time, I stick to it and gradually develop a project.

For my book *La colonie de vacances,* I was inspired by photos of my father as a camp instructor in Switzerland in the 70s. I often consult the family archives.

When I get stuck, I return to the basics, that is, to the pleasure of taking a photograph, regardless of the subject, technique or purpose. For a moment, I stop the project that's blocking me and step to the side and create purely for pleasure. Often after this small diversion, I return to my project in a more serene state of mind.

Playing is above all a source of inspiration. I love to draw characters in motion. I like the choreography of bodies at play. In general, when the work becomes tedious, I remember that drawing is a form of play, between myself and the medium, between the book I create and my readers, or between my hand and the image being drawn. Accidents have their place, the same as mistakes.

I don't know if I'm a good illustrator. But I try to be as honest and fair with myself as possible. If my images speak to people, it's a success!"

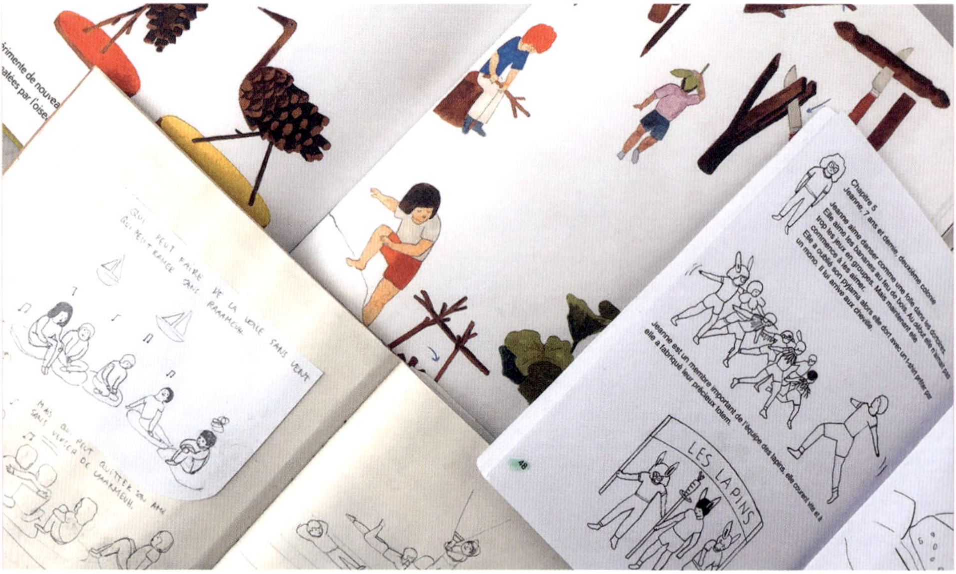
LES LAPINS
48

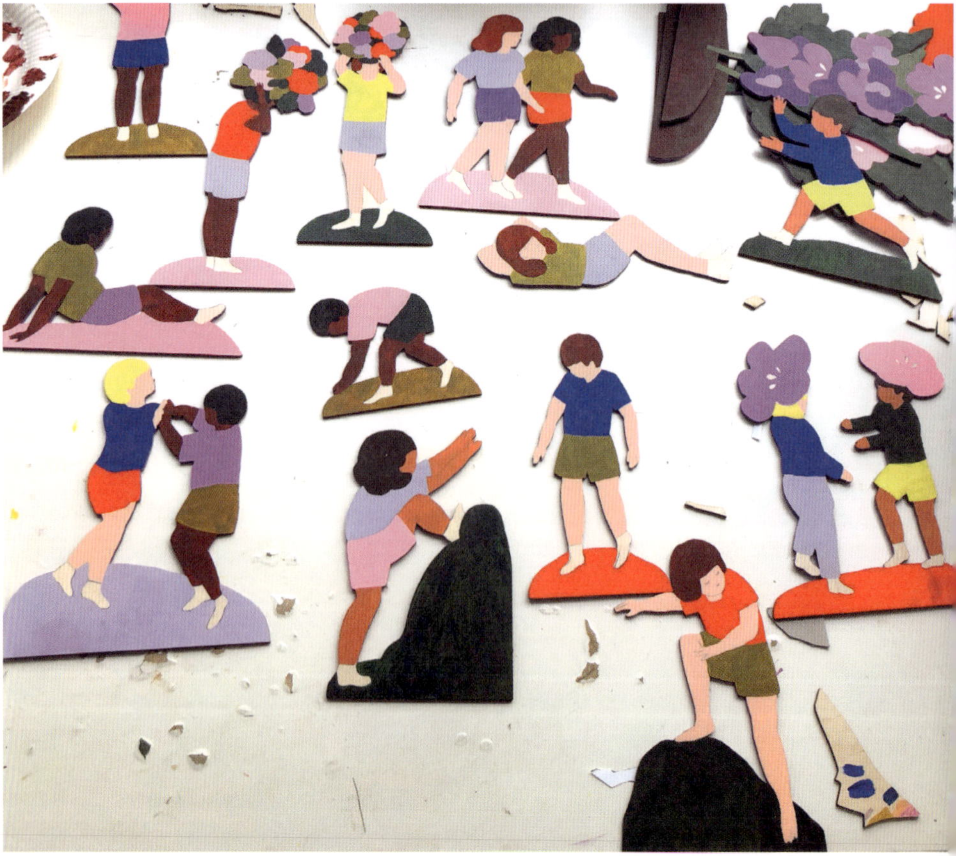

Photography: Claire Vandamme

Delphine Durand

"I've published around forty children's books in France and abroad. Although I live in France, I first published many children's books in the United States and England (Random House, Penguin Books, Walker Books) because I used to have an English agent when I started out. These books have been translated in many countries. In France, my main publishers are Nathan, Actes Sud, Éditions du Rouergue, Hélium, Milan and Les Fourmis Rouges.

If I had to mention only one of my books, as an author-illustrator it would be *My House* (Éditions du Rouergue, 2000), which was also my thesis project in art school a few years earlier. It was a milestone for me. It was like the foundation of a universe, which I've continued to expand on ever since. This book, which I didn't think would be published at the time, has become a kind of 'cult' book over the years. I'm still quite proud of it even though it's now more than 20 years old.

A few years ago, I decided to create a kind of *spin-off* with the trilogy *Les Mous*, *Gouniche* and *Ratapoil*, dedicating an entire sixty-four-page book to each of the iconic characters in *My House*. *Les Mous* was translated into English by Enchanted Lion Books (*The Flops*) in 2019.

My second book as an author (*Bob et Compagnie*, Editions du Rouergue, 2005 / *Bob & Co*, Tate Publishing, 2006) is diametrically opposed to the first. It's small, very white, as simple in appearance as the first was dense and brimming with information: a kind of genesis, it deals with the creation of the world (and at the same time it's a nod to the creation of a book). Things slowly fall into place. Some arrive late; everyone is a bit lost. It's a bit like a play, a dialog from beginning to end.

This book grew out of a small text. I wrote it in one day, in a single sitting, in a notebook while reflecting on the act of creation. The previous book (*My House*), on the other hand, arose out of my drawings, from my notebooks filled with characters."

2 fois par mois

astrapi

OSE ÊTRE TOI !

Des idées, des conseils pour être bien dans tes baskets !

SALUT

"I think the first challenge for me was to make a decent living from my passion. It's an opportunity (and a lot of work) to be able to do this.

After checking off this first box (and although the future is unpredictable), the second challenge is perhaps, for illustrators who are given assignments and earn a living from this profession, to make sure you don't stop enjoying the work. You need to keep your original passion and aspirations alive, to be alert to avoid being hypnotized by or locking yourself into systems (type of assignment, successful series, etc.) that work, at the risk of sacrificing creativity along the way.

My first choice was freedom, and to exercise it as much as possible. I didn't want to have a 'normal' (salaried) job on the side, and I didn't foresee help coming from anywhere either. Financially I had a limited amount of time to see if this was possible. I don't know if that's a good thing or not. But I think this is what led me to explore different paths at the beginning, alongside publishing. In a different situation, I probably would have spent most of my time in a tree house painting and writing stories.

These two poles of freedom/security are always present. When you choose one, you have to work for the other. For me, it can be complex to combine assignments (however beautiful they may be) with personal work, an endless surfing, a balance that has to be achieved over time."

HA HA HA HA

BOU!

"The first thing that occurs to me when I think about the notion of creativity is childhood. Creativity as something natural but also as a necessity, an active process to try and make sense of the world.

Also a need to distance oneself from things, from what surrounds us, a way of 'stepping to the side' to observe things from a different angle. I also associate creativity with a kind of solitude, being able to isolate yourself from the rest of the world. And also freedom. Limitless freedom. A place where everything is possible. I imagine it as a kind of refuge, an invisible hiding place. It's its own world that you can visit when you want to, with its own space-time and that can't be threatened by anything or anyone. A form of protection then? Or a superpower? Once again, we're back to childhood.

I remember when I was a teenager, I thought drawing was the only thing they couldn't take away from me. I wasn't in a particularly dramatic situation but, still, I felt this very strongly. A bit like a talisman. However, at the time I had no idea that one day I could earn a living from it."

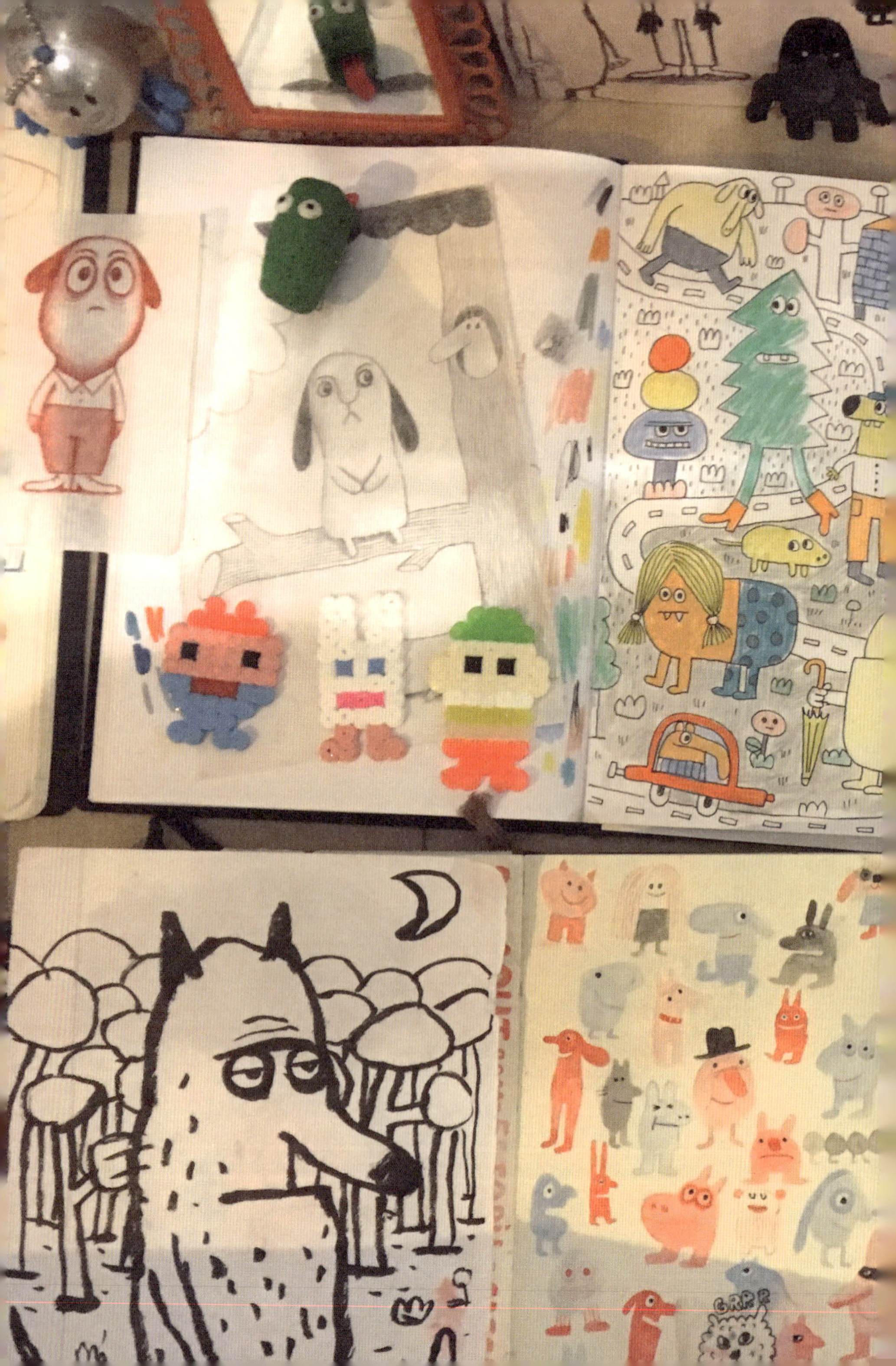
GRRR

DELPHINE DURAND asso-articho.blogspot.com

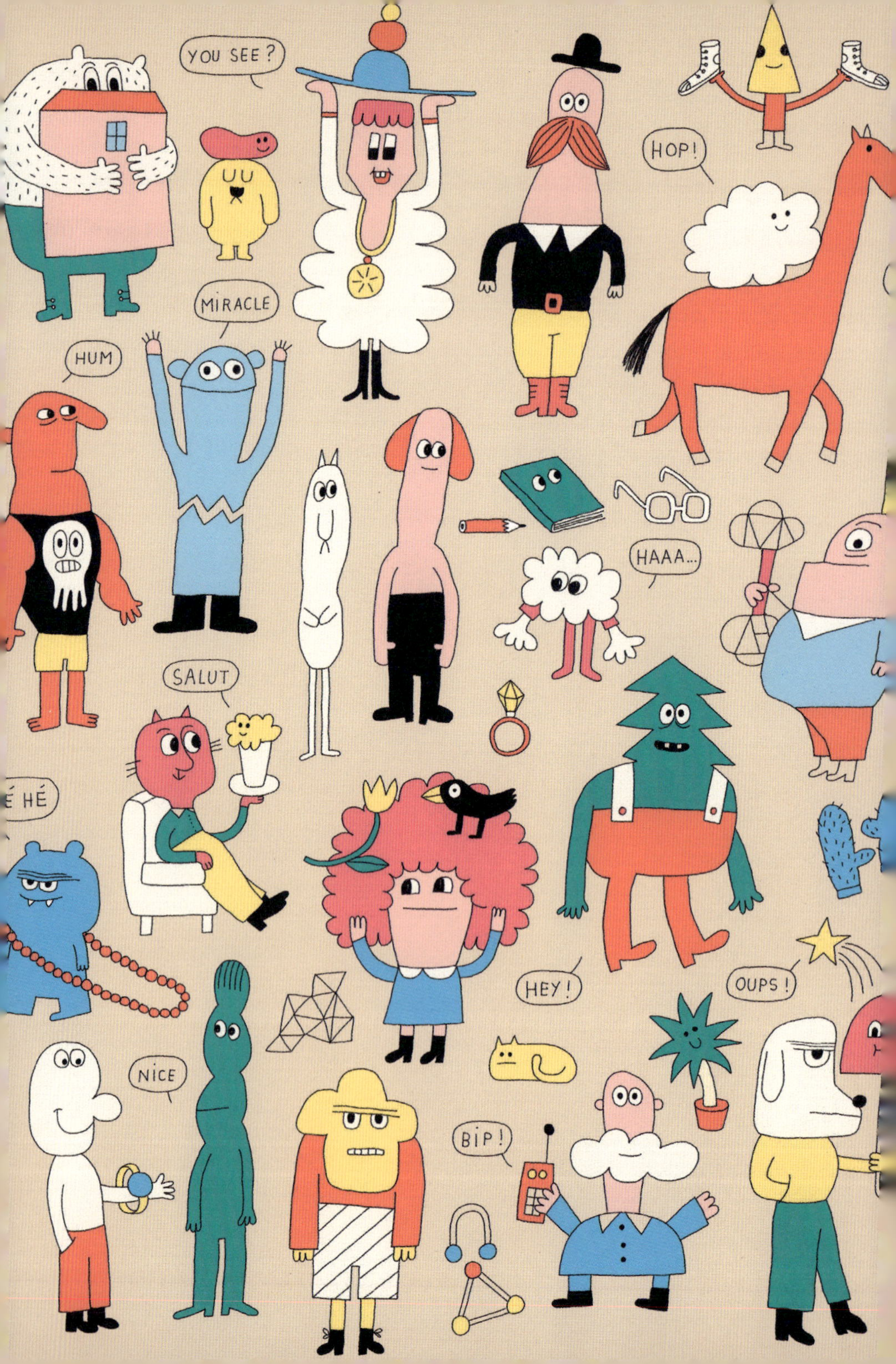
YOU SEE?
HOP!
MIRACLE
HUM
HAAA...
SALUT
É HÉ
HEY!
OUPS!
NICE
BIP!

"Maybe ideas stem from a problem with the switch... An unexpected collision of two particles, a connection that shouldn't have taken place, dust in the gears?

In my opinion, they exist in a place somewhere off the beaten track, on the side of the road, sometimes when we think we're going down the wrong road, or when we're forced to pause for a minute.

They can hide inside surprises, in astonishment, in laughter, but also in anger and exasperation. Sometimes they're in the little things of everyday life. Ideas are playful little elves. They're easy to see but hard to catch.

I don't think having ideas is the hard part. The challenge is to recognize them, to pay attention to them. Having a little notebook, taking notes.

I do it often but I also forget to a lot. For me, ideas come through words or drawing. Words are like interior monologues (or dialogs) when the brain can allow itself to wander, let itself be carried away by a situation. I often write in my head, in transitional moments such as taking a shower or when walking.

The ideas that emerge through drawing are also times to let go, like when I draw liberally in my notebook, often while traveling or when I'm sitting in a cafe...

In the first phase of work on a project, I try not to think about it. I try to avoid pressure, expectations (my own and presumably those of others). I try to slip away from my consciousness a bit to find spontaneity, a freedom similar to that of a child at play. Again, it's more a matter of removing obstacles than searching for something.

This first phase of drawing is crucial because it will remain the essence, the foundation. It contains the energy, establishes the tone.

Isolating yourself from routine, from daily life, establishing physical distance is also a good breeding ground for ideas. When I travel, I always take a notebook with me.

And of course reading, going to an exhibition, seeing a movie or a show, talking with friends, with my son, seeing a documentary about a subject I don't know anything about also generate ideas".

Fig.923 a : Vue en coupe d'une Résidence de Mous

ET PUIS IL A PLEIN D'AUTRES AMIS

"The idea of play has a key role in my work. Creating a book, a story, inventing characters, having them experience situations involves play, of course. At first. Especially for stories where humor is essential. I also enjoy the technical aspect of these books, using different tools, changing the narrative style, etc. (because they're projects that lend themselves to this).

When I was studying illustration, one time they asked us to bring our childhood drawings in to look at together and talk about with the rest of the class. I was lucky to have a grandmother who saved many of mine. She used to cover her bedroom walls with them.

Suddenly, paying attention to them, sharing them with others was a very powerful experience. It represented a reconnection between my young-adult-student self and my child self, a valuable ingredient that complemented (or completed) what I was trying to learn or un-learn at the same time.

I think that was the moment when I began consciously to search for what I mentioned before, to find that childhood state when you play, when you invent stories, when you draw. To put at the center that freedom that already existed, instead of using it. To change our perspective of what we believe to be defects, clumsiness, and instead, focus on their special details, on what's good in them. And to be like a compass when I lose my way.

The notion of mistakes, of clumsiness, of accidents in drawing is also sometimes synonymous with pleasant surprises, new discoveries, and this can lead to new perspectives. I like research, experimenting, accidents that lead us to another way of doing things that we hadn't thought of before."

Isidro Ferrer

To be something

"I don't how to define myself. Sometimes I'm an illustrator of concepts and at other times I'm an illustrator of emotions. I know that ideas, concepts lend stature to illustration, make it shine. But I also know that emotion gives it a pulse, gives it flesh and blood.

Light or shadow, idea or emotion, that's the biggest quandary I face every day. To act in a cerebral way or to act compulsively. To be disciplined and organized or to trust my gut, to be spontaneous and uncontrolled. A perpetual duel of opposites draws me from one side of the scale to the other. Sometimes I want to be a cerebral and functional illustrator and other times just the opposite, emotional and visceral.

It's a ridiculous dilemma. Because it's just as true that ideas are linked to emotions as it is that emotions nurture ideas. Still, I make it a point to contradict myself. To live in a state of permanent discontent. To always want to be the opposite.

In my case, to illustrate is to entertain the fantasy of being someone I'm not."

1

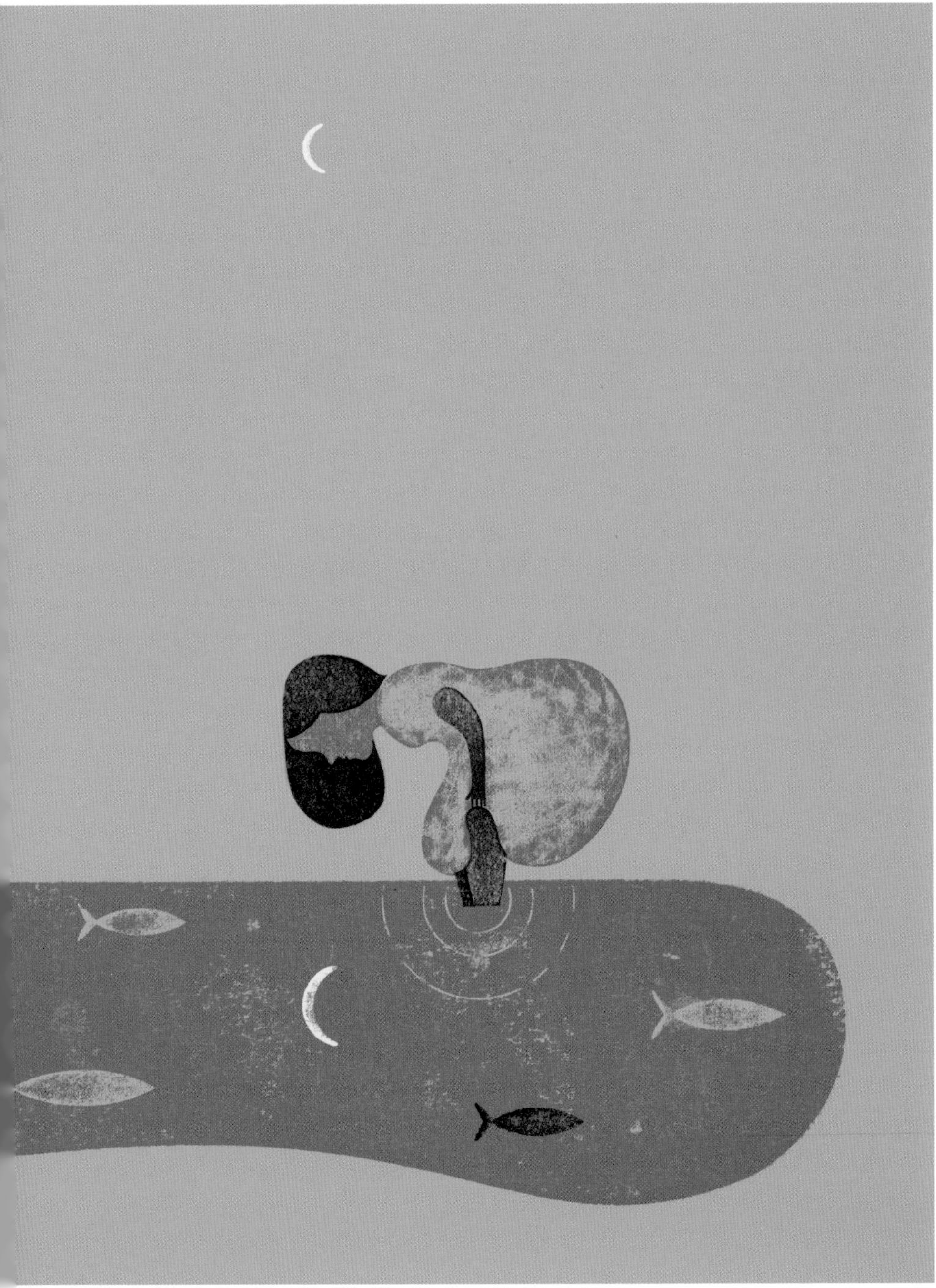

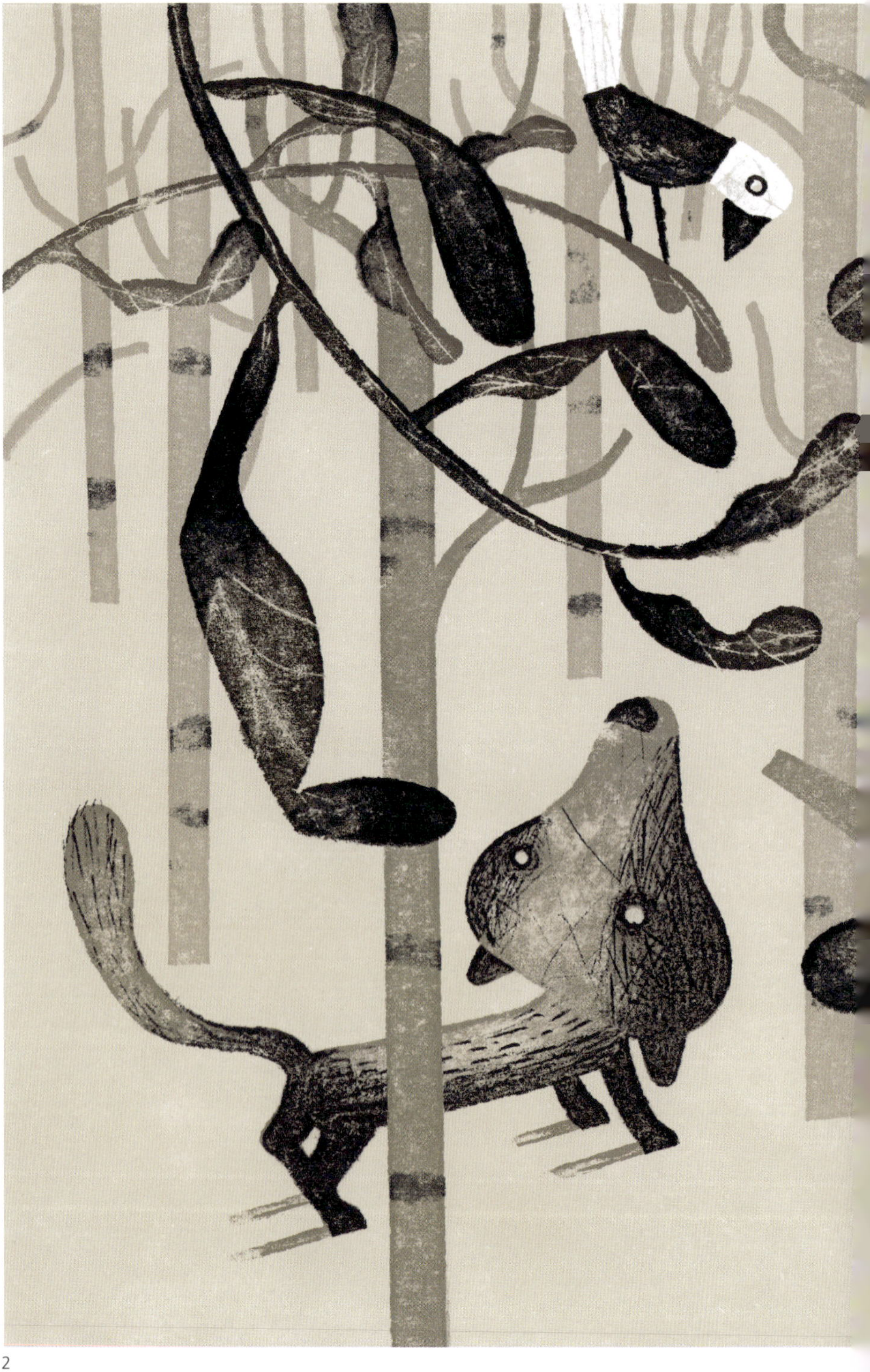

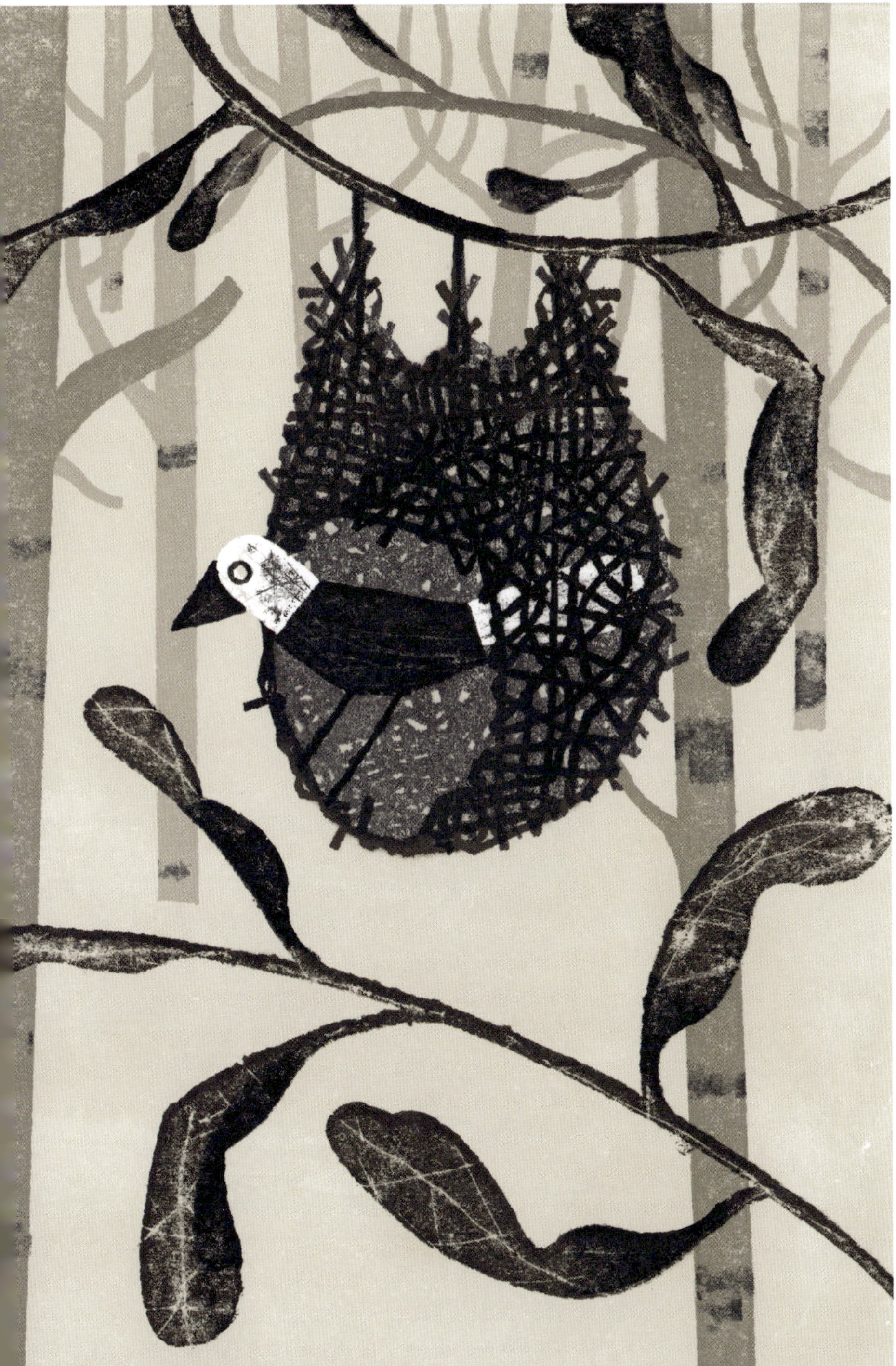

3

1. *Nocturno*. Text by Rafael Alberti, Graphic Communication Workshop and The National Council for Culture and Arts (Conaculta), Mexico City, 2012.
2. *Kipling illustrated*, Kalandraka, 2020.
3. *La casa que nos habita*, La Compañía Ilustrada, Provincial Council of Huesca, 2021.
4. Calendar for Imprenta Moisés, Barbastro, 2018.

Being a child

"In 1930, María de Maeztu invited José de Bergamín to give a lecture at the Residence for Young Women in Madrid. Bergamín accepted the invitation. Yet he warned the director of the residence in advance about the content of his talk. He was sure his ideas would be misunderstood, as they were, and his words were branded as scandalous, arbitrary and mistaken.

In this lecture, entitled *The Decline of Illiteracy*, Bergamín shared some of his ideas on creation, contrasting academic, literate values with the spontaneous illiterate values characteristic of popular culture and children.

It should be noted that for Bergamín, illiteracy did not represent ignorance but rather the essence of the word outside of the alphabetic system. When poetry is 'literaturized', it interrupts the creative flow and sterilizes thought. This literal culture, the alphabetic culture that is at the service of the letter, of letters, is set against another spiritual culture: that of thought, of the imagination, of the word.

The word versus the letter.

For José Bergamín 'all children, as long as they are children, are illiterate. A child cannot begin to learn the letters of the alphabet, he cannot begin to learn to read and write until he begins to possess what is rightly called the use of reason: a use of reason that when the child becomes, if he does become, a literate man, a man of letters, will most certainly be abused. The use and abuse of reason is, in short, its rational use, practical reason. Because it is not that the child does not possess reason before using it, before knowing what it is going to do for him or for what he is going to use it practically – you cannot use what you do not have –; it is that he has an intact reason, spiritually immaculate, a pure reason; that is, an illiterate reason. And this is the child's bliss. It is not that he is incapable of knowing the world. Rather he knows it purely, in an exclusive spiritual way, not yet literal or literate or literaturized. The child's reason is a purely spiritual reason: poetic.'

And what does the child do with his reason, if he doesn't use it, if he doesn't engage it? What does he do? What he does with everything of course: play. He plays.

For a child, as long he remains a child, thinking is a state of play. And the state of play is always, in the child, a state of grace. When I illustrate, through play I search for that state of grace typical of children. This is one of my ambitions: to be a child at least for a little while."

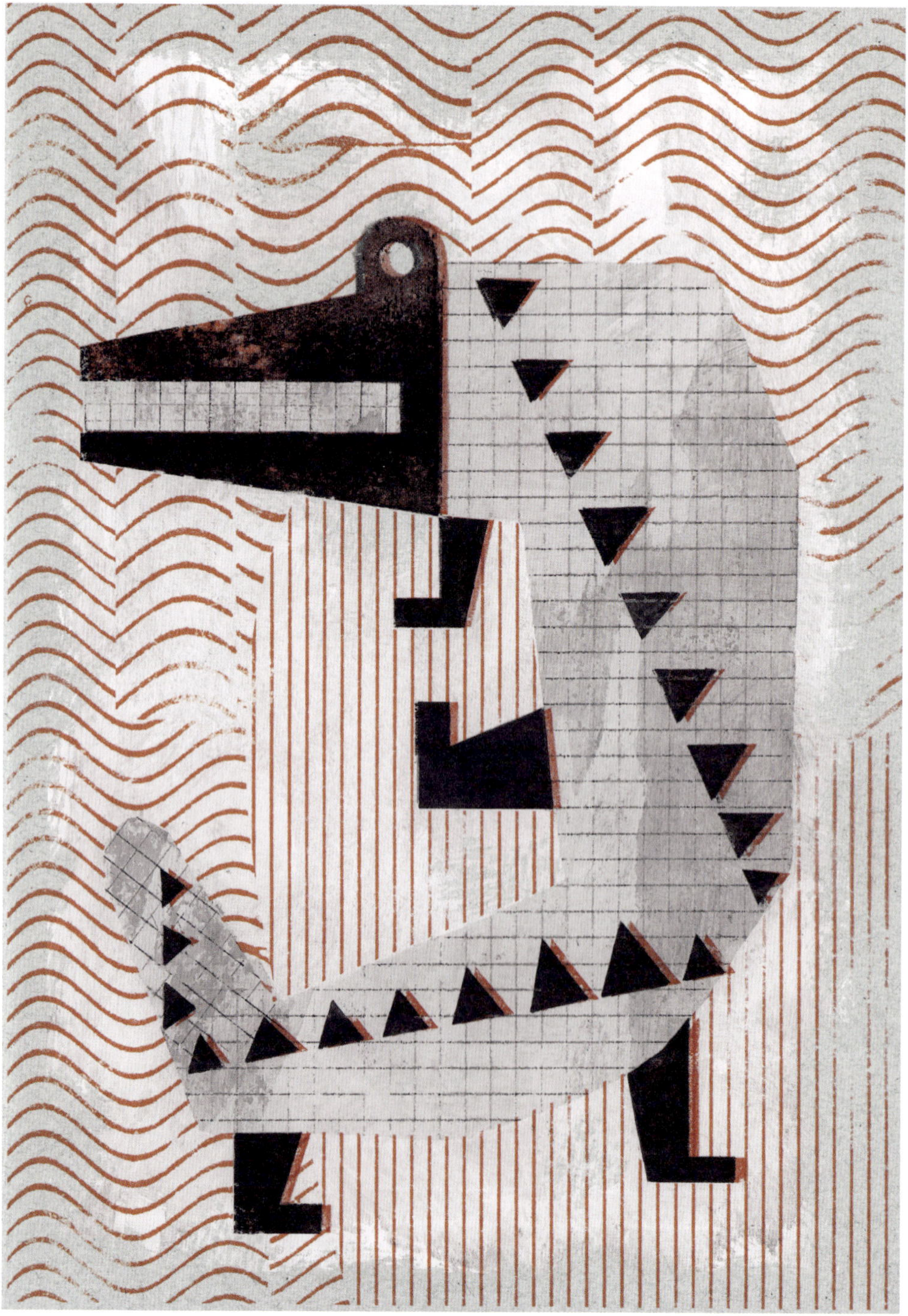

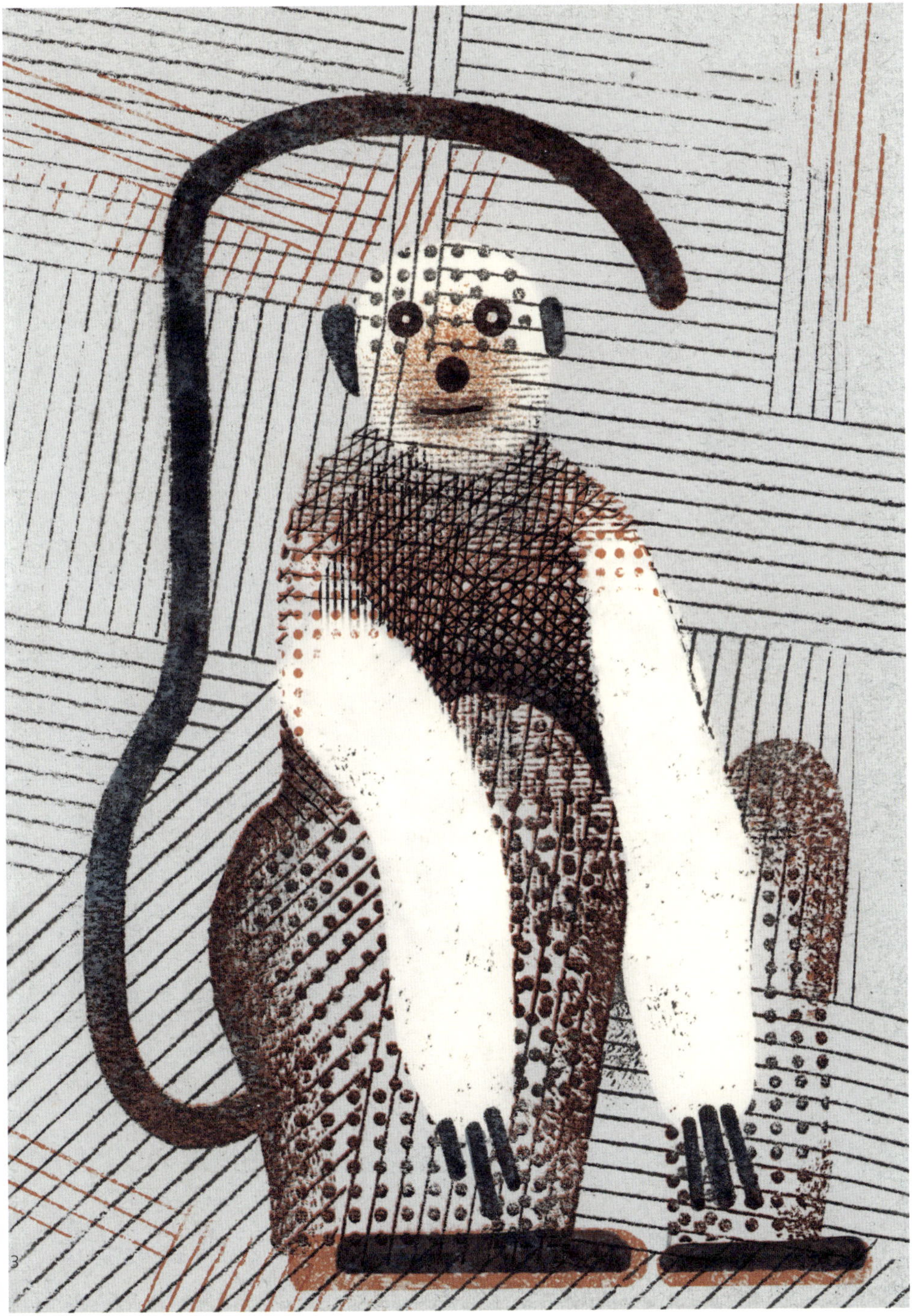

3

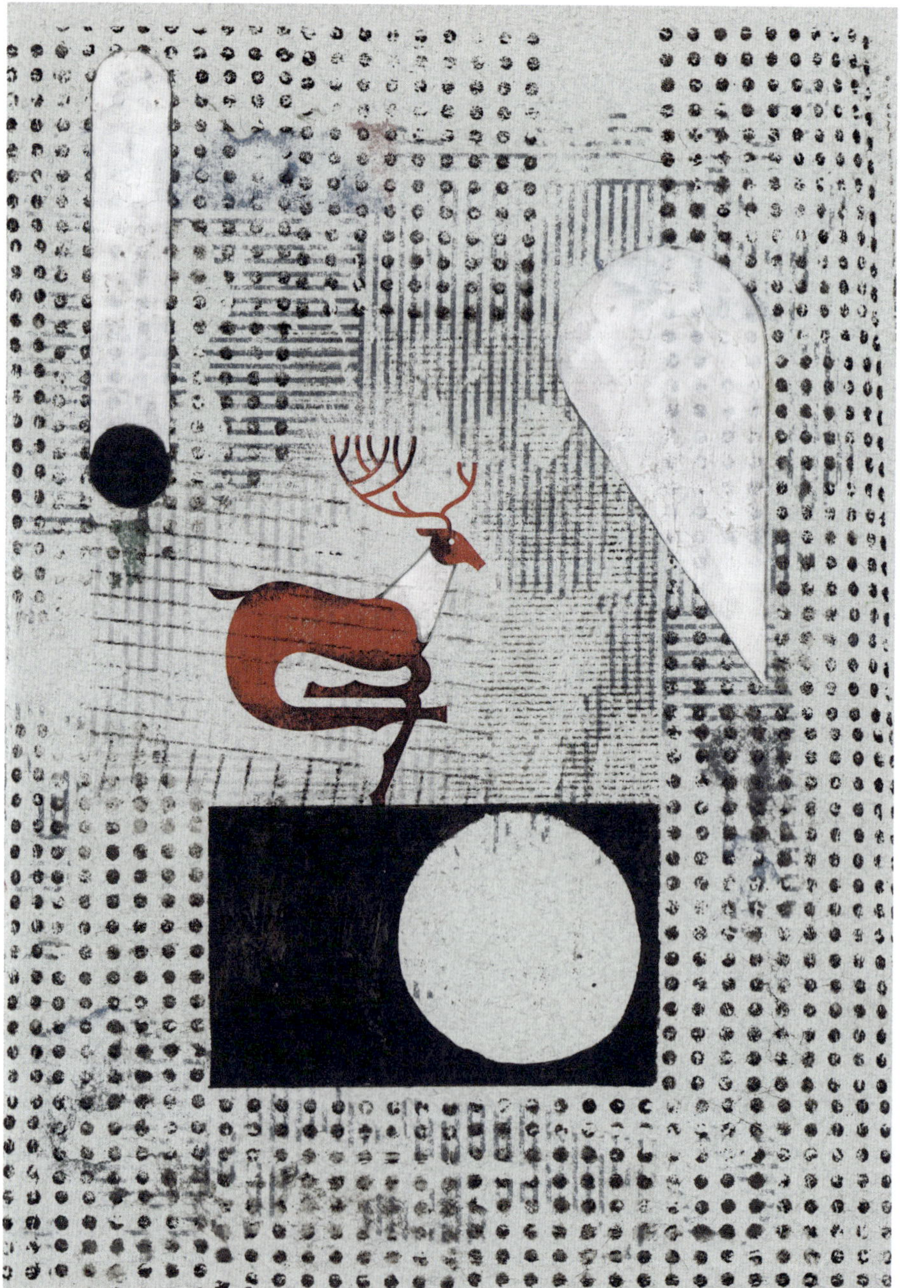

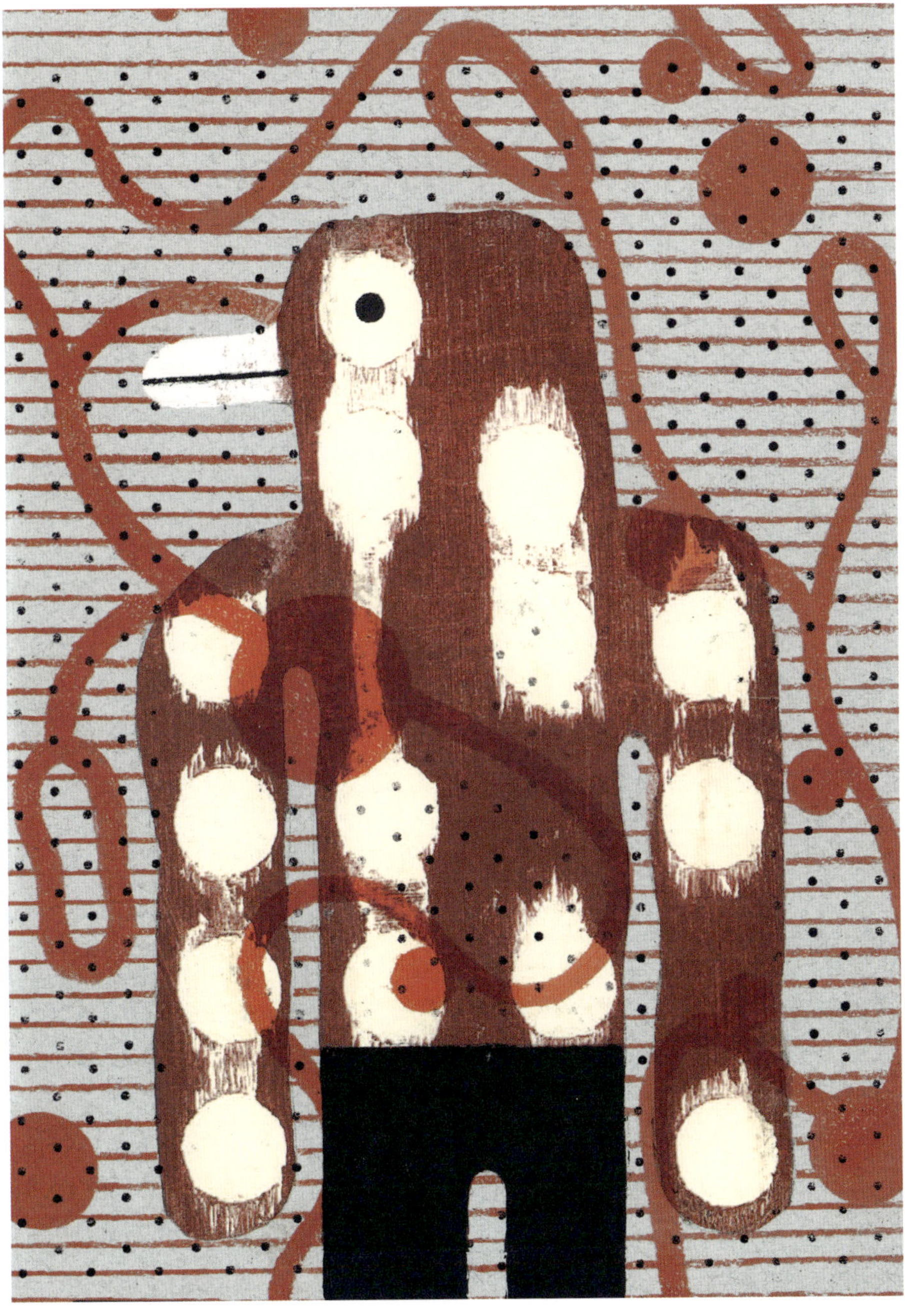

Guridi

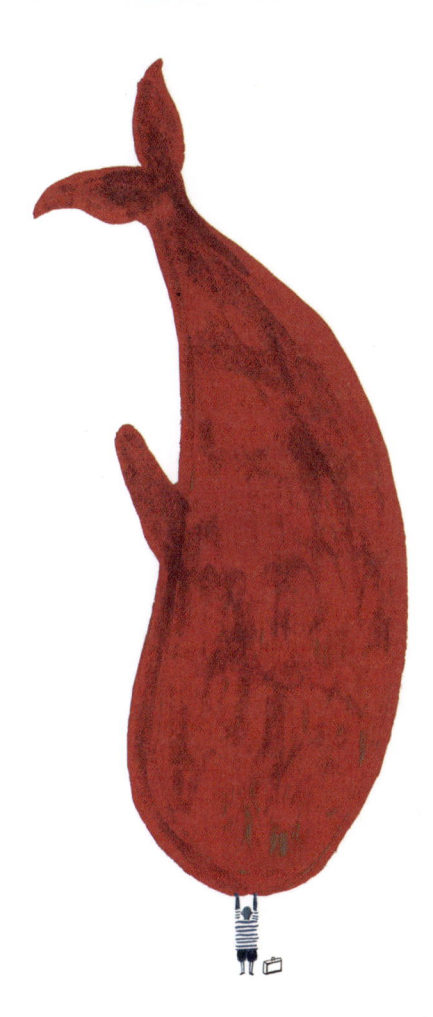

"As the son of a draftsman and a painter, I've always had a pencil in my hand. I majored in painting at the Seville College of Fine Arts. Since 1993, I have worked in nearly every area related to images, printing, graphic design and publishing, advertising and ephemeral architecture, in addition to teaching.

Since 2010, my artistic production has focused mainly on children's book illustration and posters for the theater and dance, as well as leading creativity and visual narrative workshops.

Some of my books, of which I am either the author or co-author, have been translated into 14 languages."

EL FARO

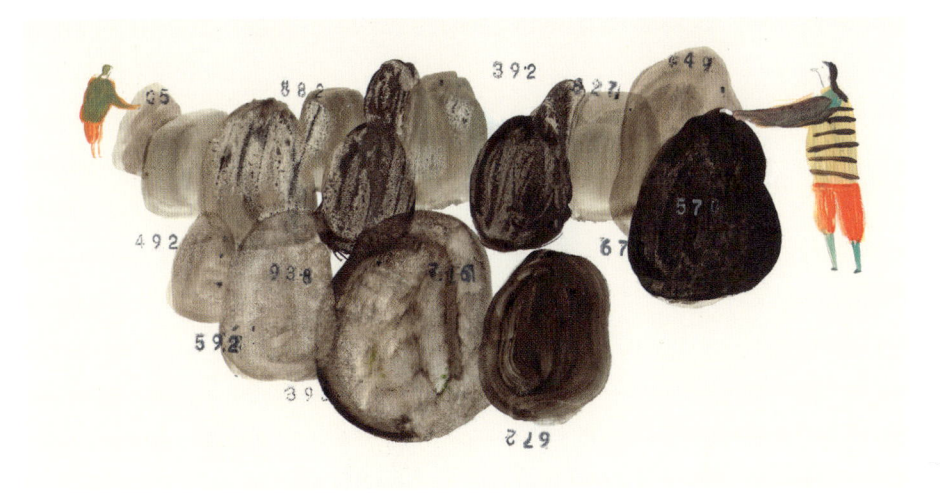

"Everything begins with a *click*, a state brimming with truth. I don't know how I get there. Maybe a strain of music, a look, a sentence, a sound... Without knowing it, I'm prepared. Then a multi-directional process blossoms filled with unexpected connections, an open map, changeable and adaptable where needed to anything. Everything always comes and goes, a tangled web filled with nonhierarchical possibilities.

You take note of everything, this and that, the logical and the absurd, and flood your mind, returning, every once and a while, to the original idea. In each and every one of these movements, you keep what interests you, in a winnowing out of the whole in which the essence of the original idea is never lost.

The narratives for my projects are created from a collection of objects, words, sounds, discarded fragments, personal experiences, people or things that affect me. Sometimes these connections lead to a discovery; other times they remain there, *on standby* in my notebook, biding their time.

The narrative starts to emerge from these discoveries, along with other things: opinions, exchanges of ideas, other people's vision... These elements are gradually filtered to the point where the basic framework of the project gets created.

It's important for the entire process to be on the table continuously, so that there isn't any timeline and to ensure that every part of the project can interact with one another. The process is, more than anything, a place filled with mistakes and getting it right, where you find yourself and lose yourself over and over again by chance, good luck and accident."

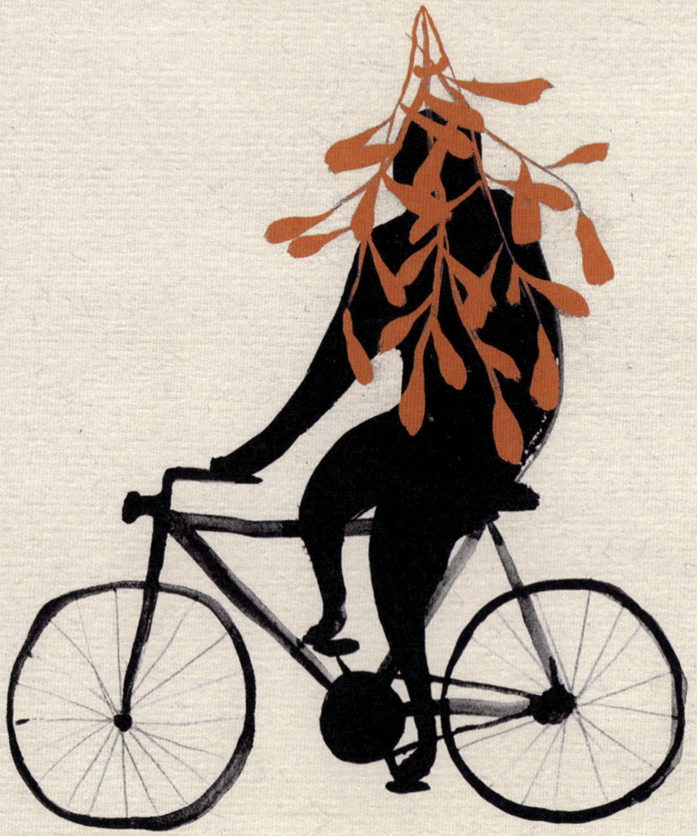

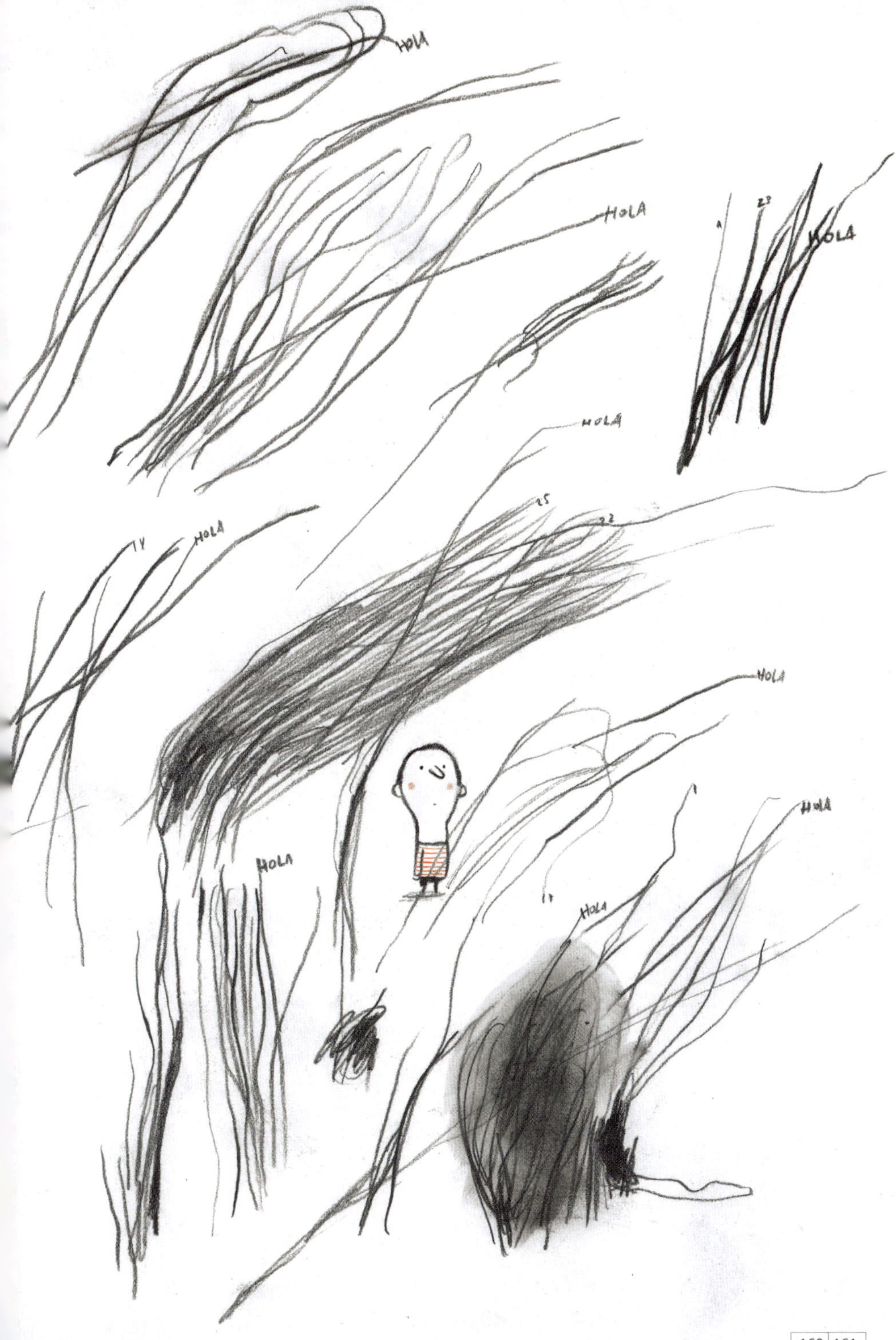
HOLA
HOLA
23
HOLA
HOLA
25
22
14
HOLA
HOLA
HOLA
1
HOLA
17
HOLA

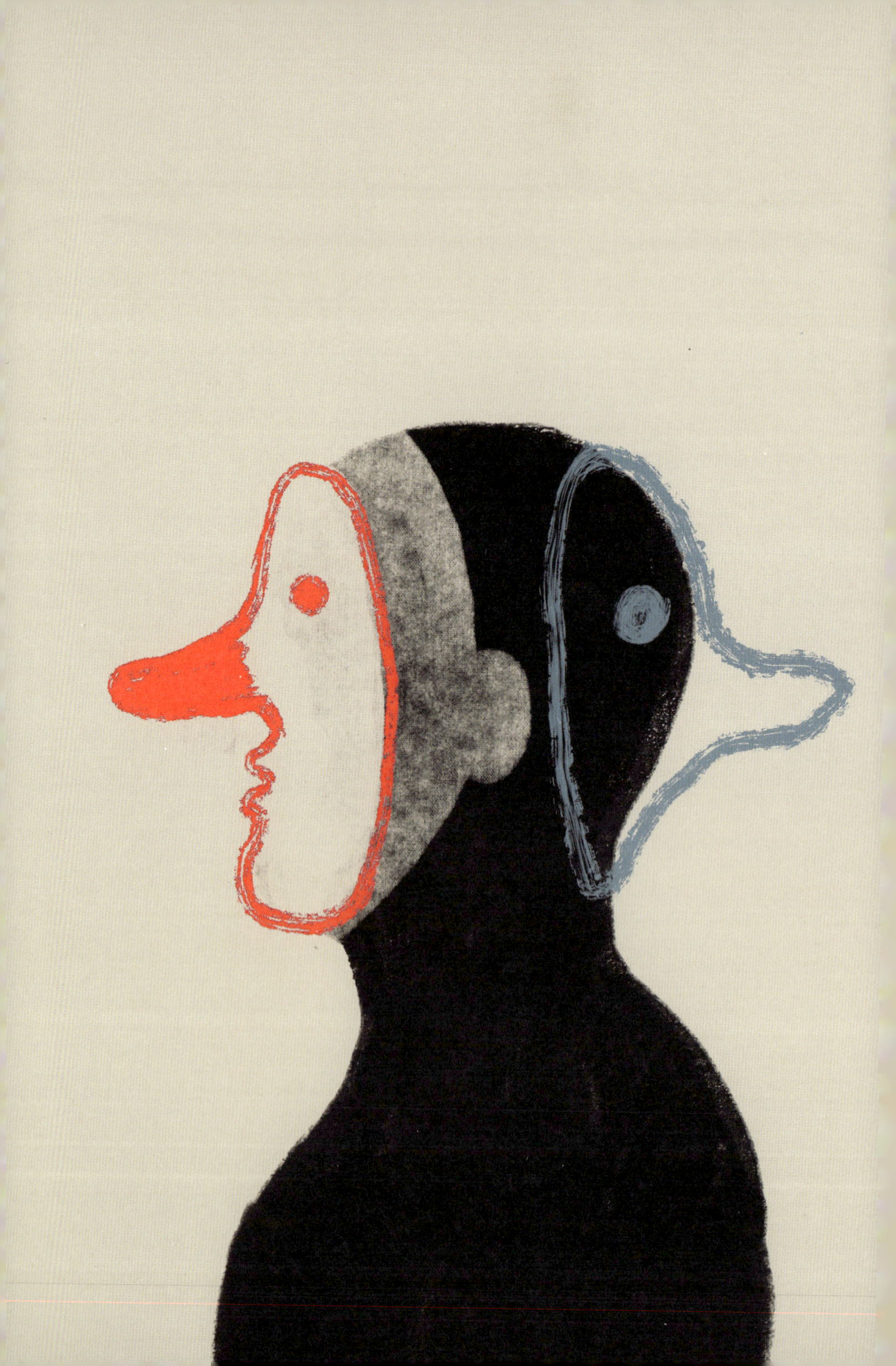

"I like to be honest with myself, to meticulously control the process knowing when to leave space for chance and when not to. I can't separate what I create from who I am."

"Graphic experimentation is conditioned at all times by what I'm trying to say, and the tools I use are my fears, my mistakes, my visual universe. It's a complex, non-linear approach to work in which improvisation, contradiction and challenges make up a structure that is endlessly ebbing and flowing, creating different paths. It allows me to address complicated aspects of reality and offer a solution through fiction and creating a dialog with the person who interacts with my work. In light of this, I like to play with reading alternatives, though with a foundation. Nothing should be left to chance.

My characters move in scenic spaces, where the placement, camera and angle are essential. I want to communicate what they feel, what they hear, what they breathe. For this reason, the space they inhabit is equally as important as the uninhabited space. Color plays a central role only occasionally.

I usually work on several projects simultaneously. As a result, the combinations can intermingle with each other as part of the whole. One project can serve as a catalyst for another. This enables me to find graphic or conceptual solutions that I wouldn't have access to if I only focused on one. Serendipity also plays a very important role, giving rise to unexpected results that open up the possibility for new projects."

Yoshiko Hada

Photography: Tomoko Arima

Photography: Tomoko Arima

"My work is like an extension of children's doodles, consisting of a simple, dynamic form and a combination of vibrant colors. It seeks to arouse the playfulness of the child in viewers' minds and make them smile.

I think my style is characterized by innocence, playfulness, a sense of humor and sensibility (atmosphere) that goes beyond technique.
It isn't descriptive but rather impressionistic. Everything is communicated through the first impression.

Regardless of the client, I'm interested in projects whose purpose and content I can relate to. I'm thinking in particular of projects that add new value through illustrations of products that are part of our daily life and our living environment. I'm also interested in things related to music and the picture book field."

The 100 days Challenge for happiness
062. Colorful bird

The 100 days Challenge for happiness
063. Tableware

The 100 days Challenge for happiness
056. Man and woman

The 100 days Challenge for happiness
027. Dots horse

The 100 days Challenge for happiness
022. Shima shima bird

The 100 days Challenge for happiness
021. Pink-head elephant

The 100 days Challenge
for happiness
059. Pocket-man

The 100 days Challenge
for happiness
057. A man with red hat

The 100 days Challenge
for happiness
063. He needs vegetables

CARROT
AND
TURNIP

The 100 days Challenge
for happiness
017. Charming face

The 100 days Challenge
for happiness
023. Trico-bird

The 100 days Challenge
for happiness
058. Daily discussion

Photography: Rie Sato / Textile design: Akane Nishimura

Photography: Tomoko Arima

"Creativity is based on innocent curiosity about shapes and colors, and on how they affect the viewer. I also believe that it's based on the basic desire to share something that seems 'wonderful' (or 'enchanting') with another person.

My ideas come from a place beyond my intention, from the unconscious when my brain is distracted. Often ideas occur to me while looking at my own doodles that I draw without thinking every day. Unintended things contain unexpected and interesting things. I think this is because to be unconscious is the most open mental state.

I'm directly inspired by my own doodles drawn freely and accidental things that sometimes happen while creating. But I'm also inspired indirectly by dance music, fashion, Tokyo's chaotic culture and great work by other illustrators and artists."

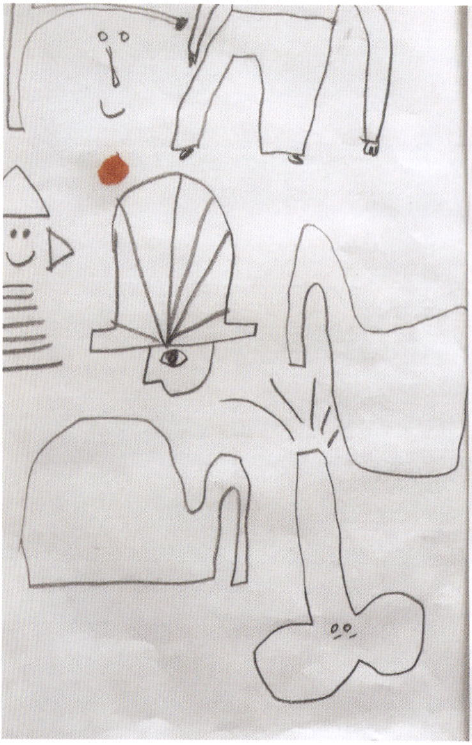

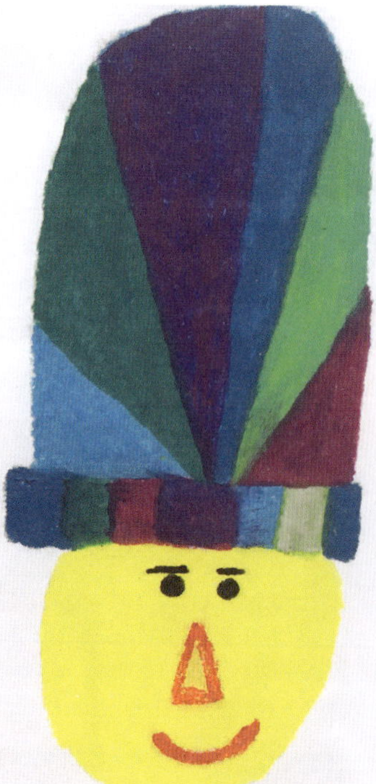

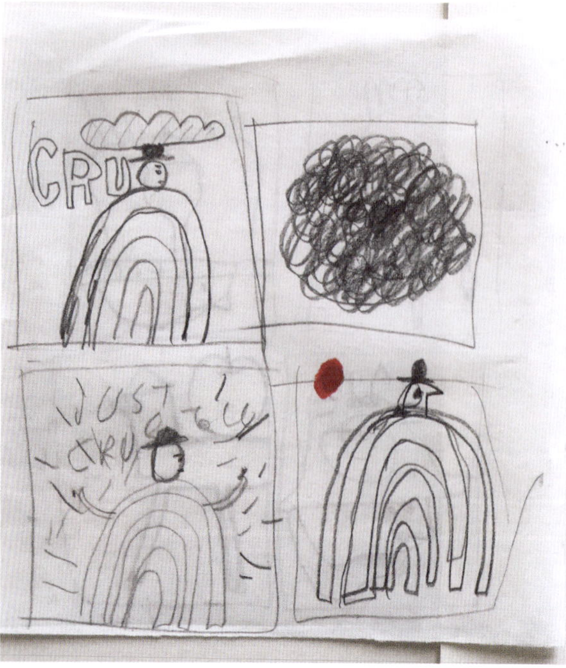
CRU
JUST

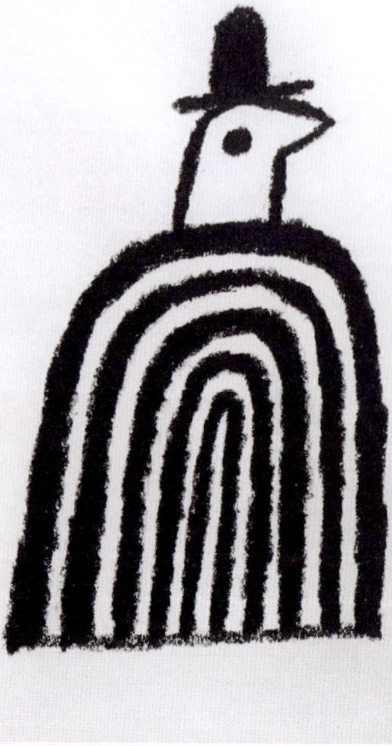

"I think the secret to being a good illustrator is drawing frequently and being led by trial and error, maintaining curiosity about graphic arts in general. In the case of clients, I think it's important to create the work by imagining the feelings of the person who will ultimately receive it. I always want to improve as an illustrator. It's a long journey that never ends."

"I tend to doodle on carbon copy paper and in sketchbooks with a STAEDTLER 6B pencil. Sometimes I choose a topic and draw it. Other times I just draw what comes to me randomly. I also doodle with oil pastels. It's not that different from the scribbling of a child. It's almost surrealistic. (Sometimes I can't help but laugh when I see them). I always keeps them as *stock*. I choose the ones that seem interesting to me or that I like the most, and I use them as basis to expand upon. Then I draw the final artistic product.

To fight creative blocks, if I have time, I take a break. I recharge my brain by watching television, watching movies, observing birds, cleaning, doing something other than drawing. Unloading my brain often gives me new ideas. I also revise my previous work and sketches. Sometimes they remind me of a feeling that I'd forgotten about in the meantime. Sometimes they contain ideas that I'd ignored before. Finally, I just keep on moving my hand (I draw and draw and draw).

I think that the work of an illustrator is similar to that of a translator. I communicate what my client (or somebody else) wants to say to the final user (or someone else) through my own filter. Adding something creative, exaggerations or a slightly different perspective, I try to communicate it more poetically and make it more memorable. In addition, I think my role is to recall for viewers the innocent feelings they had when they were children and make them feel a little happier. It's also like alchemy."

STRANGE Direction

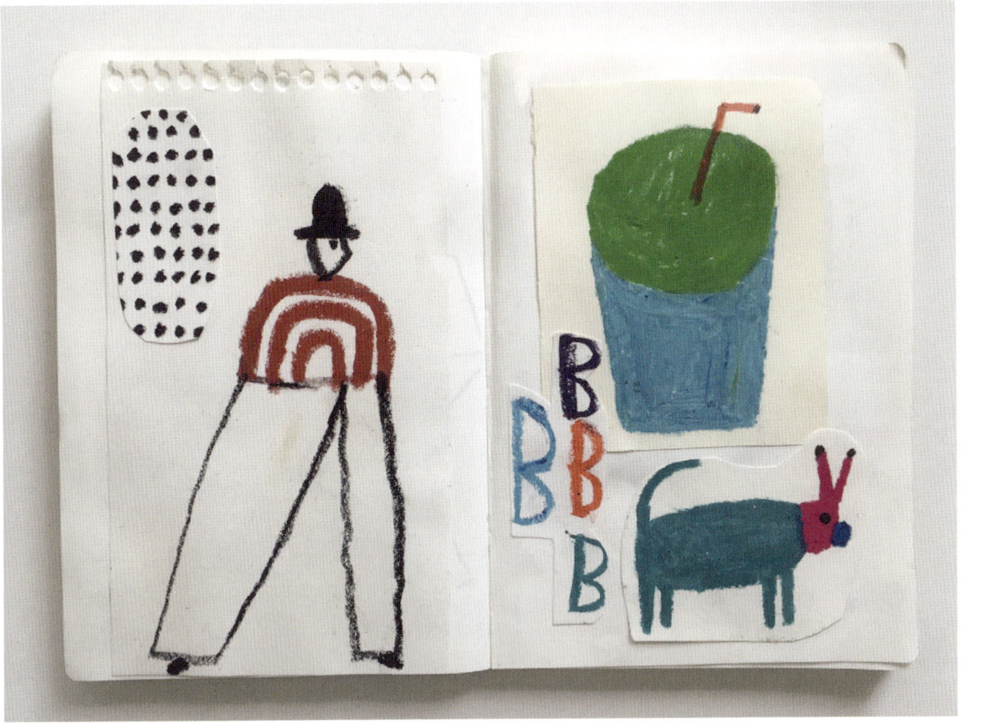
B
B
B
B

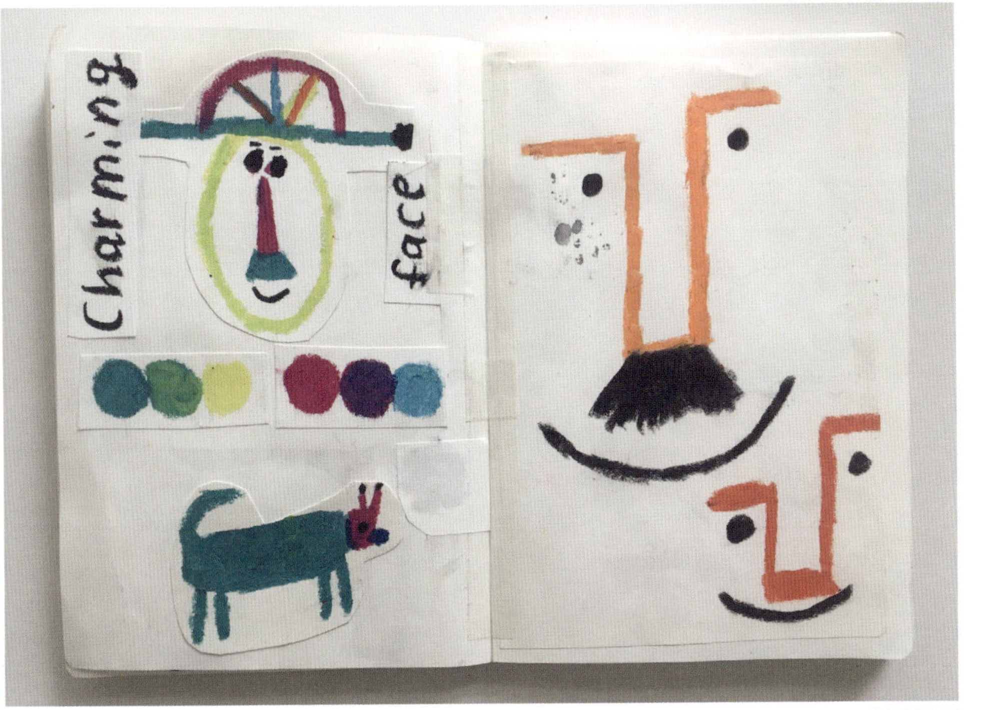
Charming
face

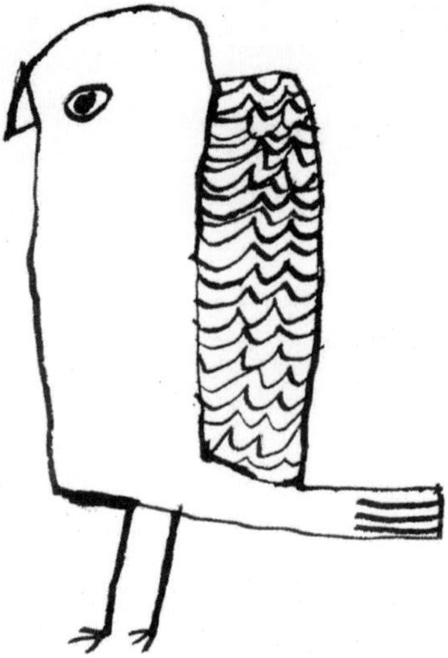
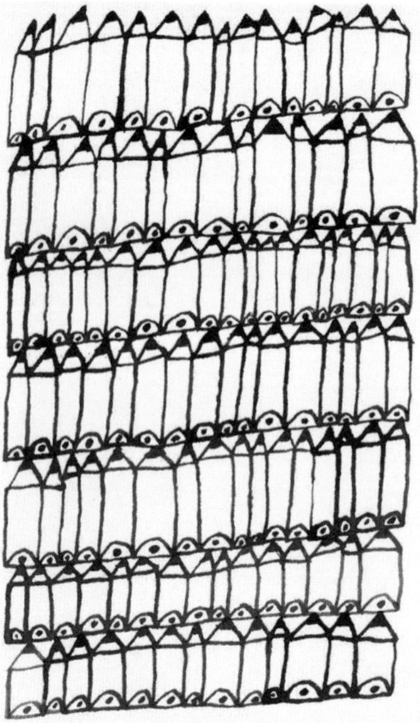
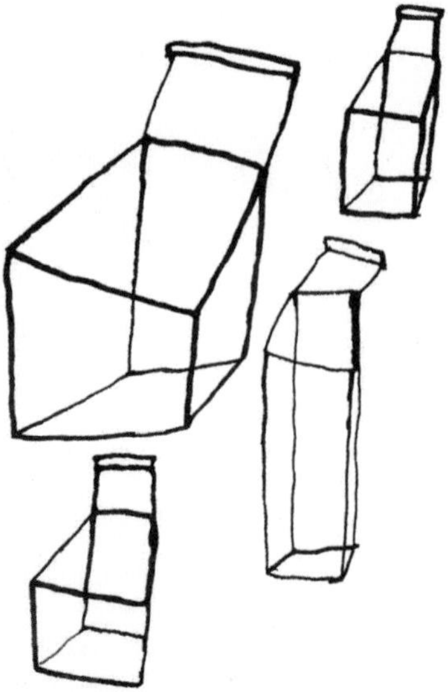
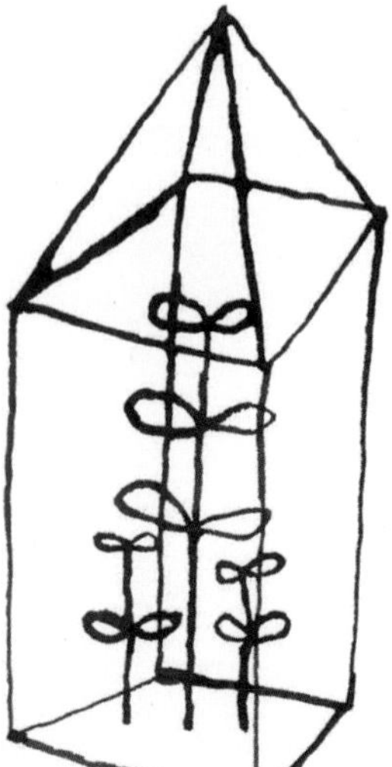

Go Forward

Elizabeth Haidle

Photography: Rebecca Feder

"As a lover of surrealism and a practitioner of sketchbook therapy, I like to peak under the superficial layer of mundane reality and discover hints of wonder. Art is a way of paying attention, of inquiring, of investigating, and often of resolving my own problems. Sometimes these things materialize in collaboration with other artists, an example of true joy in this life.

I'm attracted by comic books because of the immersive experience they offer. I'm particularly drawn to non-fiction comic books for their ability to transform information into something memorable and convincing.

I chose the path of illustration because my goal is to communicate, delight and intrigue."

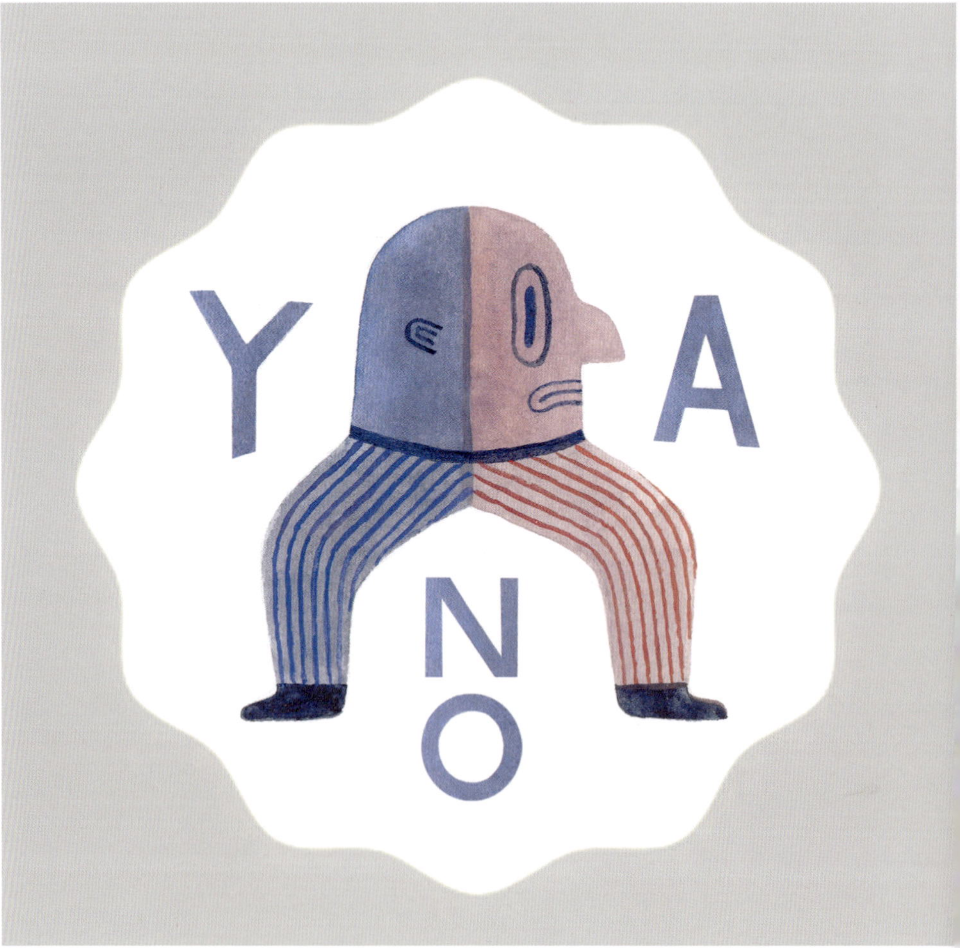
Y
A
N
O

eh

FLOWER-HAND

Just imagine

MEGA CROCS

We are paradoxical.

"An illustrator needs to wear a lot of hats these days, which is something I like. Sometimes I'm a writer, sometimes a researcher and other times I'm an editor and art director.

Something unusual about me is that I'm comfortable with paradoxes: I like to combine non-fiction with surrealism, whimsicalness with seriousness, a dose of mysticism along with the practical.

Most of my ideas come from my daily routine. I write and draw every day. Time doesn't matter: sometimes I create an image devoting just five minutes a day; sometimes it takes me a week or two. Other times I can spend one or two hours on it. What matters is the stimulus. And the volume. For every idea that finds a place in the world, there are easily twenty or more in my trash can or forgotten in some sketchbook.

Creativity is based on the ability to remain curious, to ask oneself questions. I create visual riddles in my sketchbook that are reflections on the Why, the What and the How.

I'm inspired by other artists, musicians, writers and thinkers. Poets, dancers, interpreters: all human beings who truly bring their curiosity to the situation at hand. Recently: RuPaul and Lynda Barry. Both have given many public lectures. They've taught. They've shared their wisdom with ingenuity and humility.

The Surrealist movement is the one that has impressed me the most: artists such as Remedios Varo, Leonora Carrington and Dalí. Also mystic painters: Hilma af Klint and Hildegarda de Bingen."

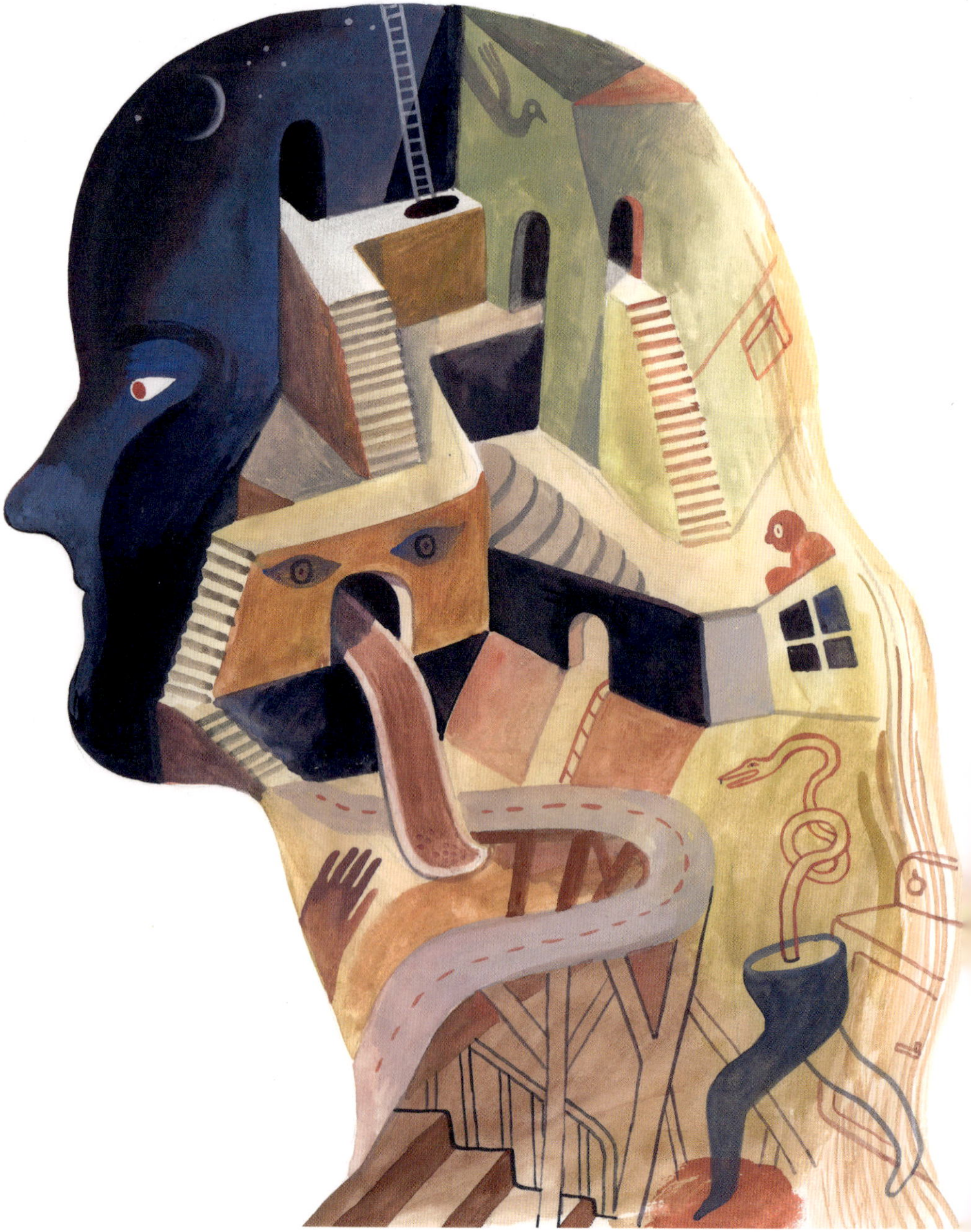

"**What's the secret to being a good illustrator?
Well, I'd have to define what 'good' means to me.
But I see it as an artist in 'evolution', one who is always
open to experimenting."**

"To come up with ideas I read, I watch movies about faraway places, I travel. When I start a new project, I tend to go to a different place to think, even if it's just sitting beneath a tree with a little sketchbook, to see what comes out on the page. I like to see how the drawing is influenced by my surroundings.

How do I fight through creative blocks?

Technique no.1: Juggling!
When I started to have multiple series for which I was doing research (anything, from painting emotions to daily comic strips, futuristic hair styles and fantastical boots), I realized that when I hit one of those familiar 'blocks', I didn't have to put my pencil down and stop drawing that day. I rummaged through my files, looking for things I'd already begun, until I found something else that I wanted to pick up again.

Technique no. 2: Total distraction!
This isn't a good idea all the time. But when I'm bogged down by a project that I can't seem to make any progress on, I get something to eat, I put on a mystery in the background, I call a friend and put on timer and work for 20 minutes straight, with frequent breaks. In a way, distractions make the time fly by, and I don't have room in mind for worries. It's as if I literally push my fear out the window by embracing so many distractions... there's no space left for doubt.

Chris Haughton

"When I graduated from art school, I wanted to get a job as an illustrator. The only way to pay the bills was drawing for advertising. I liked this commercial work. It's rather satisfying from a creative point of view, and I was able to have my illustrations appear on billboards and in magazines. But at the same time, it didn't really excite me, and I began looking for other avenues for my work.

A friend was working for a fair trade company called People Tree. I ended up becoming a volunteer and doing illustrations and design work for them. This became a productive collaboration. The line of children's clothing that I designed with them sold well. They asked me to do more and more and it became a big part of my work for many years. Not only that. I became known for my fair trade work, and other social-oriented companies and environmental organizations hired me to illustrate for them.

In 2010, I traveled through India and Nepal for eight months. I met with a lot of fair trade organizations that had been working with People Tree and started to collaborate with them directly. One of the most fruitful collaborations was a social responsibility company that I created (madebynode.com) that manufactures rugs in Nepal. We've had exhibitions throughout the world, including a large exhibition of eighteen rugs at the London Museum of Design in 2012.

I studied visual communication in art school. I think my work has its roots in visual communication.

I always wanted to illustrate books, but I felt like I didn't have the ability to write. Or at least I felt uncomfortable doing it. So, when I tried to create a picture book, the only way to do it was by telling a purely visual story. In many ways, I think this is what makes my illustrated books work. My disadvantage became an advantage because I was forced to tell a story visually."

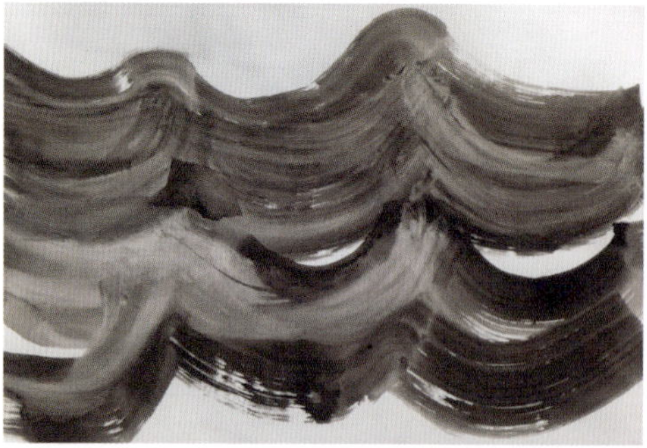
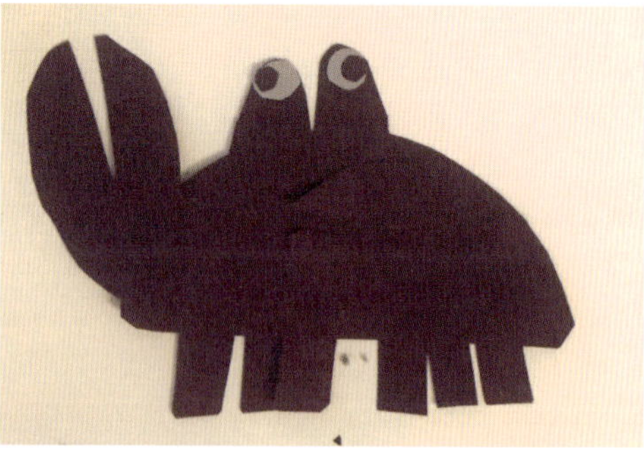
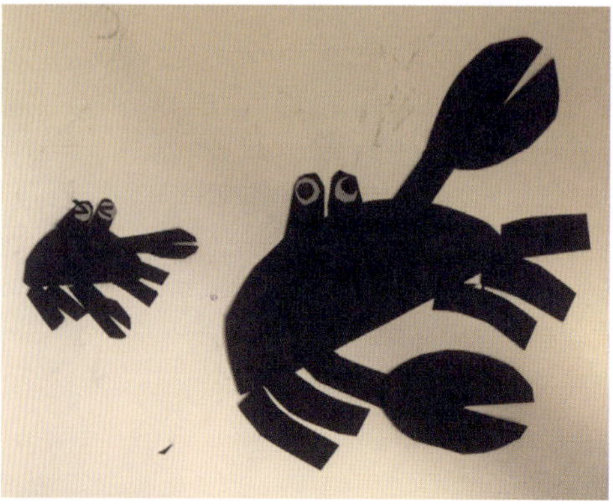
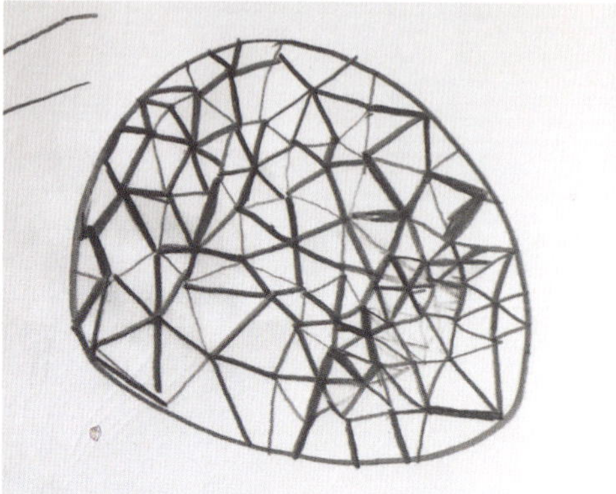
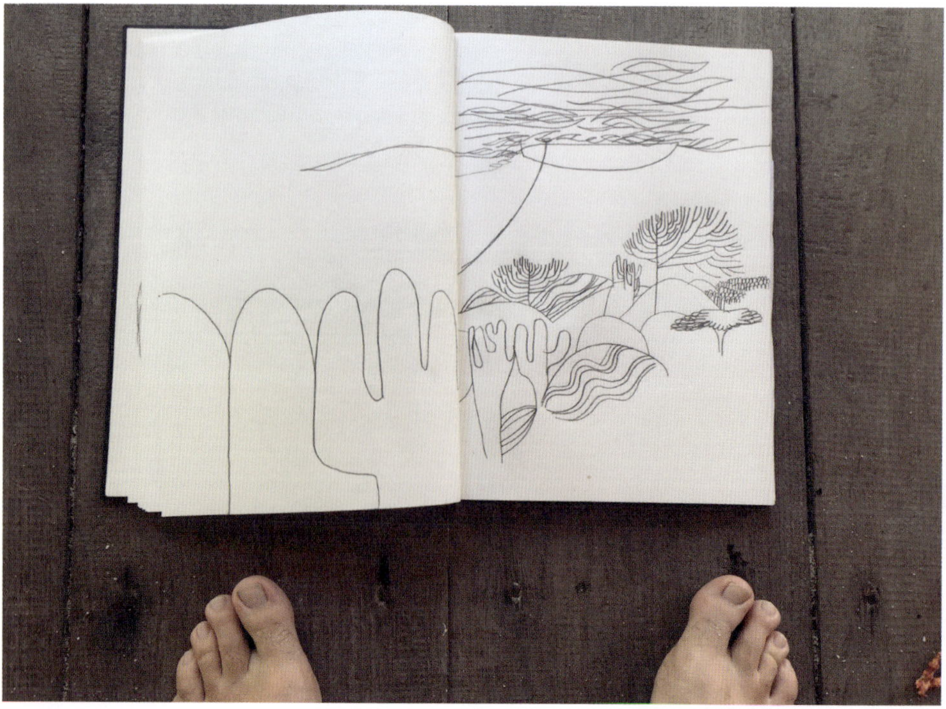

"The advantage of stories that are narrated in a purely visual way is that very small children can understand them. Also, they translate easily into other languages.

An important visual communication technique is to focus your eye, what's known as 'visual hierarchy'. A designer or an illustrator identifies the most relevant elements of the information that are intended to grab the viewer's attention and designs them in a way that draws our attention to them. Then, once you've caught the viewer's eye and they're focusing on the design, the layout should reveal the following important elements, then the next, and so on. In the case of a magazine article, we could have a title, then the subtitle, and finally the text. In the case of a concert poster, we could start with a photo and the artist's name, then the date of the concert, and lastly the information about the venue and tickets.

In my picture books, some of the elements must be communicated immediately. Some elements are secondary; others might not even be apparent in a first reading.

For example, on this page of *A Bit Lost*, the first thing we see is a small owl falling to the forest floor. I drew the character of the owl in black and white against a color background. This helps the eye distinguish the small main character on the color pages. Maybe the second thing the reader notices is the squirrel in the corner. The last thing is the other forest animals hidden in the background. They're the same color as the background in this image to help make them more visible, although physically they're bigger than the owl."

"Well, how about we go the long way home?"

"Can we go up this way?" asks Little Crab

"I think illustrated albums is a very interesting medium. They're a combination of images and words; so in a way they're both art and literature. And since they're usually read out loud, they also make use of interpretation. They tend to be a child's first introduction to art, literature and performance. To human culture, in fact. This is surprising when you think about it. When I look back at my books, I realize, without doing it consciously, that in each one there's some kind of main action and that this action is narrated through some type of prelinguistic exclamation: 'uh-oh', 'oh, no', 'shh', 'ahhhh' (a yawn), 'whoosh' and 'hmmm'.

Prelinguistic sounds are so universal they seem to suggest where language evolved from. Yawns are universal. In fact, all mammals yawn. It seems to be a primitive form of communication. The sound 'shh' is the same in all languages into which it has been translated. There are slight variations in 'whoosh' and 'uh-oh' in different languages, but the meaning can be understood in all languages."

"I think the possibilities of picture books for children are infinite. My goal is to create books for increasingly younger children. At the same time, I'm also interested in visual communication for adults. I've been working on a virtual reality application and now augmented reality that communicates the immensity of space."

1. *Don't worry, little crab,* Walker Books, 2019.
2. *A bit lost.* Walker Books, 2010.
3. *Shh! We have a Plan,* Walker Books, 2014.

3

Isol

Photography: Marcelo Cugliari

"My work is very specific. I create images that tell a story, that are related to the written word, and which appear mainly in children's books. This format is exciting because of the enormous amount of possibilities it offers. I combine visual images in sequences (like in comic books and film), and my work is also related to literature, visual poetry and design. Very often I draw and I write the text. This makes me feel like a movie director, where some things are shown and others are spoken. Sometimes it isn't a story. The book can be a cookbook of dreams, a spelling book with different scenes or two stories with the same images. Working from images in combination with words is what works best for me. It's there where I encounter surprise, a certain shift from the predictable that moves me. For this reason, I don't like to show them outside of the context in which they were created, because I think their best quality is how they're related to the sequence and text. My images aren't 'pretty' in themselves. I strive for an expressive and plastic quality that has to do with evoking something, communicating, making a strong impact, the search for personal aesthetic solutions, always in harmony with the story I want to tell.

In my stories, an idea of estrangement from the ordinary emerges. It's a way of seeing that allows me to search in simple and recognizable situations for the mysterious, the absurd, the questions I ask myself outside of what is considered normal or conventional. I see things a bit like child does, in terms of a certain wild impunity of the imagination, as if I were seeing situations, realities for the first time. Also, the narrator of my stories is often a child who shares his desires, questions, fears and experiences with the reader. And if the voice is not identifiable as that of a child, it's related to a story free of formality or moral teachings; it's an unbiased voice expressing something surprising, trying to understand it, to move through it. I think something that defines my work is a kind of humor that proceeds from a place of asking questions, accompanying the characters without judging them.

1

YA NO TEMAS

2

Sería agradable comer sin sobresaltos.

—Amor, mira qué rico el pescadito...

¡PUAJJ!

ESCUCHA

3

LA TARARA, SÍ, LA TARARA, NO, LA TARARA, NIÑA, QUE LA HE VISTO YO

4

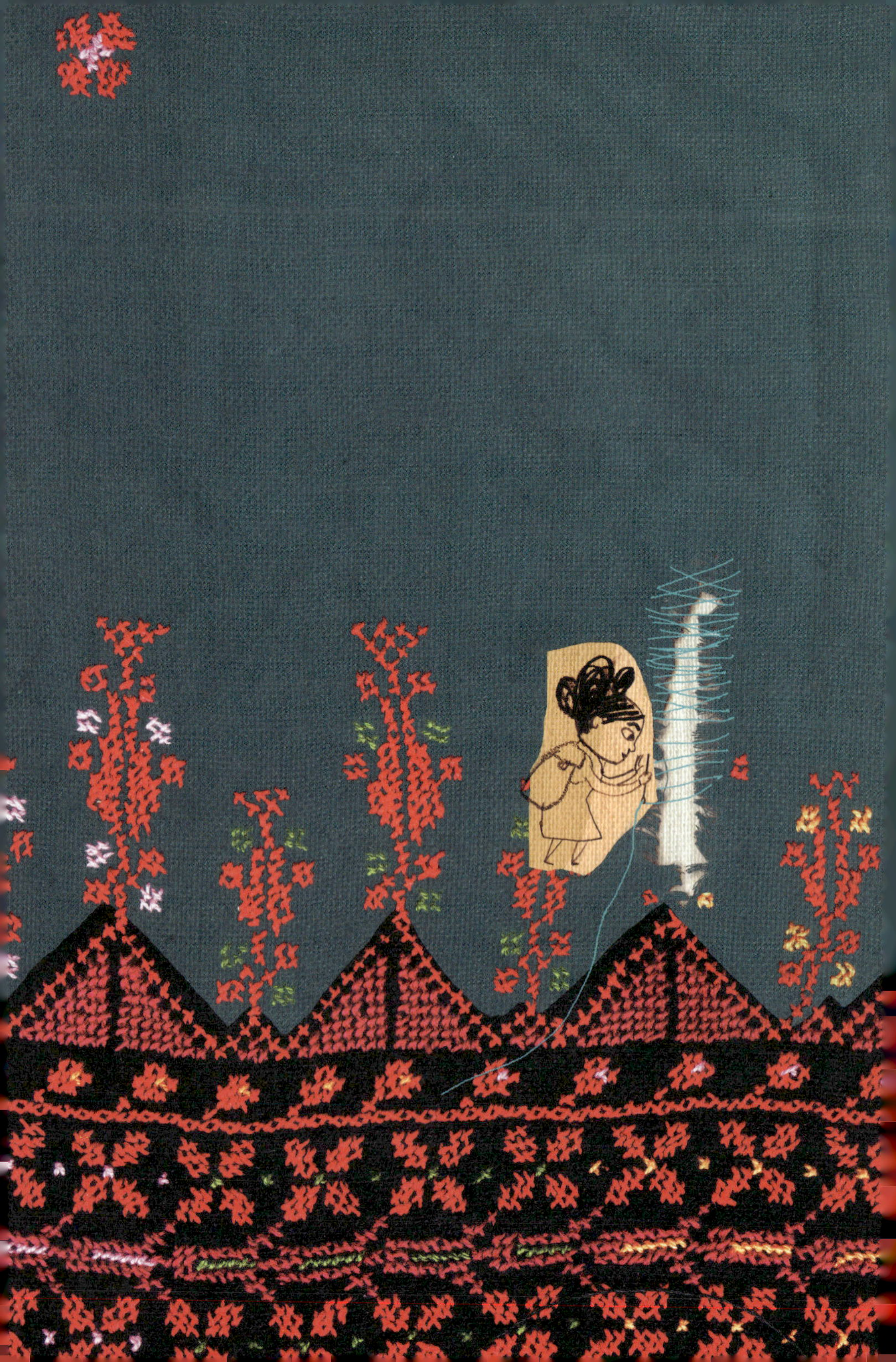

"I studied fine arts. This left an important impression on me in terms of the materials I use: graphite, *collage*, grease crayons, ink, ink stains, different papers. I enjoy working with these materials, getting dirty, trying things, cutting, gluing, twisting a brush, combining things... experimenting. Often I scan the drawings and backgrounds and assemble them on the computer as if they were layers in an etching. I love the look of printing presses from 50 years ago, the separated colors, and I use offsetting... I think the things I saw in my childhood in my parents' books, the covers, had something of that aesthetic, and it has influenced me to this day. Graphics as a vehicle for thought is also something very Argentinean. The use of humor and irony synthetically with drawing has always had a strong influence on me (Quino, Fontanarrosa and Oski are some examples).

In my own narrations and when illustrating other writers' texts, I aim for a personal vision, a way of illustrating that is graphically interesting and that relates to what I'm saying in a way that enhances the story. I also love to sing. I've recorded some albums, performed in concerts with different groups (baroque music and experimental pop). This is related to connecting with other people and evoking a dream space, a cathartic space, a certain transcendence I feel when something inspires me and feeds my soul. It's what I search for and what expands the boundaries of my world.

I've published 27 books, more than half with my own words, in 17 languages. I work with a few publishing companies with which I have a standing relationship. I published my first book as well as my latest one with Fondo de Cultura Económica. They have almost all my books in Spanish. I think it's good for the books to be together in one place because they help each other. But from time to time, I publish with other publishing houses, depending on the project."

1. *Ya no temas*, paper, ink, pastel and *collage*, 0,60 m x 1 m, 2017.
2. Illustration from the book *Imposible*, text and drawing by Isol, 2018.
3. *Listen*, graphic work for the Aguascalientes Book Fair, Mexico, 2020.
4. Illustration from the book *Paisaje de un día*, with poems by Federico García Lorca, 2020.
5. Illustration from the book *La Costura*, text and drawings by Isol, project for the Palestinian Museum, 2021.
6. *El rescate*, acrylic on canvas, 0,80 m x 1 m, 2018.

"I take notebooks with me wherever I go and jot down sentences and drawings in passing, without thinking too much. This helps me to connect with myself, with what's going on me with at the time. It makes me laugh; sometimes it becomes the seed of a story.

Traveling is the time when I fill my notebooks with the most ideas. Because of the waiting, the hotels, the solitude, the different routine, I tend to look at things from the outside. I love this foreign place. But the truth is I'm pretty messy and sometimes I can't remember where I left one of these notebooks... Lately I started to mark some pages to keep track of these hints at ideas. My workspace is filled with books, papers, sketches. I'm pretty impatient and move immediately on to the next thing. So stages of different projects, workshops, etc., accumulate on my four tables. I'm not very happy about it, but it seems like I don't really have a choice. Besides, I have two small children and sometimes I can't choose the time I want work. It's limited.

My ideal day is to spend a long time in my studio with a nice cup of tea, high quality paper, and the smell of oil pastel, ink and pencils. I work at my own pace, a little slow perhaps, without rushing to do something specific. I look for the place of play and desire. I think play is extremely important: to be in that place of freedom without fear of making mistakes. This leads to what later appears in the work. It's noticeable. I think that to enjoy my work you need to have a sense of humor, really, an appreciation of surprise, of the unexpected. I create my books and designs for someone who seems like me, whether a child or an adult. I couldn't create for an audience that didn't include me. I wouldn't know how. It has to move me first. It's true that sometimes you can get a little confused in the middle of the process. At that point I talk with friends who can offer an honest and interesting point of view, which can enrich my work. This can be a very solitary job at times. For this reason, I also like to create music and collaborate on projects with other people sometimes (theater, murals). It fills me with a fresh, new energy. I look for what nourishes me. That freedom helps me to be satisfied with my work and my life, shedding light and grace on what I do as an artist."

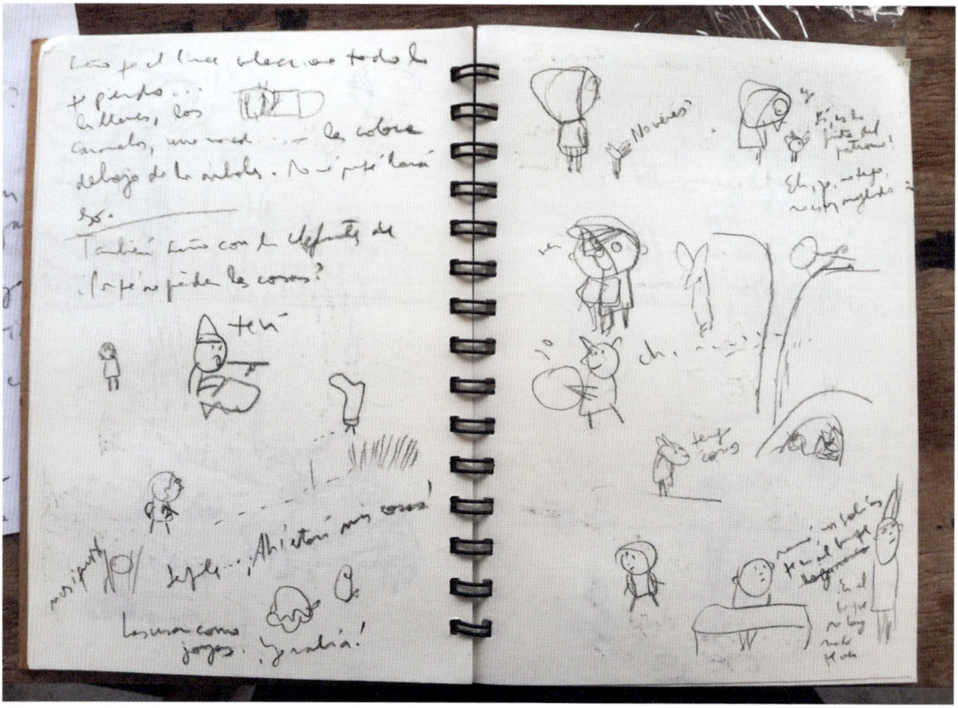

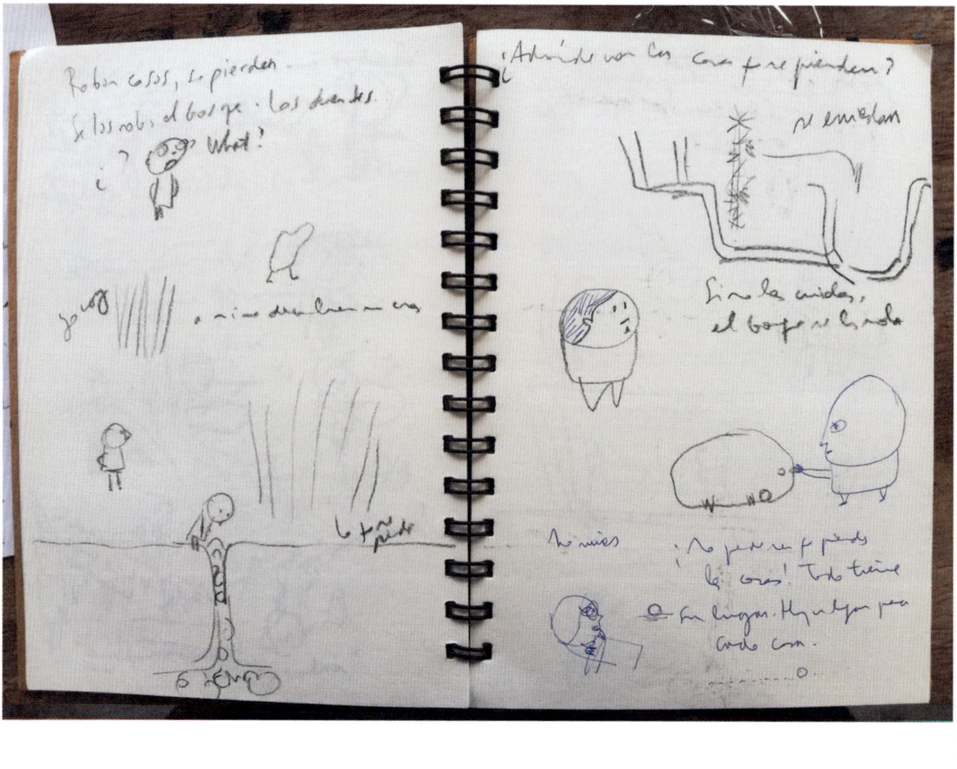
What?
¿Adónde van las cosas que se pierden?

DORMIR

PIECITOS

Martin Jarrie

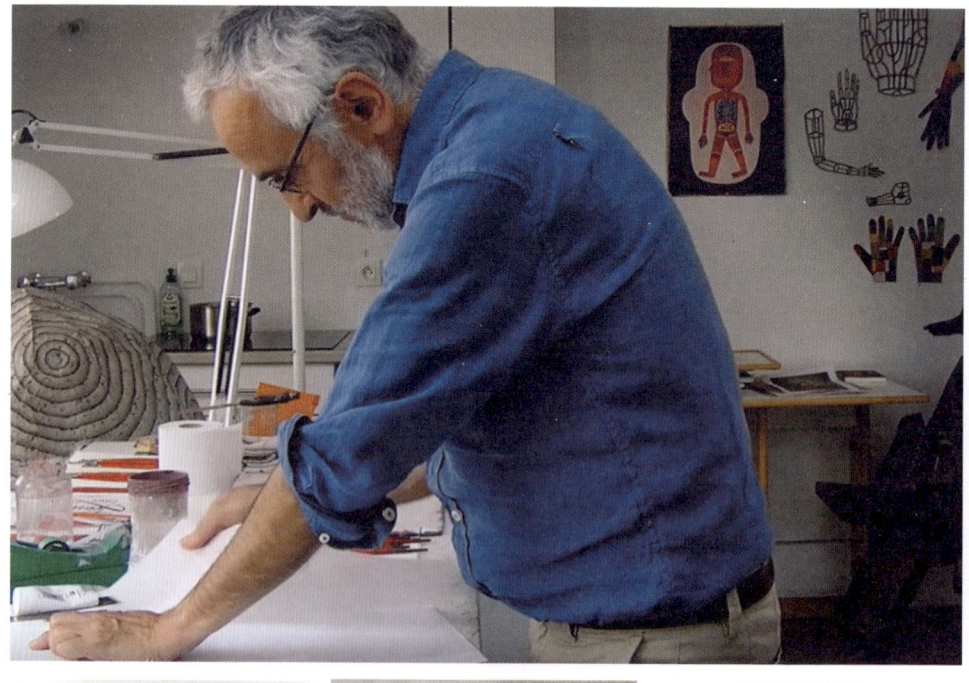

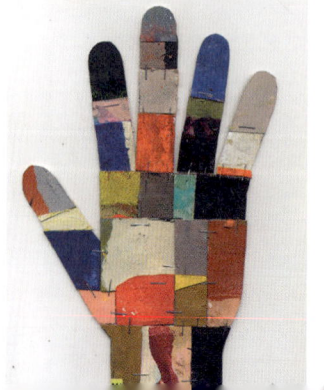

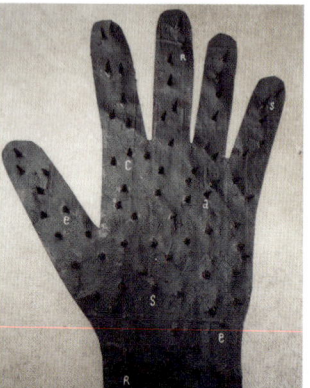

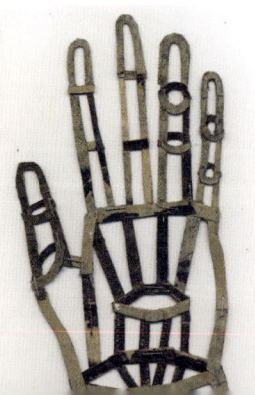

"I'm an illustrator driven by the desire to paint. I think this best defines my work and maybe is what distinguishes me from other illustrators. As a child, and then as a teenager, I wasn't very attracted to illustration. I liked comic books and especially the painters whose work I'd see reproductions of in dictionaries and later in art catalogs. My eye was trained thanks to my deep interest in and awareness of the plastic arts.

I don't know if the work I'm going to talk about is the most representative, but it's what I have the most physical and psychological investment in. I'm referring to what I call 'The anatomical factory', which is my work on imaginary anatomies. I started this project in 1996, after going to an exhibition at the French National Library featuring etchings in black from the 18th century in four-color process printing by an artist named Gautier d'Agoty, which were life-size anatomical studies. I was blown away. Back in my studio, I wanted to translate first by drawing on big sheets of paper the feeling of well-being and discomfort in the body without relying on a realistic representation of the human anatomy. Then I did a series of drawings, paintings and sculptures that ultimately became the illustrations in a book entitled *Le colosse machinal*.

I created some of this work practically in a trance, as if it involved magic rituals. I felt a great deal of happiness and confusion, as if I was in the presence of something sacred. I continued this work later and still return to it when I feel like it. I use different materials such as wood from boxes, reinforced bitumenised Kraft, candle wax, nails and also acrylic paint."

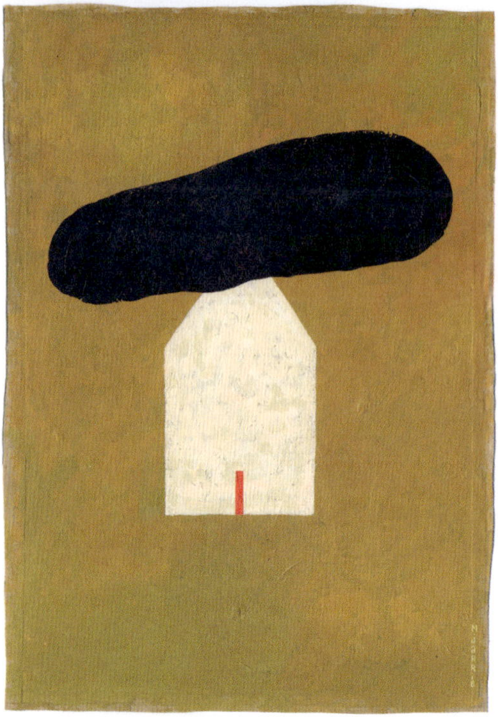

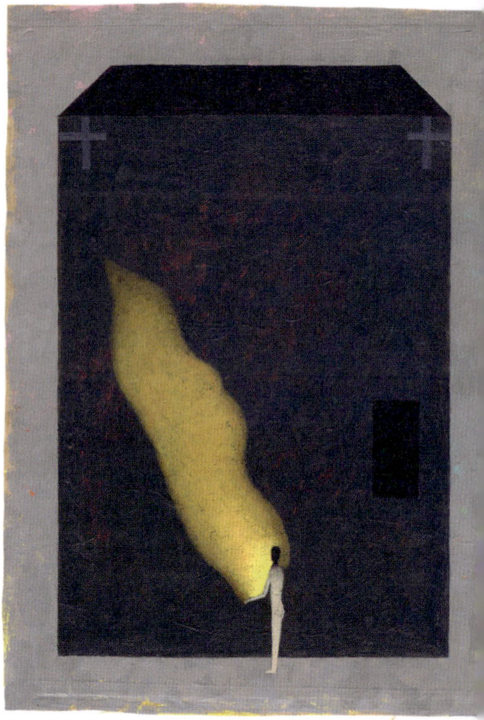

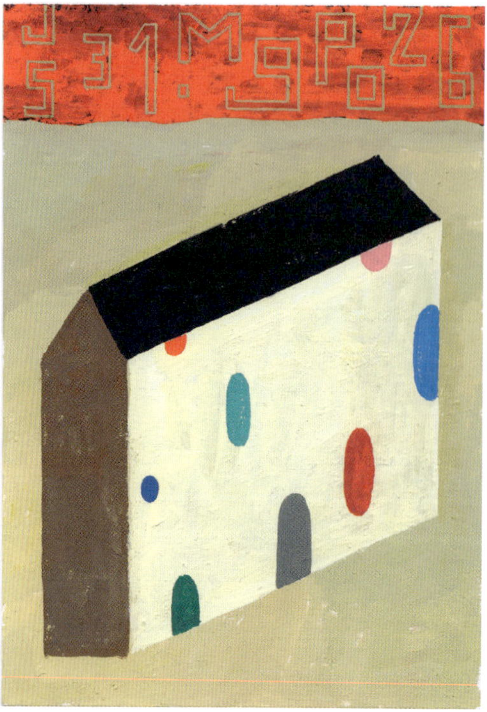

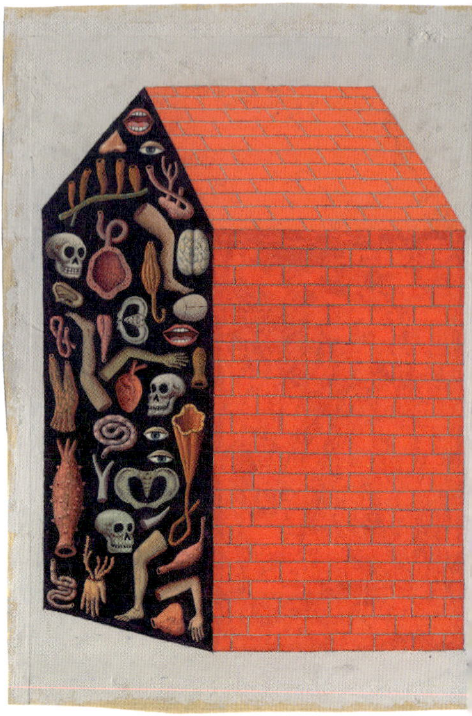

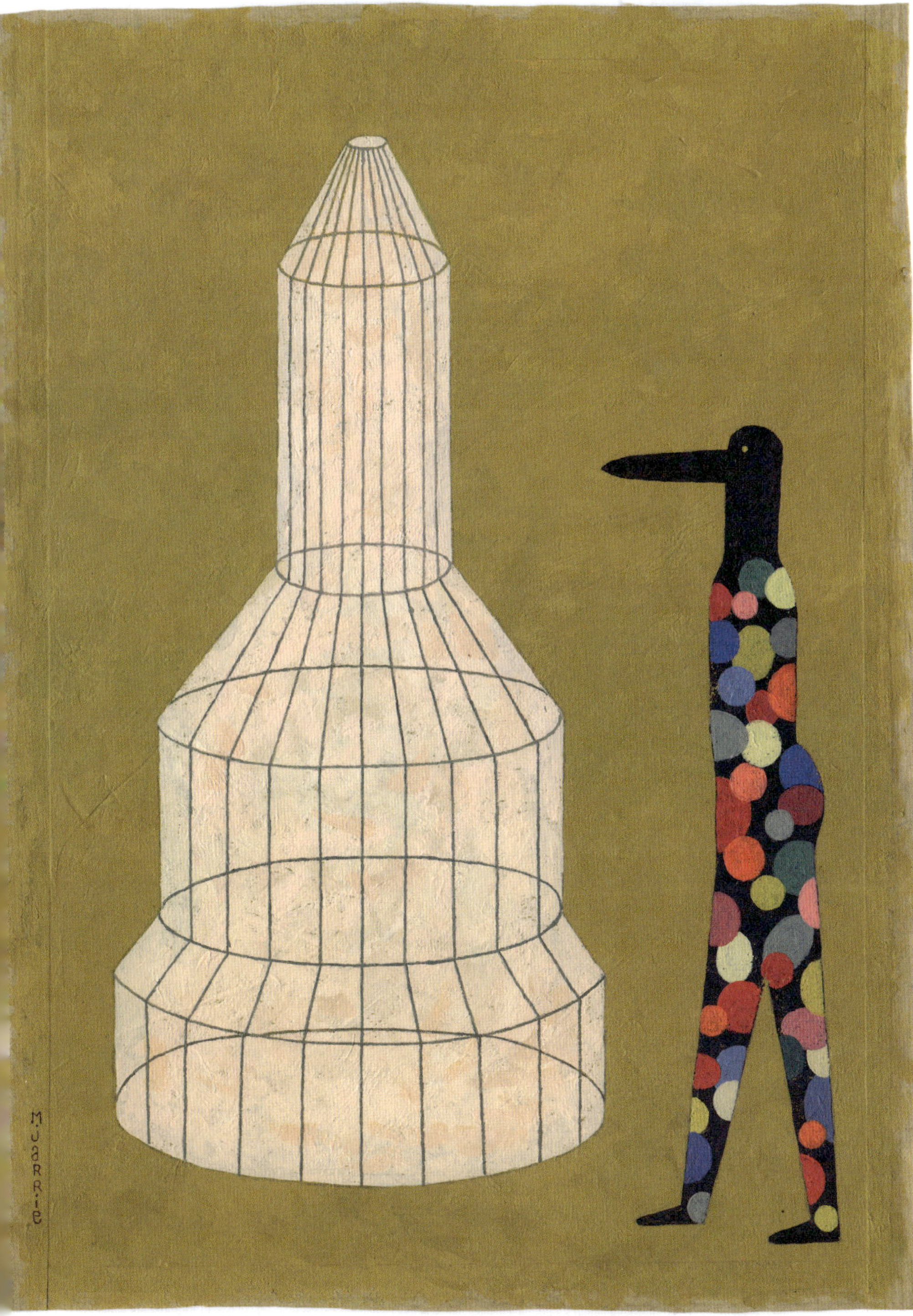
M.JaRRie

Mjarrie

"I draw, I search, I feel my way around, I scribble in my notebooks. There are a lot of failures, a lot of unfinished drawings. I've saved all these notebooks over the course of thirty years. When I get stuck, I look at them and sometimes I find a solution in drawings that seemed wanting to me but suddenly open up new avenues."

"The desire to create is deeply rooted in childhood. In my case, the boredom and loneliness I experienced as a child fueled my desire to create, to draw, to play with shapes.

I think you have to like drawing and painting and be as personally invested as possible in this work. I have the feeling that most of the time I recognize myself in the images I create. I don't see any difference between the activity of an illustrator and a painter or a visual artist.

As for sources of inspiration, they're numerous and varied: the landscapes of my childhood in Bocage Vendéen; my sisters, some of whom worked in sewing shops; my father's workshop which was a repository of all kinds of different things: old bicycles, tools and machines that I didn't know how to use. Later, there were dictionaries, the art catalogs that my older brother would bring home, the mail order catalogs that I discovered while I was studying Fine Arts in Angers.

And then, whenever I have a creative block, I leaf through the books in my library: art books, exhibition catalogs, nature books, animal books, maps of the sky, old nautical maps. I use them like a compass."

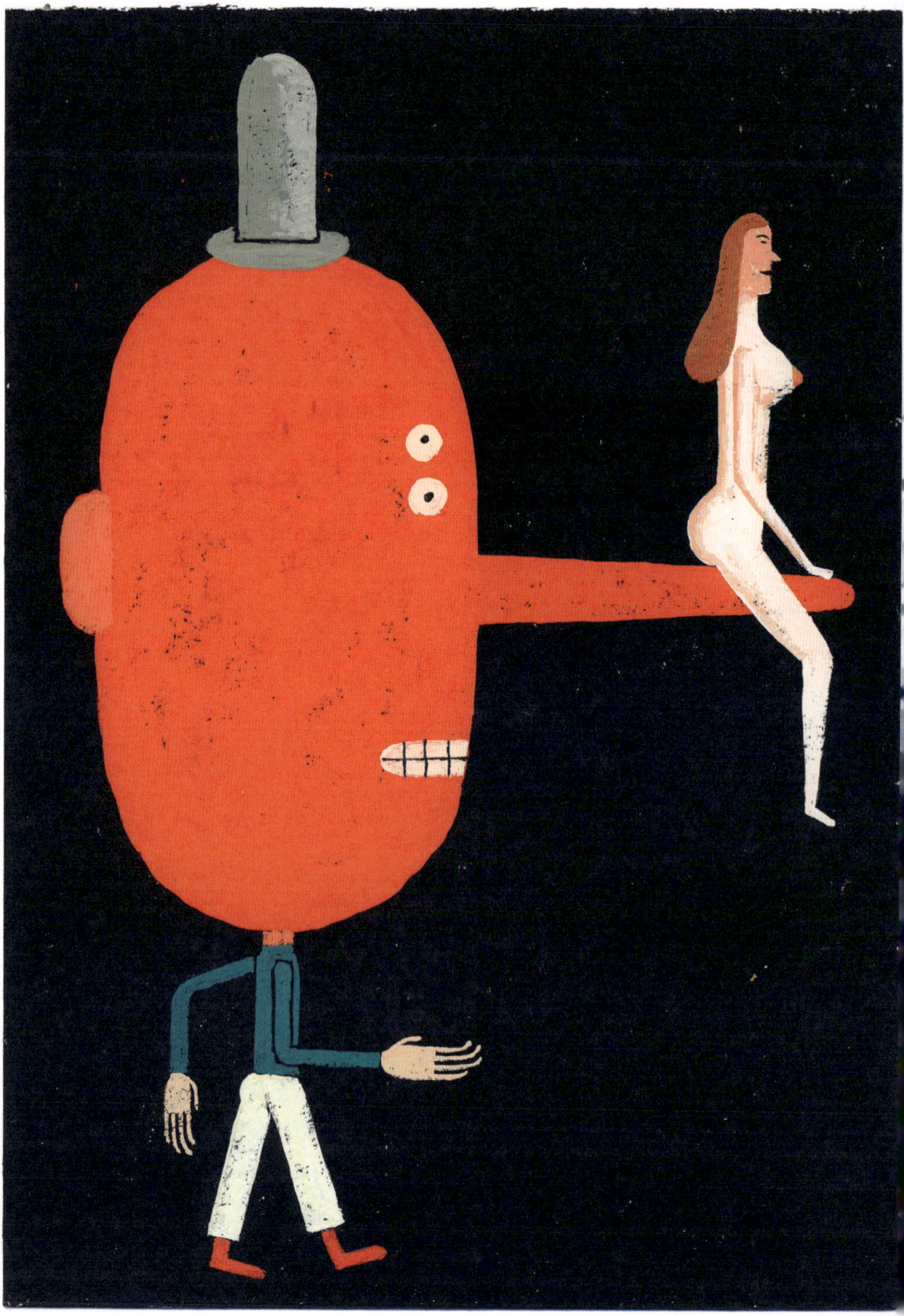

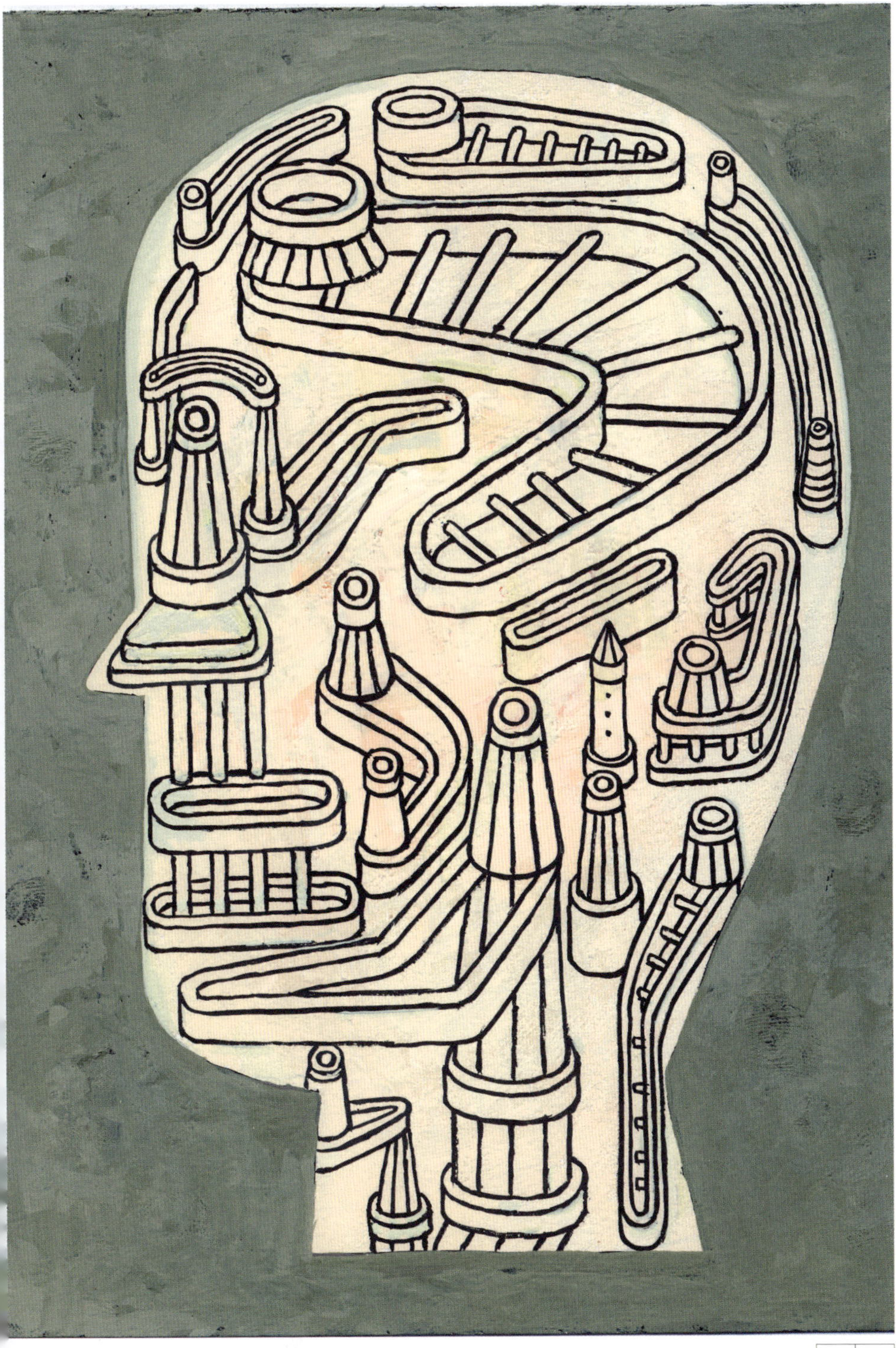

"A friend recently asked me two questions:

The first:
Both in painting and in drawing, how do you know or feel when you've found your 'personal style'?

My response: The question of style is a question I don't think I've ever asked myself but probably it's a mistake.

I think admiration for certain artists has a lot to do with it. It's a slow, a very slow process, a maturing that is never complete.

When I was a child and a teenager, I liked reproductions of works by Goya, Boucher, Géricault, and I didn't like El Greco. Later, I discovered the original works of artists in galleries and museums. I got a better idea of the gestures of painters and I fell in love with some of them. I made my own honey from all these works: seen, swallowed, devoured. But it took a long time for me to recognize myself in what I drew and painted. For ten years, from 1981 to 1991, I lost myself in hyperrealism because I was attracted to highly precise and highly realistic drawing and because this style was in high demand in advertising. I took a long time and psychoanlaysis (for other reasons) to rediscover the joy of creating that I felt as a child.

More than style, I want to talk about physical gestures, the use of specific tools, a way of working deeply rooted in the body.

I think it comes from far away and from the body, what is set down on paper or on the canvas and what we call style.

The second:
How does painting allow you to express something different than drawing?

My response: Drawing, for me, is the intellect, the search for an idea, the translation of a thought, a text, a sensation into lines. It involves fixing an image on paper in a few lines, letting let the pencil run across the page or trying to because the eye is there to control it. The pleasure of drawing lies in surprising yourself, allowing something to come out.

As for color, it's a bit banal what I'm going to say, but it's sensuality, working with the material. It's more regressive. The pleasure of covering a surface, combining colors, more liquid or thicker materials that results in happy or unhappy surprises. It's also like a caress, spreading the paint like a skin over the surface of the page or canvas.

Most of the time I proceed like this. First I research in a sketchbook, usually sketches consisting of a just a few lines, and then I decide on the format and medium (paper or canvas), and then I move on to color. I transfer my drawing to a sheet of carbon copy paper in the desired format.

I never paint on a blank background. It's always already smeared with paint (palette debris, the dregs of paint tubes, etc.).

Over the last few years, I've worked differently by choice or because I've been forced to. During the lockdown, since I couldn't leave my studio, I began to make highly elaborate drawings, more advanced in details and in the expression of volumes. Curiously, I didn't feel the need to express them in painting for the moment. But then the desire began to come!

Also, in 2015, I felt disenchanted with the way I painted. I couldn't stand to look at my paintings and illustrations.

To try and overcome this, I had the idea to work with a material other than acrylic paint. I bought some tempera tubes and I began to paint in small notebooks without doing a pencil sketch beforehand. It was very gratifying, and I felt freer.

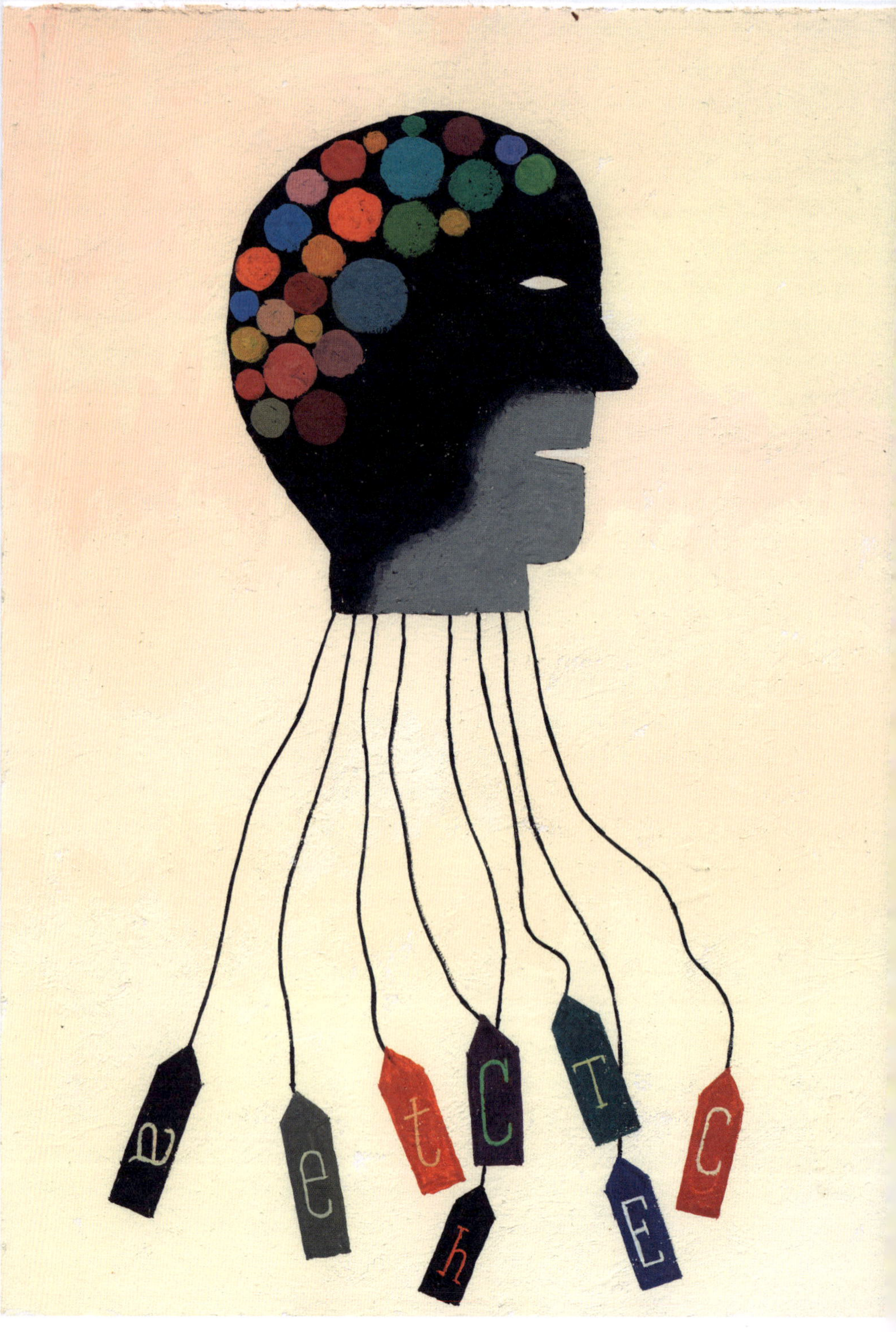

212 | 213

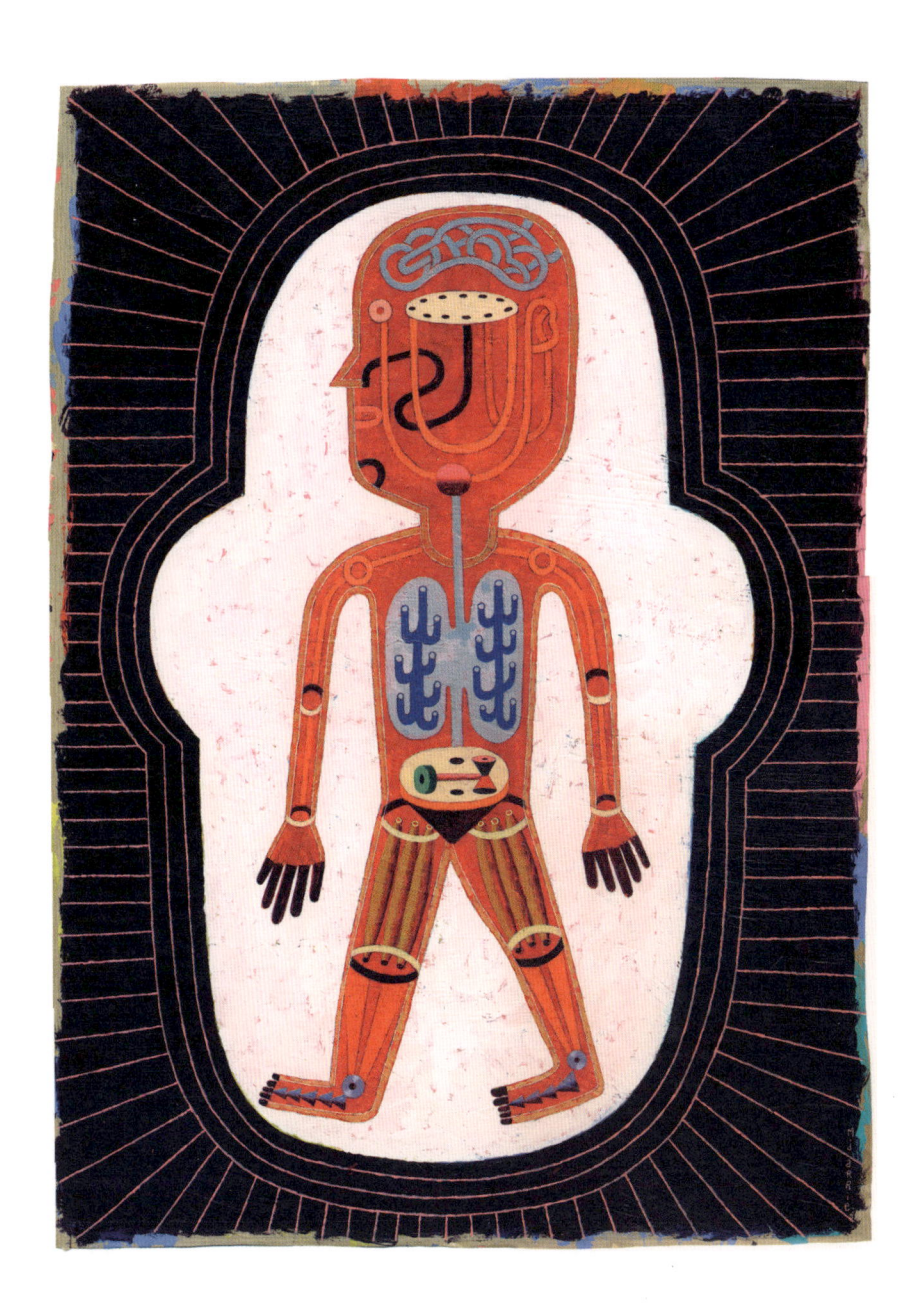

Anita Kunz

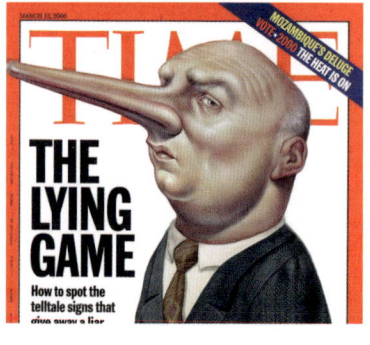

"By way of introduction, I would define myself as an artist and illustrator. I've always liked drawing and I always wanted to be an artist, so I went to art school. My first influence was my uncle Robert Kunz. He was an illustrator whose motto was 'art for education'. From him I learned that art had a function and was not merely decorative. Later, I fell in love with artists whose work addressed political and social issues. I loved the idea that they could comment visually on what was happening in the world, or at least help start some kind of dialog. My biggest heroes have always been artists like Ralph Steadman and Sue Coe. There's a passion in their work and a concern for the human condition that I find infinitely inspiring.

My assignment work (illustration) is different from my personal artistic work. I've done a lot of covers for the magazines *The New Yorker*, *Time* and *The New York Times*, and my publishing work has appeared in numerous magazines. The illustration work I've done for the *The New Yorker* and the magazine *Rolling Stone*, for example, has a specific purpose, whether it's to create a conceptual portrait of someone or to articulate an idea graphically. There's always a client and a public. It requires a series of specific skills such as the ability to work within a deadline and the willingness to collaborate with others. I really like to illustrate for magazines and books because I always have the feeling that I'm learning something (often I'm illustrating something new). It's a challenge to create an attractive image and, at the same time, to make some kind of observation. My personal work is exactly that, very personal. I've shown my work in galleries, but I don't like the idea of art as merchandise. In my personal work, I make paintings that interest me, and I'm my own critic. Most of my personal work deals with such subjects as anthropology, human narratives and gender; things I'm curious about. I don't need to work with a deadline. This way, I can take as long as I want with the project. Lately, my projects have been books. I love the idea of creating a series of works about the same subject. I can really explore in depth something that interests me.

Recently I've written and illustrated three books. The first is called *Another History of Art*. It's a revisionist history told through the eyes of a modern and secular woman (me). The second celebrates extraordinary women, many of whom history has forgotten, called *Original Sisters: Portraits of Tenacity and Courage*. And I can't talk about my third book. All I can say is it will be mischievous.

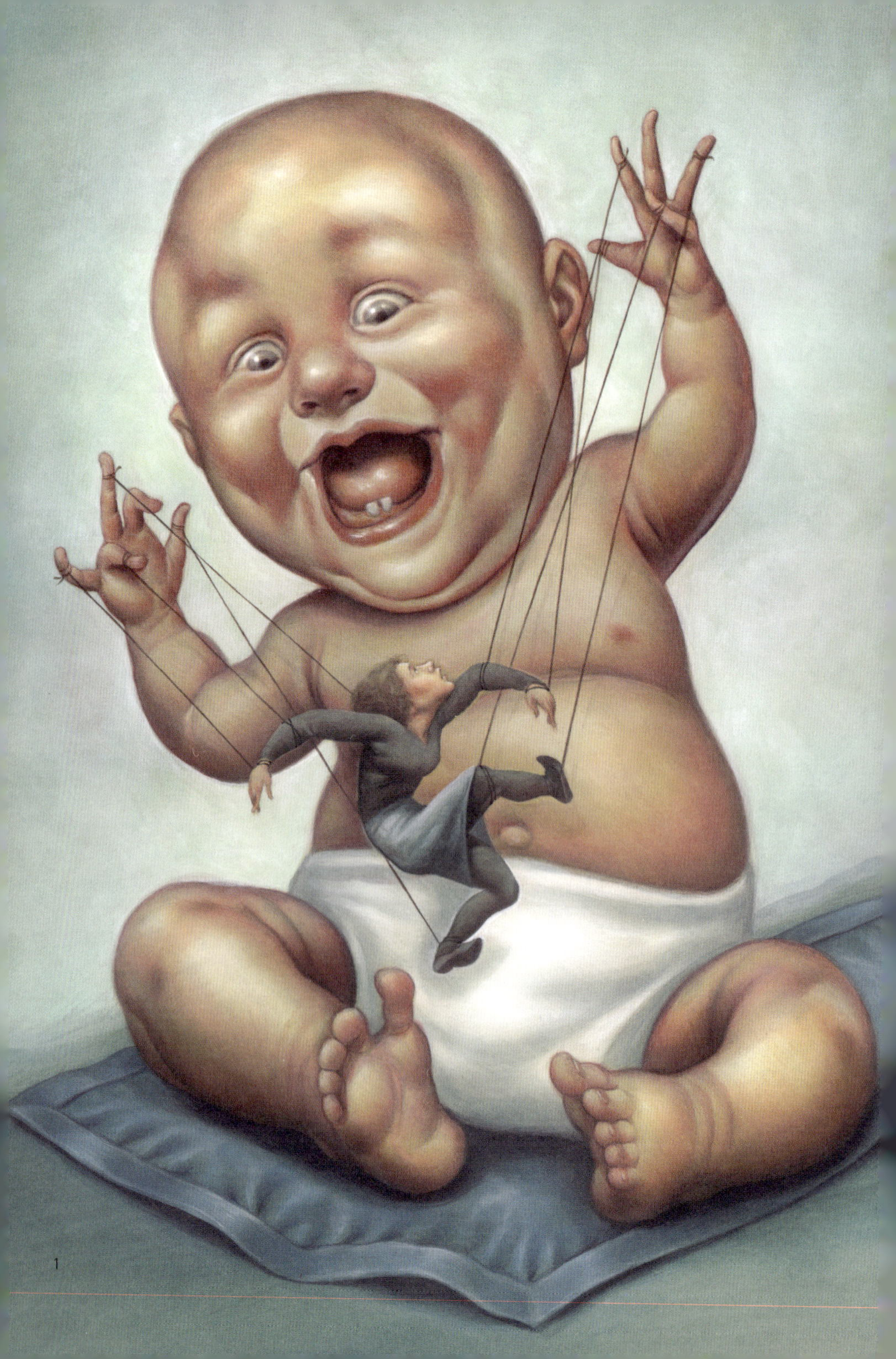

1

"I think being an artist is a way of life and not a job. And the secret to being a good illustrator is the ability to give form to ideas in functional visual narratives."

"I think that creativity is nothing more than curiosity. It's seeing things through different, sometimes new lenses. It's making new and unusual connections between things. Ideas are really just questions that emerge from our own experiences in the world. My ideas come from my own experience and tastes and are translated into visual commentaries on what I see occurring around me. My inspiration comes from politics, science, anthropology and the narratives human beings tell ourselves.

Ideas come to me in many different ways. Sometimes they have to do with linear thought. Other times ideas occur to me when I'm thinking about something totally different from the project that I have in my hands. Sometimes things come to me in dreams, or just when I'm falling asleep or waking up.

Creative blocks happen. I think they can be overcome by resting. Or doing something completely different, experimenting with a new technique or trying a new medium. I always tell my students that mistakes are extremely important. They're the best way to learn. If we don't take risks, we don't learn and we don't improve.

In my own work, I give myself a lot of creative freedom in my personal artistic projects. I do what I like. But when I work with a client, I have to behave and be professional. As an illustrator it's important to work well with others, to be able to meet deadlines and recognize the client's needs."

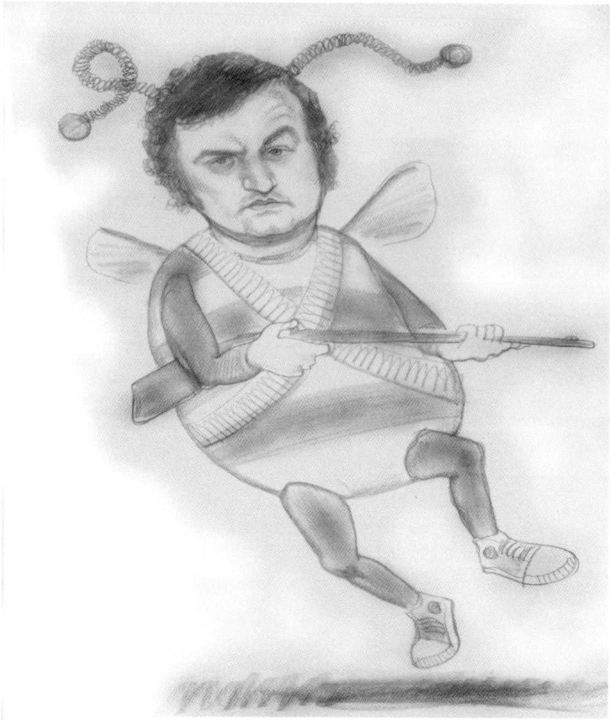

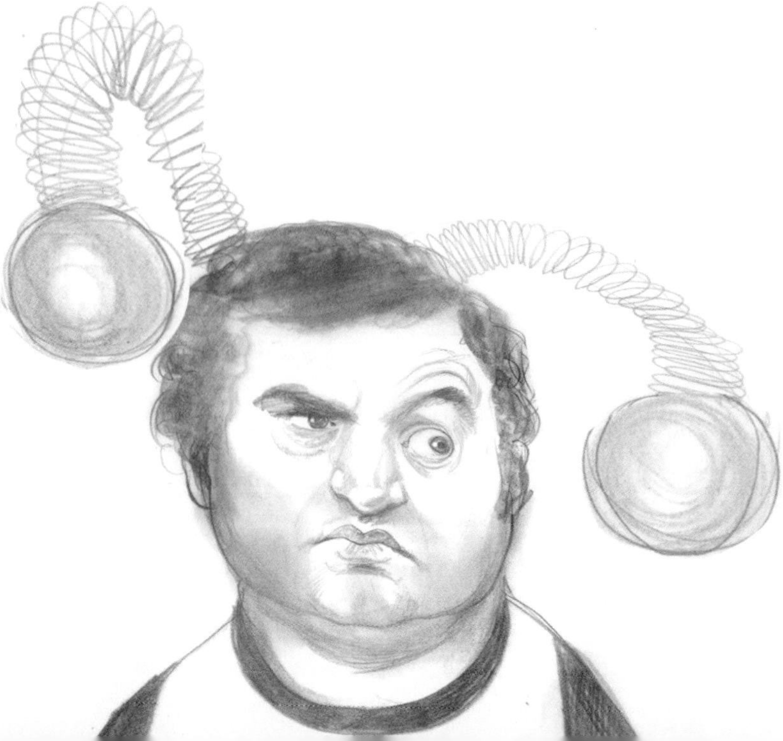

Rolling Stone

THE PENTAGON VS. CLIMATE CHANGE

40th ANNIVERSARY

Saturday Night Live

WE RANK ALL 141 CAST MEMBERS

RAY DAVIES
MY LIFE IN 15 SONGS

TREY ANASTASIO ON THE DEAD REUNION

FATHER JOHN MISTY

Issue 1229
February 26, 2015
$4.99

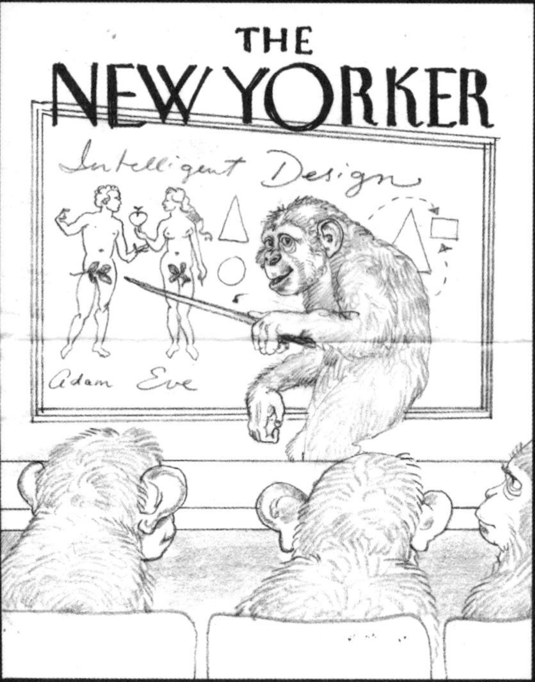
THE NEW YORKER
Intelligent Design
Adam Eve

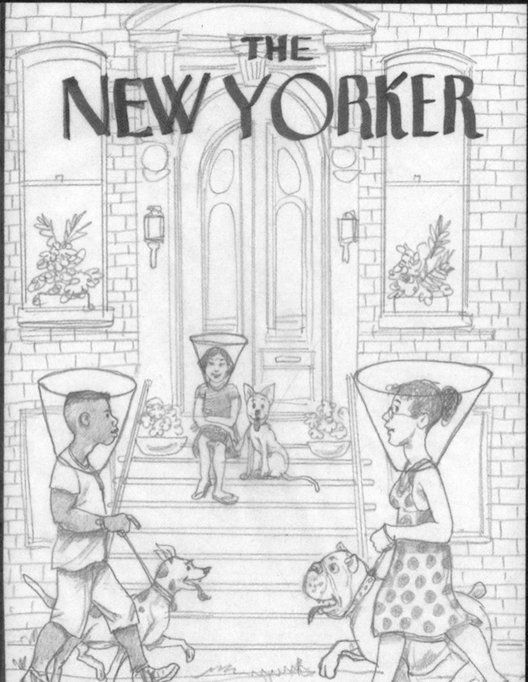
THE NEW YORKER

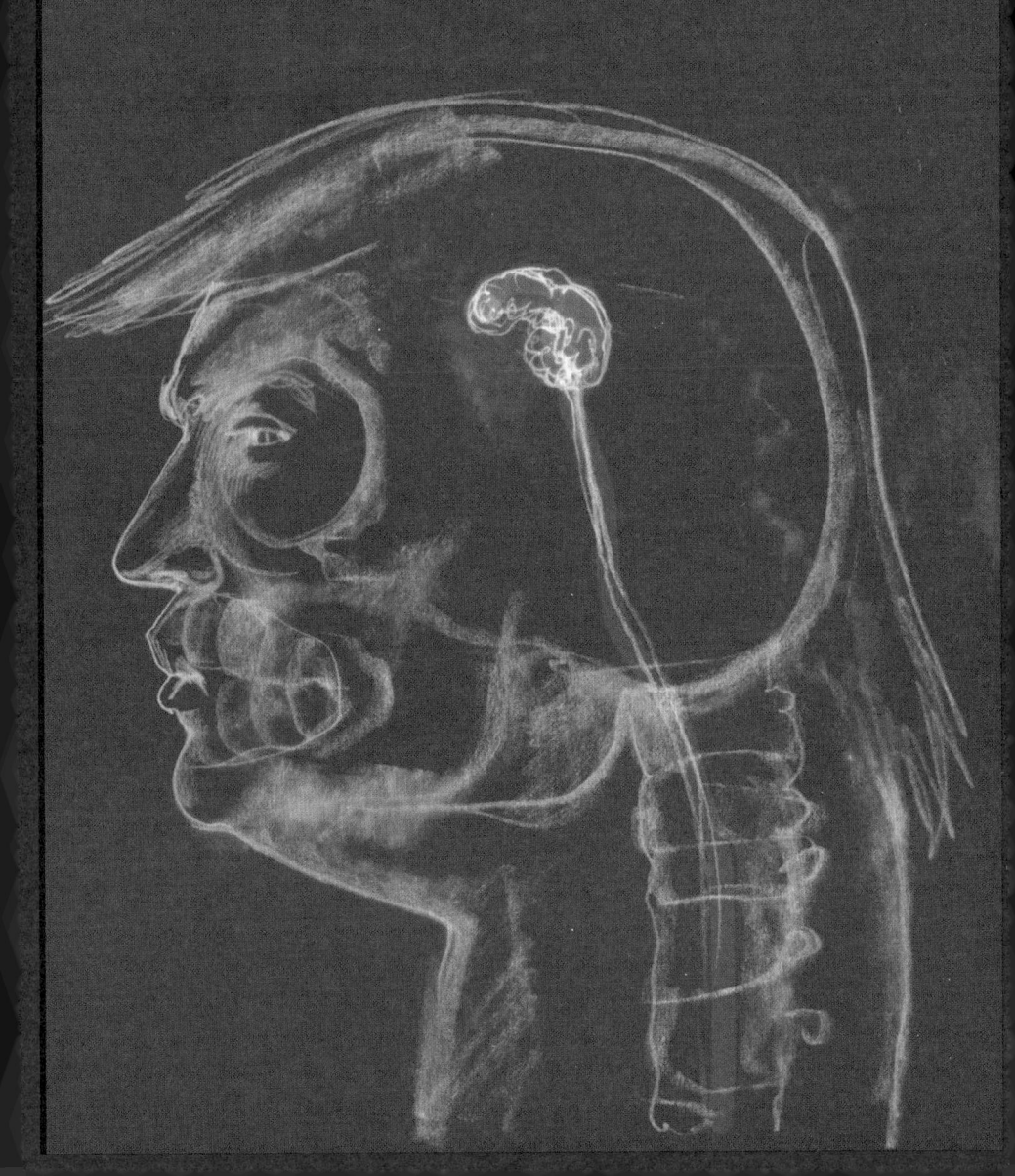

THE NEW YORKER

3

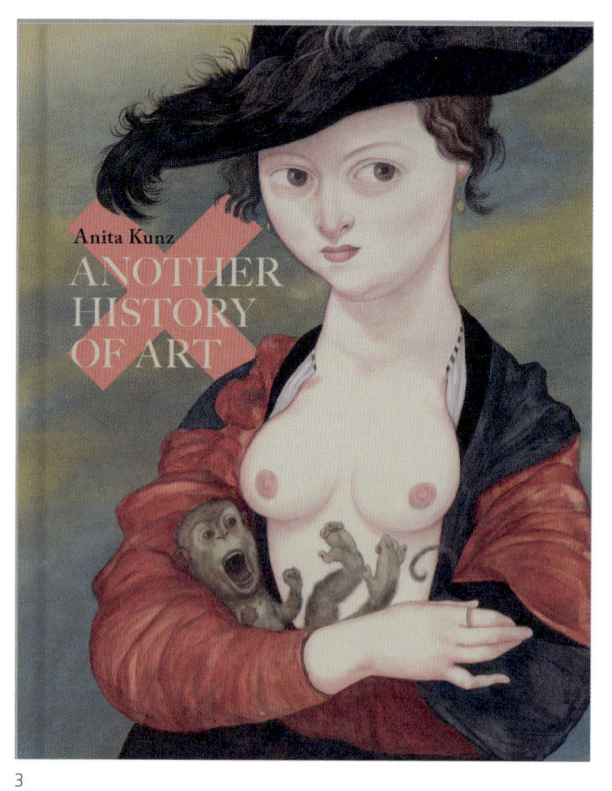

1. Image of a cover for *The New Yorker*.
2. Rejected ideas.
3. Personal projects.

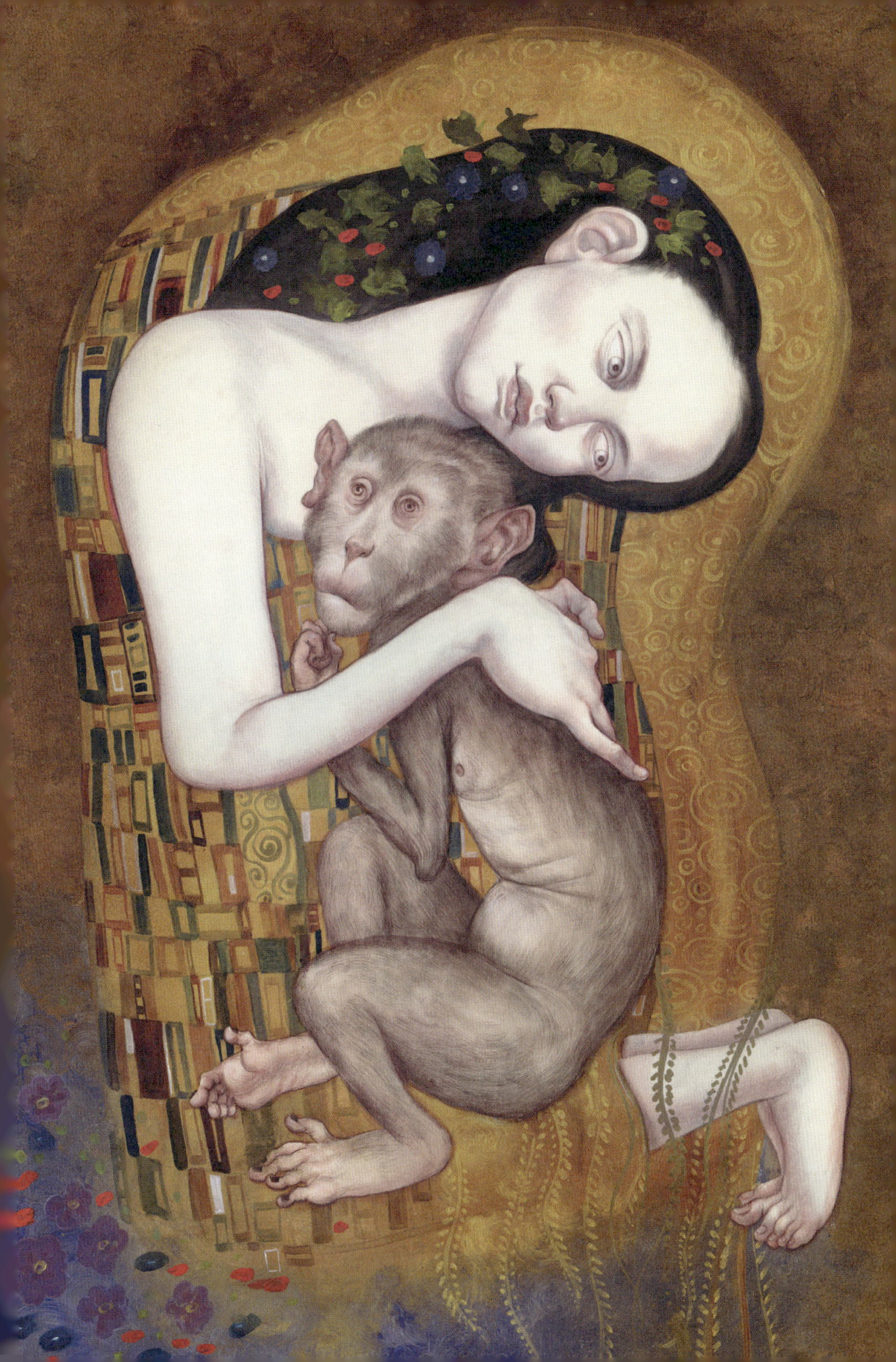

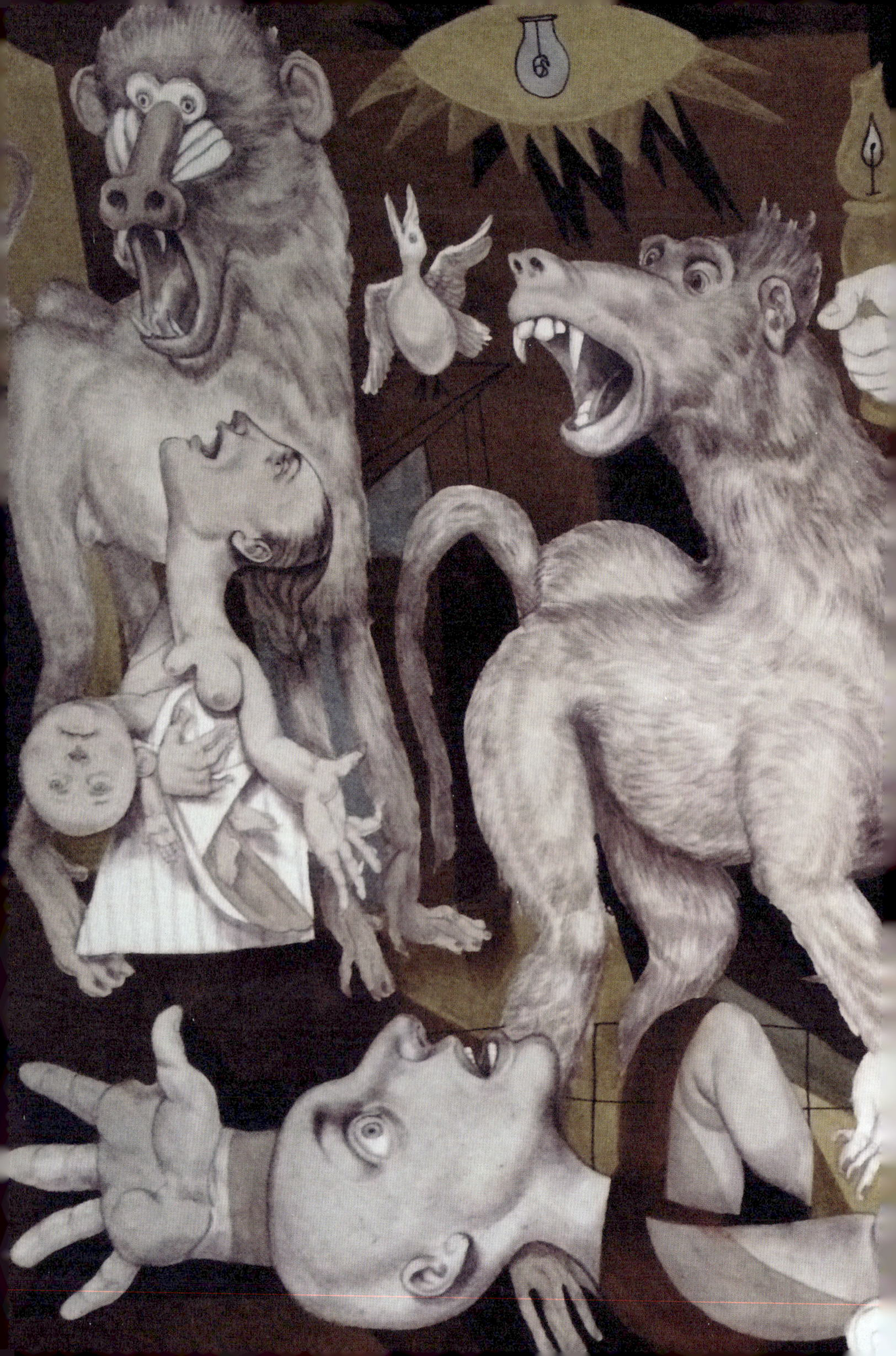

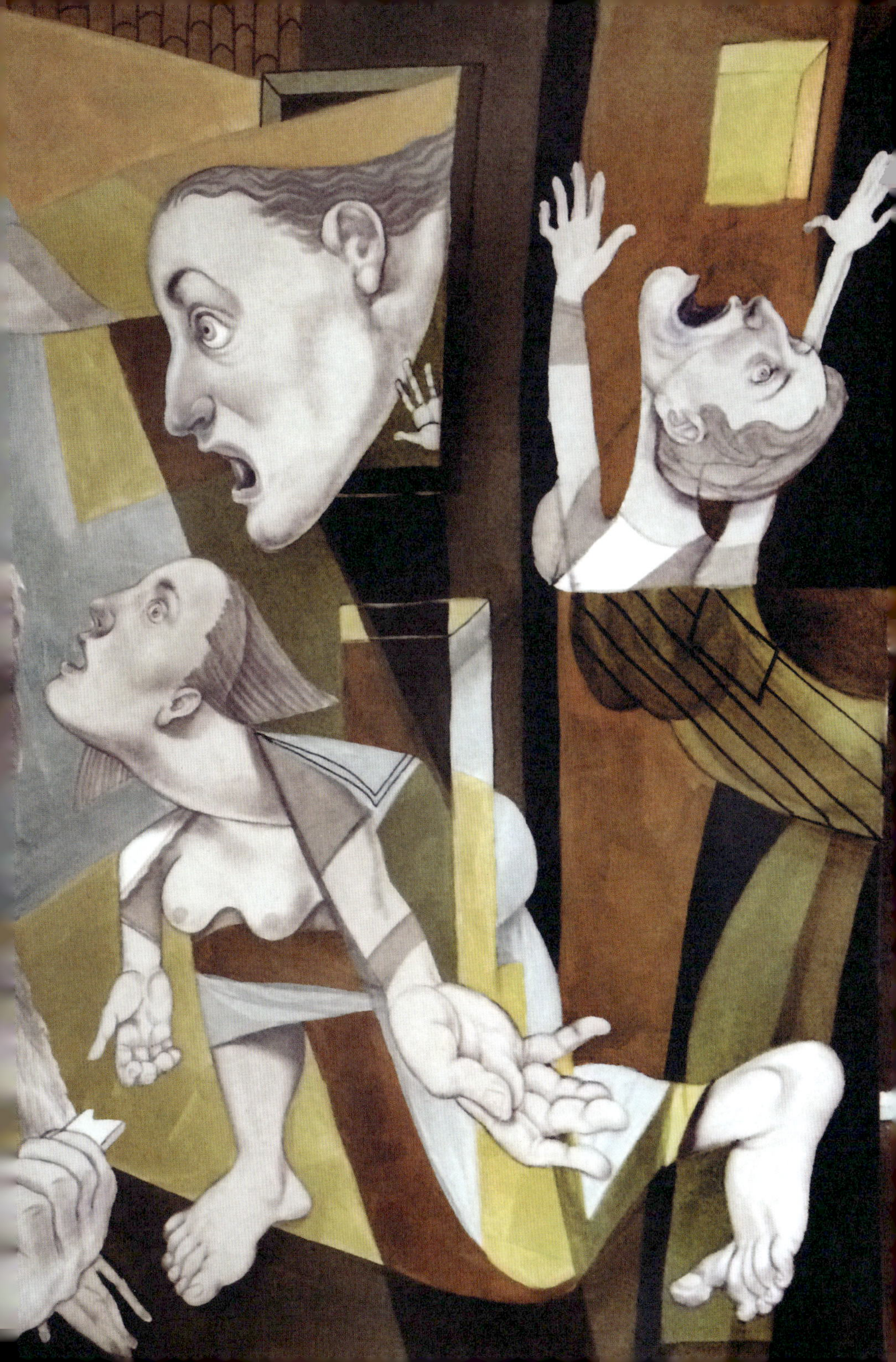

Manuel Marsol

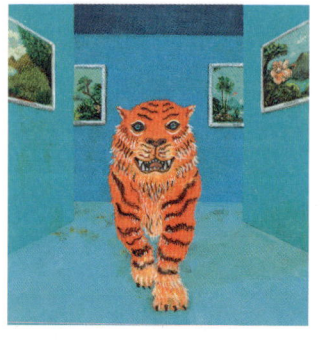

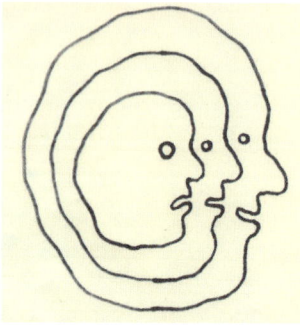

Manuel Marsol (Madrid, 1984) has in just a few years become an international point of reference for illustrated albums. He won the renowned Bologna Children's Book Fair International Illustration Award, the Ibero-American Catalog Award, the Amadora BD in Portugal and the Pépite Livre Illustré and Prix Sorcières in France.

With a degree in Advertising and Audiovisual Communication, he worked for three years as an advertising copywriter, winning awards in Cannes and San Sebastian, but left to focus on illustration. He pursued a postgraduate degree in Children's Illustration at EINA in Barcelona and published his first book after receiving the Edelvives Illustrated Album Award with *Ahab y la Ballena Blanca (Ahab and the White Whale)* (2014).

In Spain, most of his work has been published by Fulgencio Pimentel, with such titles as *El tiempo del gigante (The Time of the Giant)* (2016), *Yôkai* (2017), *Duelo al Sol (Duel in the Sun)* (2018) and *Mvsevm* (2019). He has also illustrated such novels as *The Metamophosis* by Kafka (Astro Rey, 2015) and *Venus in Furs* by Sacher-Masoch (Sexto Piso, 2016); as well as covers for Anagrama, Babelia (*El País*), Libros del K.O and Barrett, articles for the magazine *Líbero* and album covers for Jonston and El Palacio de Linares.

He has given lectures and workshops and has had exhibitions in France, Portugal, Taiwan and Mexico.

Richard Ford

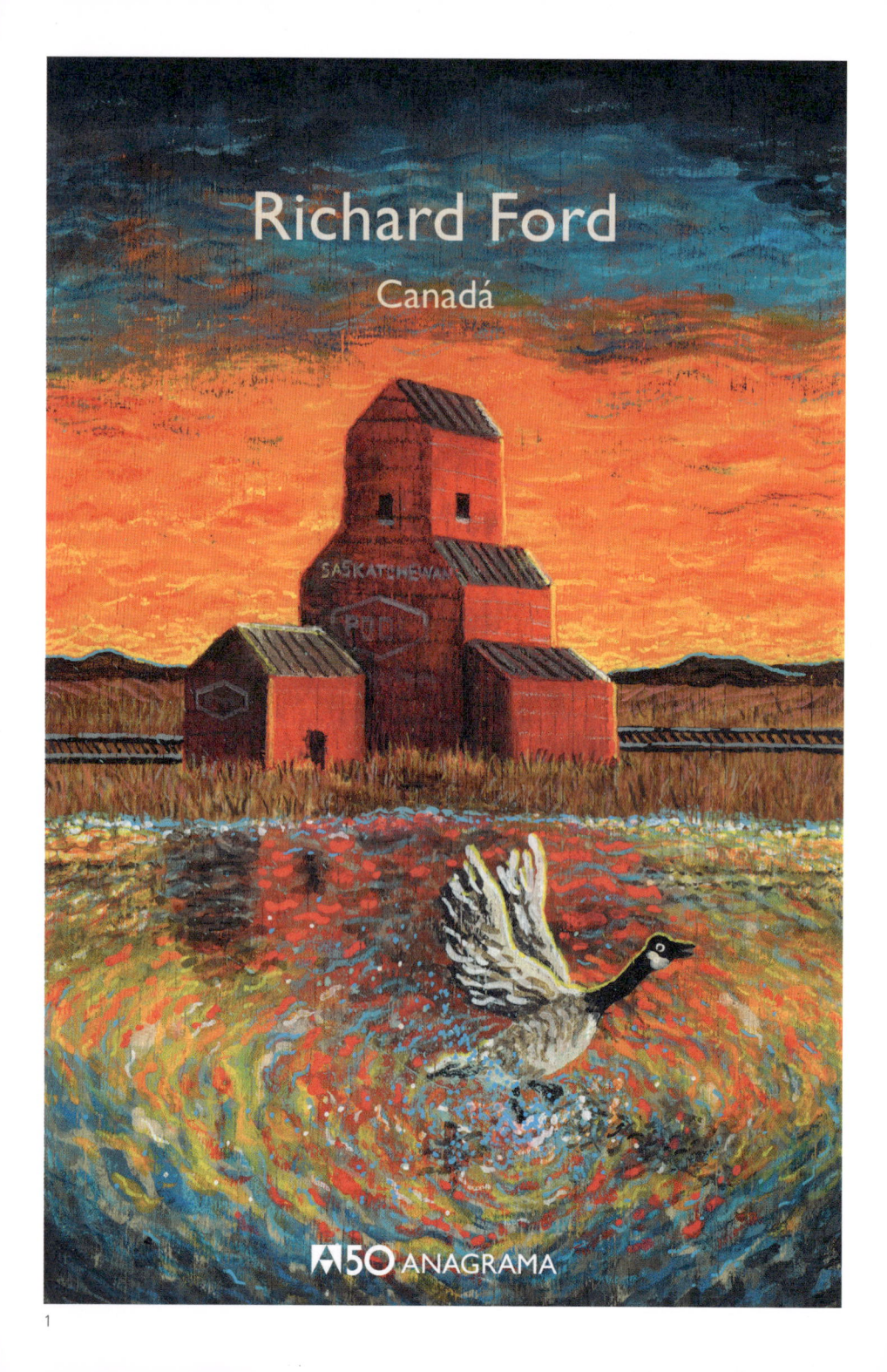

Canadá

ANAGRAMA

"I remember the excitement as a child when I would open a book and literally want to explore that world. I wanted to be there, to walk down those roads, to feel those textures, to talk to those characters. I wanted to inhabit those worlds. And I try to make sure that my albums have a similar effect on readers. If they contain anything, they're secrets to discover and time to be and to lose."

"Within fiction (film, books, video games, etc.), mystery, what is not fully understood, and even fear trigger children's imagination. I can give you a very specific example from my childhood: the impression that the image of the phantom airplanes scene in *Porco Rosso* (Hayao Miyazaki, 1992) had on me. There's a moment when a plane shot down in the war rises above the clouds and joins a long line of pilots marching in procession: they're the souls of pilots who have fallen in combat. The scene was of incomparable poetry and beauty, and I wasn't used to seeing things like that in cartoons. Such a poetic treatment of death had a profound impact on me. I couldn't understand it. I remember that I felt afraid but, more than anything, fascinated. And I had a lot of questions: Where were all of those planes going? Would they stay there forever? If they were in heaven, where was the other heaven? Now when I see that scene from *Porco Rosso*, I continue to be moved and to ask questions. Other scenes in Miyazaki that I discovered when I was older, like the trail that leads to *Totoro's* hideaway and Kodamas forest in *Princess Mononoke*, connect directly to my feelings when I was a child. The ones I had, for example, when I'd wander into the pine forest to gather pine cones for the fireplace. I'm convinced that experiences with fiction like this are the reason why now in my work I try to recreate the same atmosphere, the same degree of mystery.

I read something by Bolaño where he talks about the danger of writers who are understood. Or rather writers where everything is understood. I don't try to be deliberately cryptic, not in the least. In fact, a lot of my work consists of making my universe accessible, not only enjoyable and understandable for me. But, at the same time, I don't want to over explain it or for it to be repetitive. Not everything needs to be seen. Not everything should be understood (not even by the artist himself) because if everything is understood, there aren't any surprises or questions Striking the balance between what's boring because it's accessible and what's boring because it's inaccessible is the author's biggest challenge."

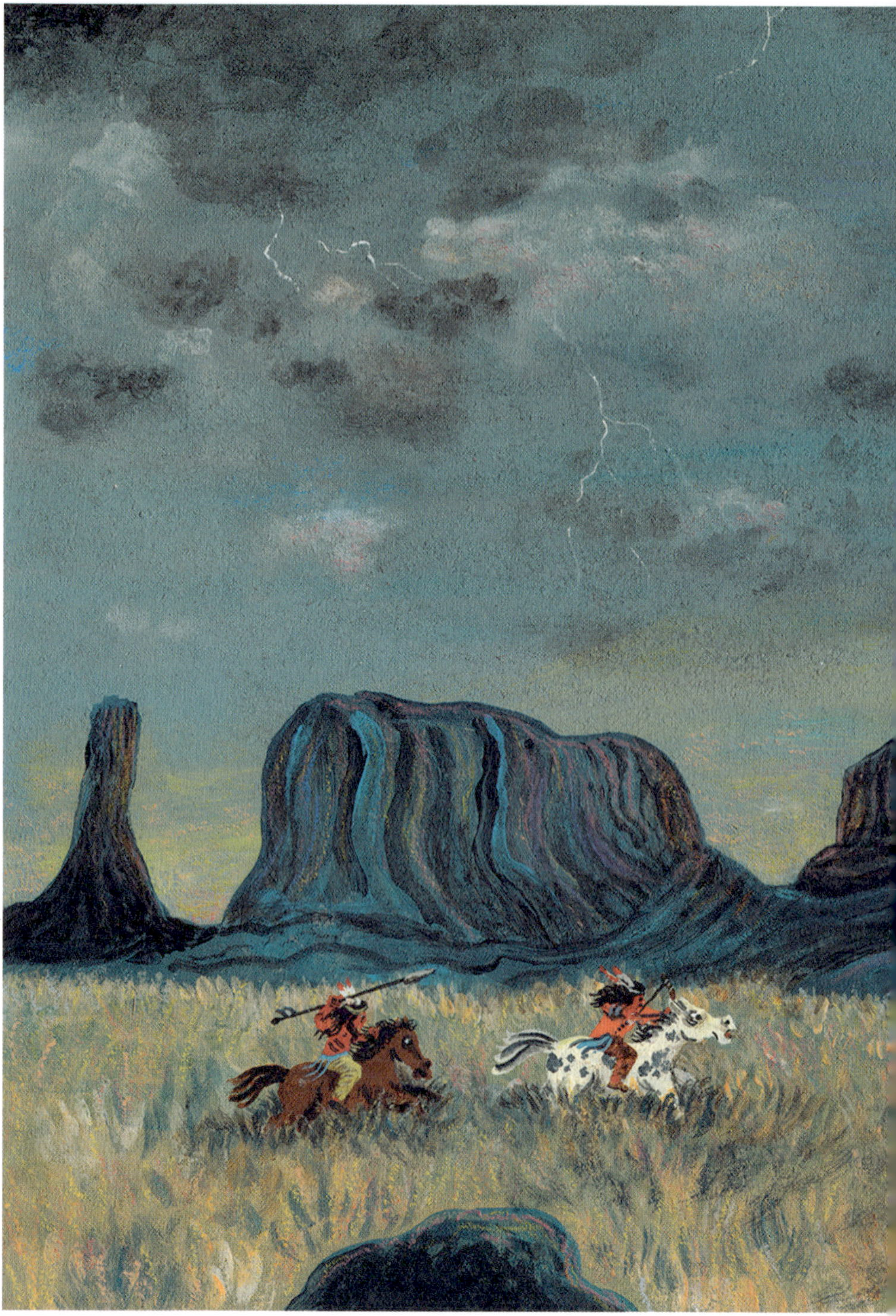

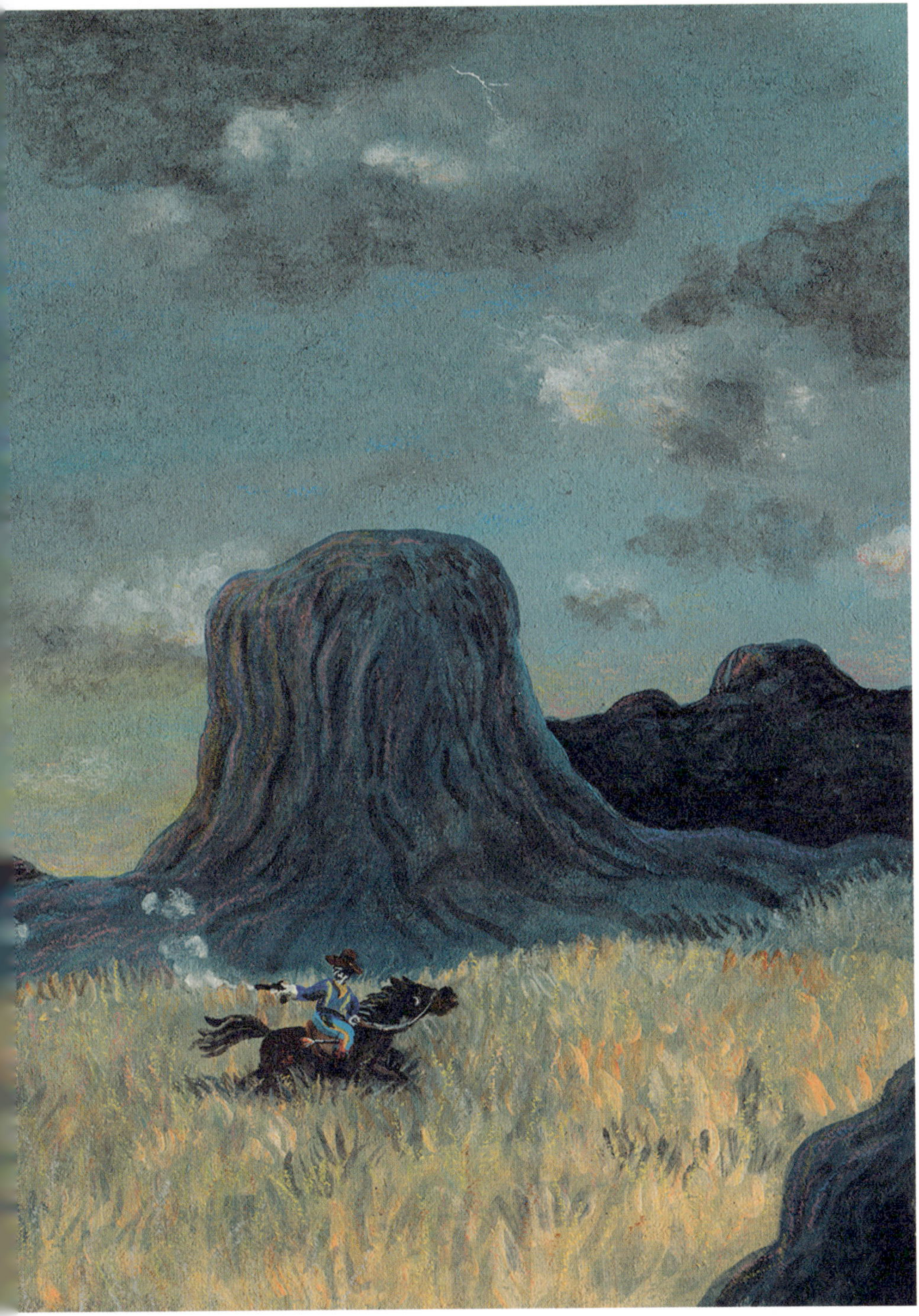

1. *Canadá*, Anagrama, 2019. Text by Richard Ford.
2. *Western Scenes*, Project in preparation.
3. *Mvsevm*, Fulgencio Pimentel, 2019. Historia de Javier Sáez Castán.
4. *Yokai*, Fulgencio Pimentel, 2019. Creative process and illustration.
5. *La leyenda de don Fermín*, SM, 2018.

"There's an interesting essay called *Saving Beauty* by the South Korean philosopher Byung-Chul Han that criticizes the tendency in today's aesthetics towards the hyper-polished and the perfect, embodied by the sculptures of Jeff Koons and smartphones. The philosopher argues that 'we like this demand for positivity because it doesn't hurt and doesn't put up any resistance but leads us to things that are increasingly banal and superficial. When, in reality, what shakes us up is the unexpected, contrast, opaqueness, mystery, irregularity, negativity.' The essay is very nuanced. Yet in a world where childishness seems to be invaded by the demand for positivity and by the uniform and 'polished' aesthetics of mass products, it doesn't hurt to rediscover less conventional forms that can still be found in many illustrated albums of yesterday and today. Because as much talk as there is about a publishing boom, it's still a minority (and somewhat precarious) market, and therefore not really guided by the logic of consumption, which anesthetizes rather than aestheticizes. For this reason, it's good to keep in mind less 'polished' work such as that by masters of children's animation like Vladislav Starévich and Yuri Norstein, of whom Jim Henson was a worthy heir, and illustration album authors like Atak, Stepán Zavrel, Kitty Crowther, Etienne Delessert, Javier Sáez Castán, Jesús Cisneros and Józef Wilkon, to name a few."

25 - AGOSTO

Álbunes
- Viaje carretera
- Montaña
- ~~Fútbol~~

Un escalador?

MONTAÑA

Caballo gigante

montañas a lo lejos

El montañista va subiendo, y se va parando a contemplar el valle, descubriendo cosas, etc.

Pero su meta es la cima.
¿Qué habrá allí arriba? ¿Será capaz de alcanzar la cima?

Algún animal le acompaña.

Una montaña mágica, con la capacidad de modificar las cosas a su alrededor.
- Caballito blanco - Caballo gigante.
- La cima se convierte en el valle
- El barco que sube por ella (Fitzcarraldo)
- Las gambas que florecen en los árboles.
- La roca que cambia de lugar.

Su mano se transforma en la de un monstruo, o animal, etc.

La importancia de "el otro lado"

Caballo mete cabeza

túnel mágico

Una cueva que lleva al otro lado.
Al cruzarla cambia el tiempo, o la luz, o teletransporta una m... o la cabeza de u... caba... o tr...

túnel Noche

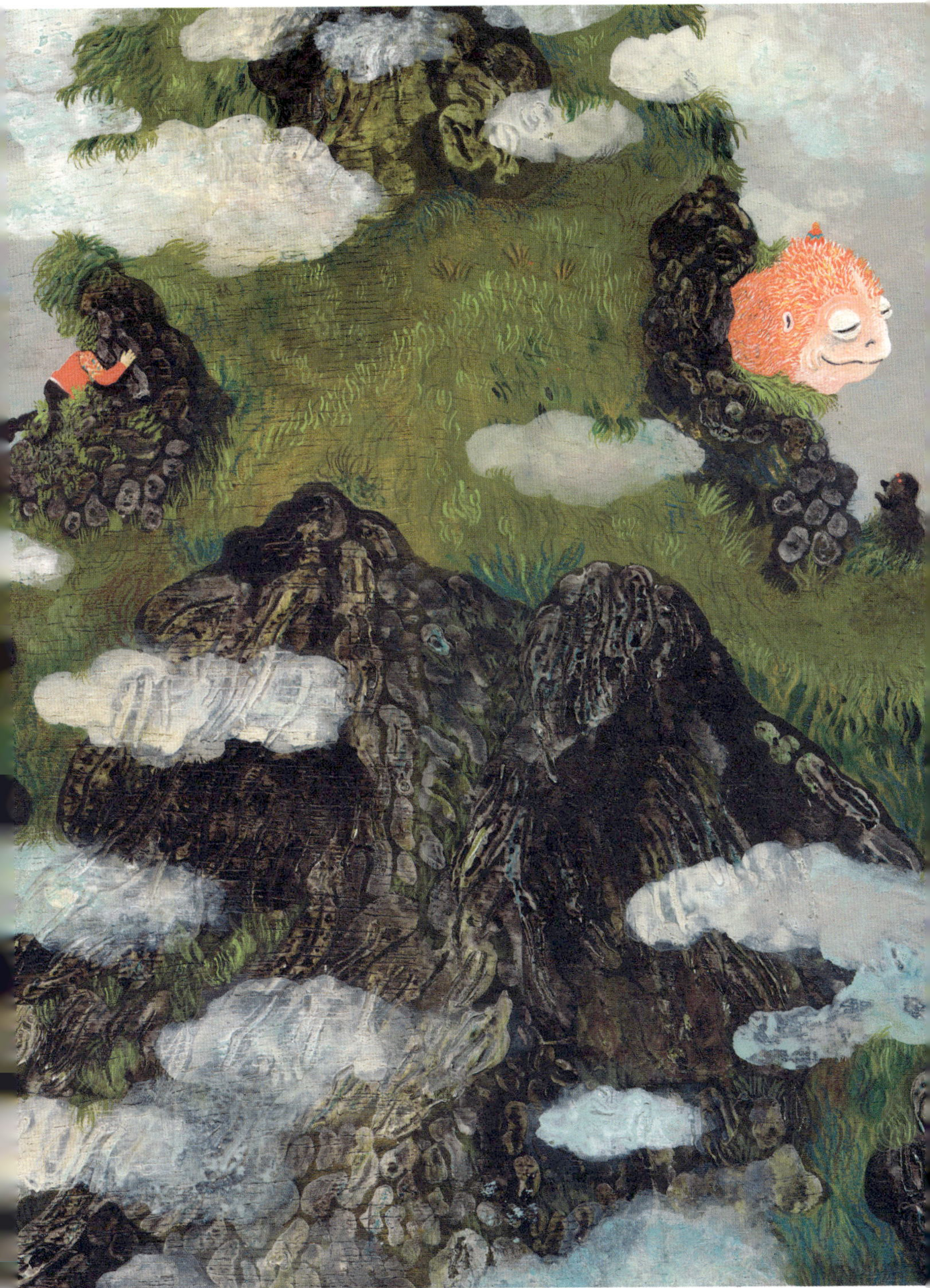

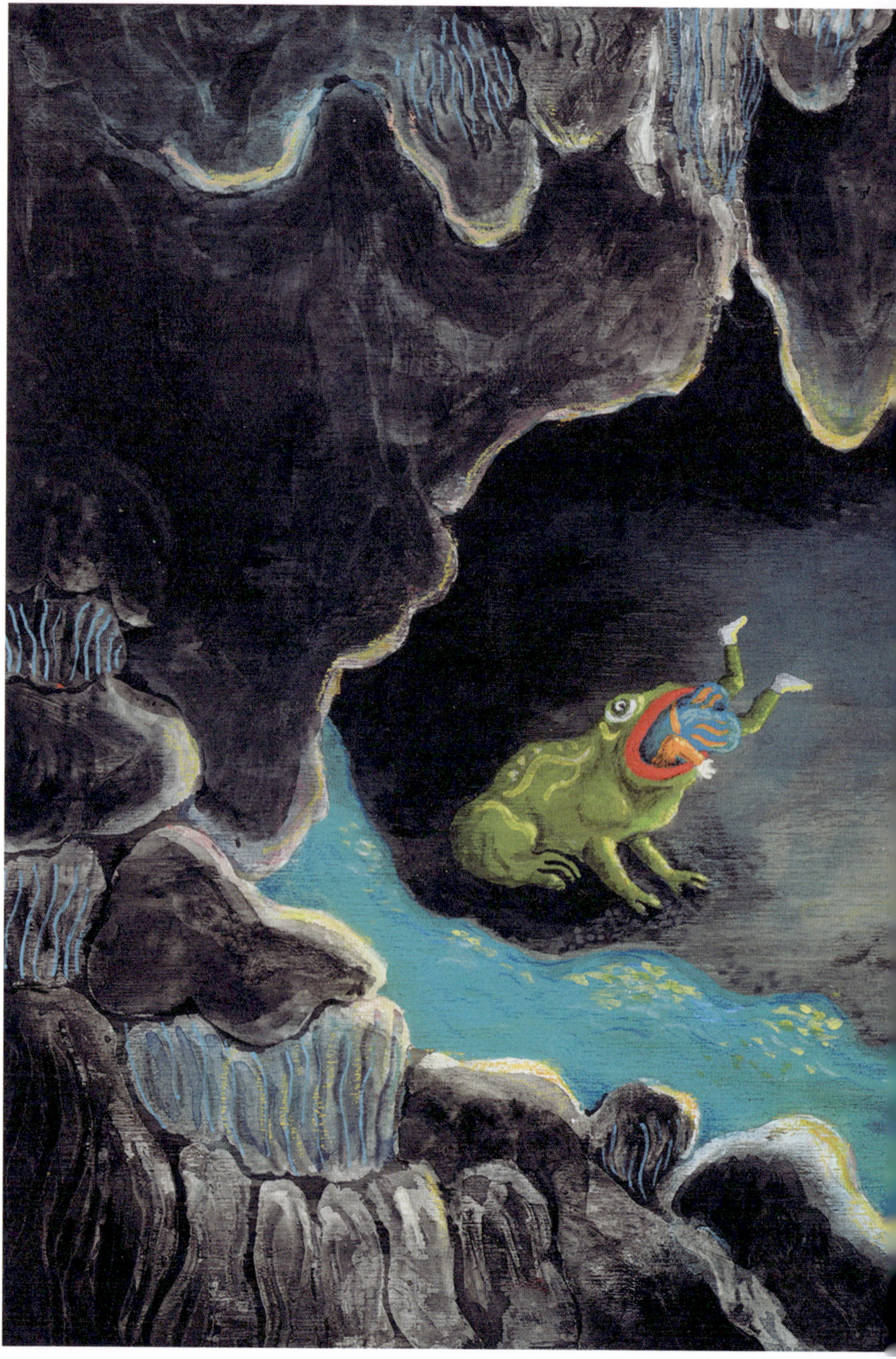

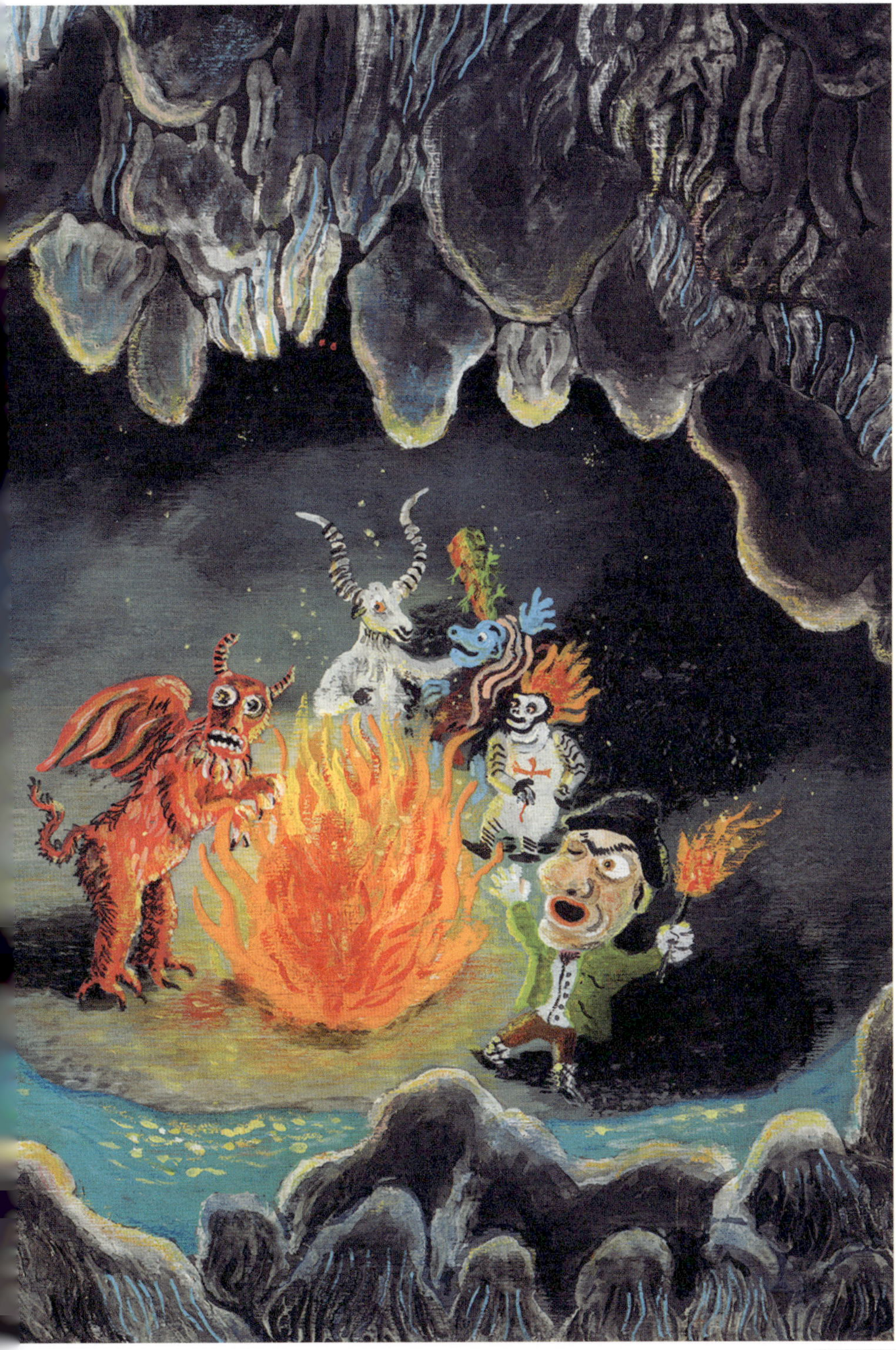

Flavio Morais

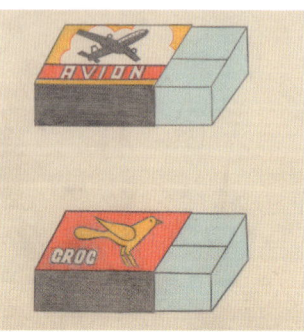

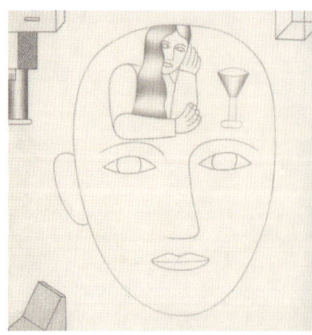

"I've had the opportunity to use my illustrations in various formats including magazines, newspapers, murals, design projects and animation... for clients such as *The New York Times*, *La Vanguardia*, Canal+, *Los Angeles Times*, Fundación Joan Miró Barcelona, Vamos Festival Newcastle and *The Financial Post*.

At the same time, I've always experimented with personal projects. In addition to fueling my commercial illustration work, they allow me to look inside myself and find freer spaces, which always leads to individual or group exhibitions in art galleries such as Casa de América de Madrid, Fundación Miró Barcelona, Galerie T Dusseldorf, Galerie Anatome París, Pentagram Gallery Londres, and Abject Gallery Newcastle."

INTO THE
Birria-VERSE
QUESADILLAS
Birrieria
¡Deliciosas!
Ricas
GONZALEZ
TACOS
HOLLA
LA TIJUANA
MULITAS

PICOLE
LOVE
RED
Boi ESTRELA
yes
CHILLI POWDER
here
MC
DISCO VOADOR BRASILEIRO
BUS
QUE LUZ
funk
FM

"I'm inspired by music. And life for me is pure music. So you could say that absolutely everything inspires me. All is worthwhile if the soul is not small, said Fernando Pessoa. Although I also like the idea of doing work that has nothing to do with inspiration, something ordinary. It's a relief."

"I don't know if can define my work, since it's always in motion and changing in each different setting. Maybe for that reason I prefer not to try and define it, so as not to confine it. Instead of defining it, I'd rather describe it.

I alternate between commissioned illustration work and personal experiments. Many of my illustrations are heavily indebted to the woodblock prints of northern Brazil, known as Cordel Literature, from the two years I lived in Salvador, Bahia, where I immersed myself in the local popular street culture. It's basically a re-reading of Cordel's woodcuts, though currently I'm exploring a more personal path and experimenting with pencil drawings and wood volumes. The illustrations are based on the typical commercial storyline, with a text or a concept as a starting point and with the objective of communicating something and a financial compensation at the end.

The personal experiments aren't corrupted by profitability, pragmatism and commercialism. It's an experimental exercise in freedom.

It doesn't mean this or that. It's a finger that points in a direction without any prior intentions, a game of intuitive and random improvisation in order to be able to forget names and lose myself in more open spaces where meanings aren't important".

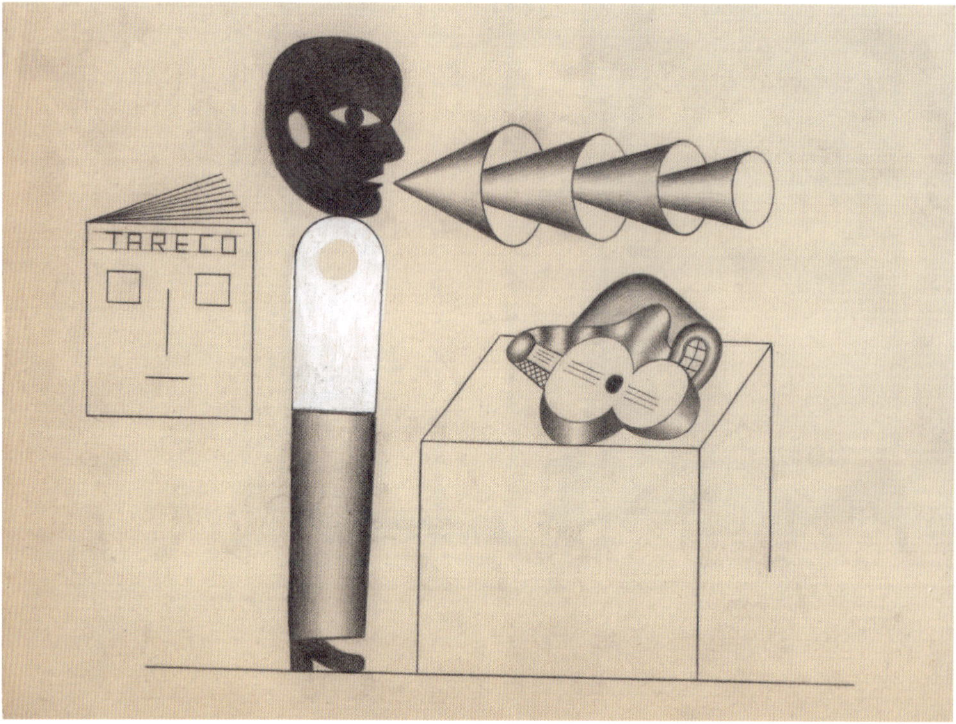
TARECO

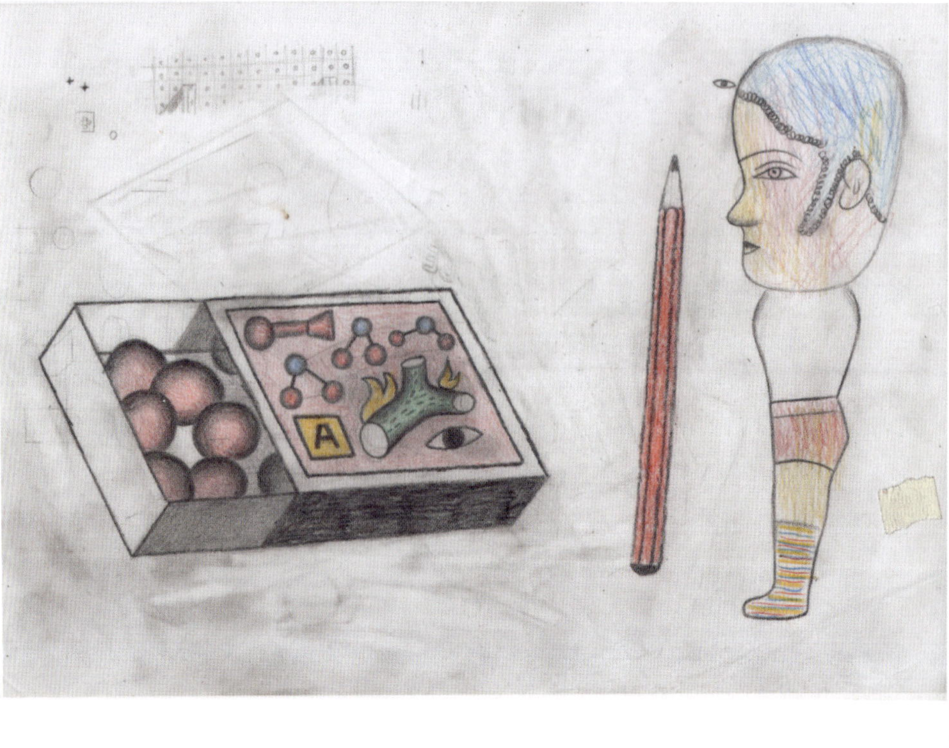
A

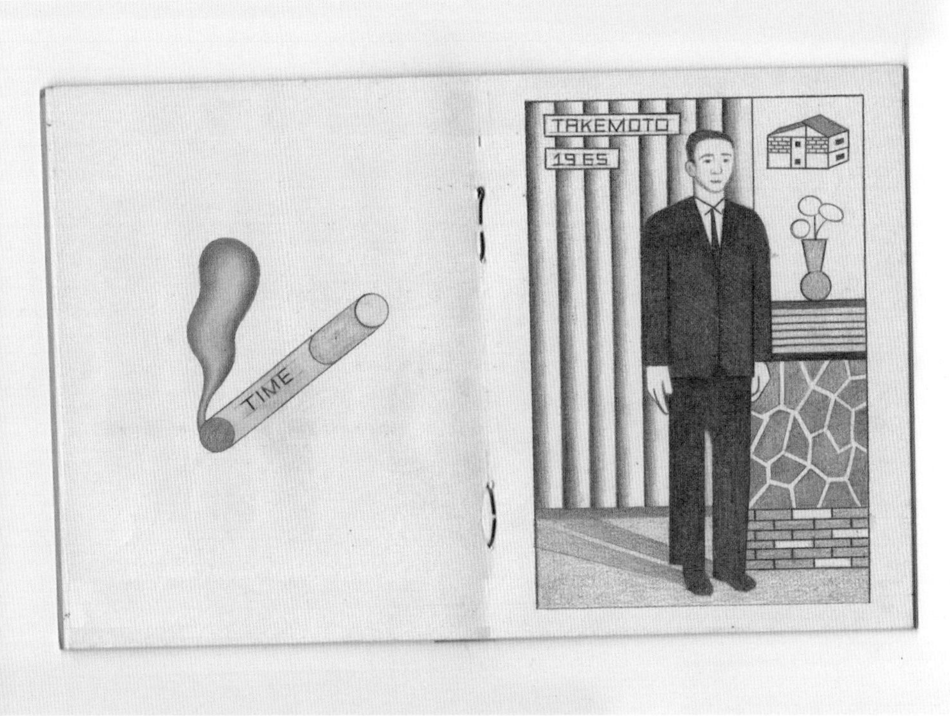
TIME
TAKEMOTO
1965

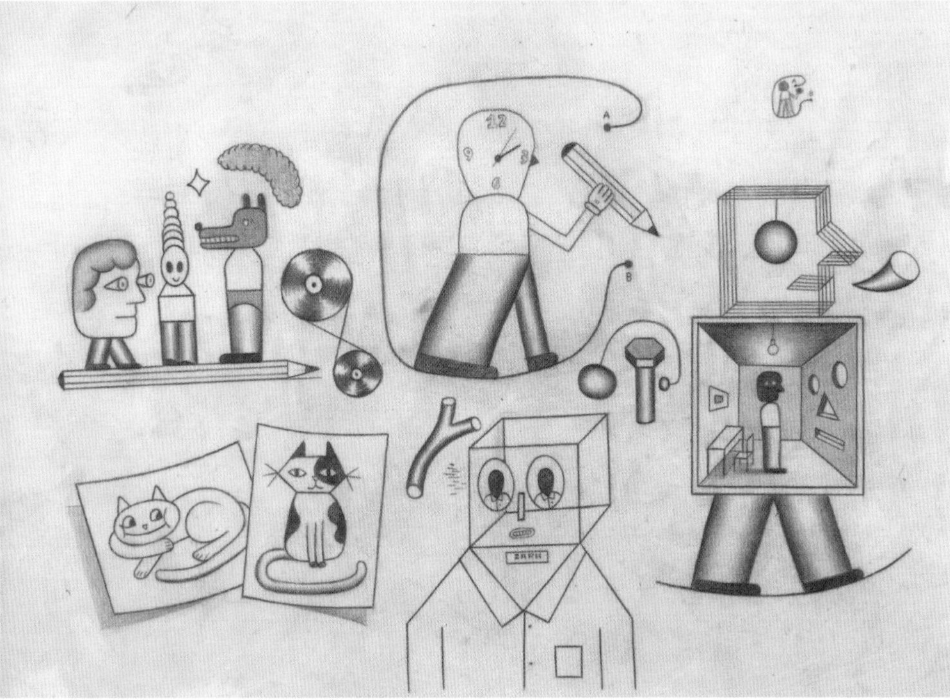

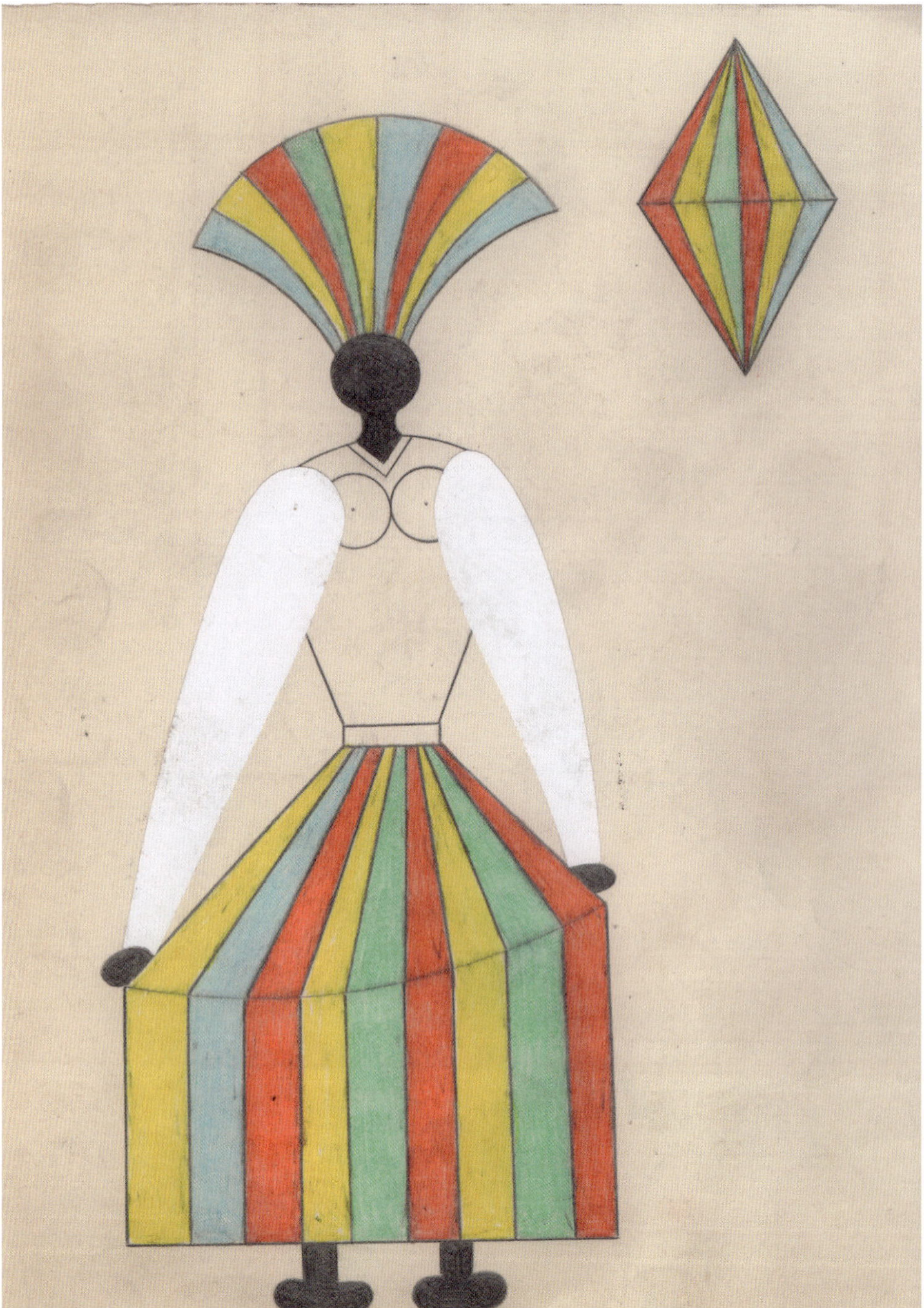

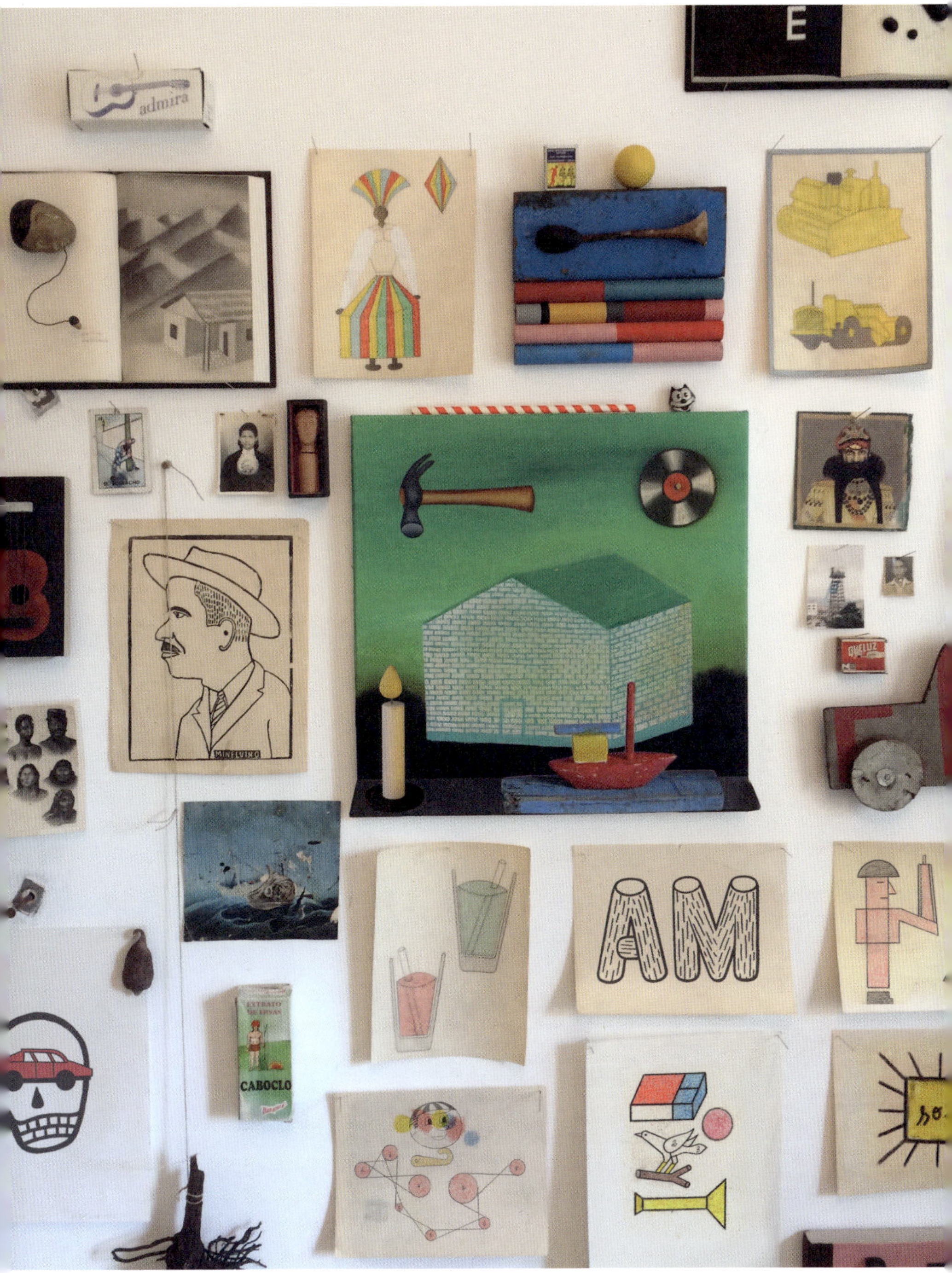
admira
E
AM
CABOCLO

Pérez Arteaga

1

"When I was six years old, I remember my first year at school, my first patron saint feast day for Brother Polycarp, and my first drawing contest in his honor. I never could draw. I lacked the ability, the patience and the interest. But after transforming Polycarp into both a saint and a superhero who could fly and appear in different places at the same time, I was chosen as the unanimous winner of the contest. This changed the way I looked at life. Doing something that others couldn't do, and even more so if it was an artistic matter, granted you a certain aura of superiority, a kind of magic power that you couldn't squander.

When you are good at drawing, your future is determined: you study Fine Arts, or Design, or Illustration, you meet people with the same artistic sensibility, and if you're lucky, you make a career out of it. Since this wasn't the case with me, I studied economics."

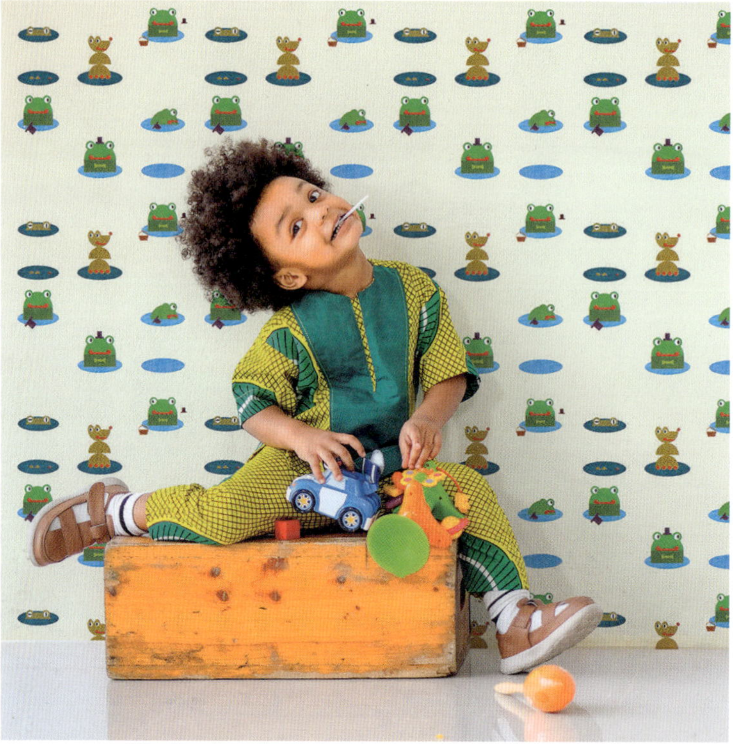

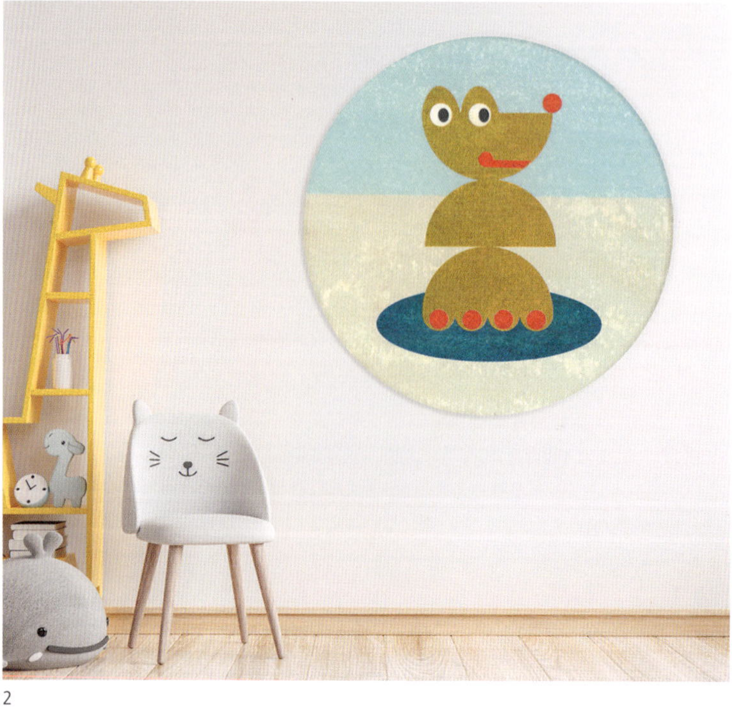

3

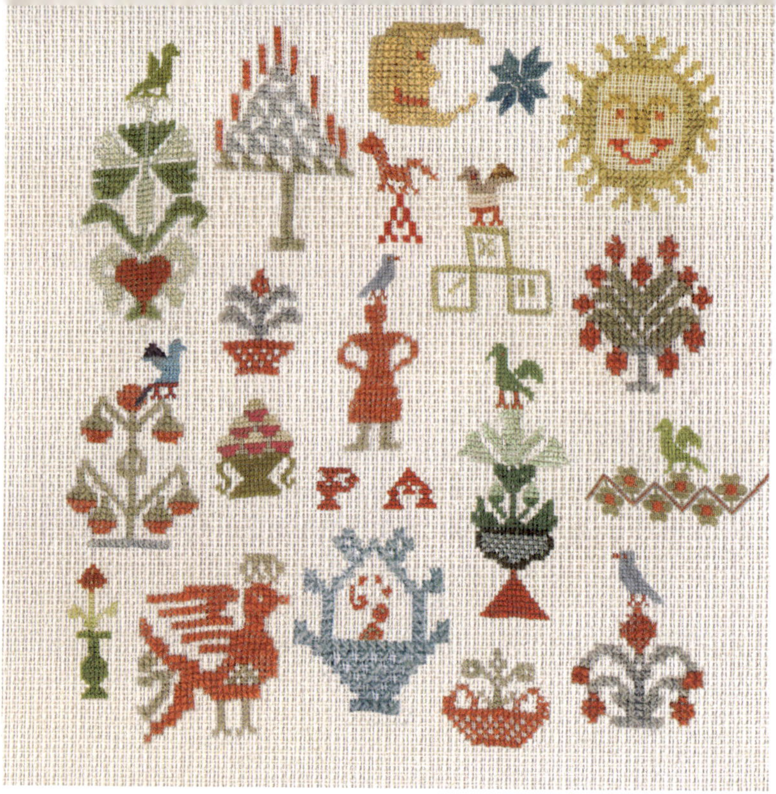

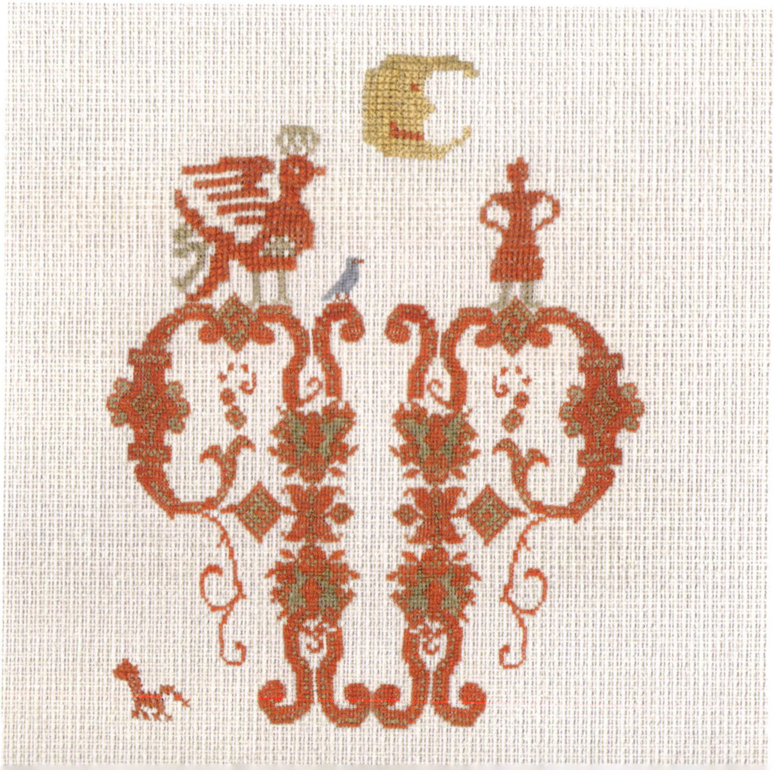

"My field is graphic design. In my case, this includes creating corporate images, graphic design for exhibition projects and book layouts. There's not a lot of room for illustration, and even less if it's personal, but I try and do it whenever I can.

Illustration for children's stories is another matter. In general, I don't have a very defined style and I've never been good at adapting to market *tastes*. In spite of this, I've published ten stories that have received some recognition. These are personal projects that for the most part I've illustrated and also written. They've been published in Spain, Mexico and Brazil by OQO, Milrazones, El Naranjo and Yekibud, small publishing houses that support special books.

The stories appear out of nowhere. They pop into my head effortlessly. When they appear, they become obsessive. You could say that I have no choice but to bring them to life, and I almost always do it compulsively.

It rarely happens to me and there's always a trigger. Holding my son in my arms when he was born inspired me to tell a story about *dreaming with little angels*; a piece of wood found on the beach leads me to search for an African legend that deals with death; the sun reflected in my eyes at the beach makes me think of characters lost in the world of *dreams*. I don't set out to make a book. I don't research techniques. I don't labor over the process of creating an illustration. It just appears and I have to capture it before it slips away.

***Práscedes. Me gusta dibujar*, Yekibud, 2019.**

The needlework lay there for years, in a corner in the living room of the house in the village.
Barely hanging on in a corner of the frame was a black-and-white photograph of Elvigia, my father's only sister, who died very young. We always thought the embroidery was something she'd done at school.
When it's a rainy day and there isn't very much to do, it's easy, at least for me, to return to these mementos, to take up the photograph for the first time and discover a date – 1898 – written in a corner and the initials P.A. And also to notice for the first time what I'd seen on countless occasions: a glove, a small ladder, a peacock and some plants. Quickly I find a sheet of paper and begin to write a story, almost as if it were a dictation.
Later I learned that P. A. was Práscedes Alastuey, my great-grandmother Pascuala's little sister.
As a girl, she left the village to work in a priest's house.
I don't know why I envision an erudite priest, one who gave her the opportunity to study and who opened the doors to a world of needlework, of those designs that were so fashionable in wealthy European households and that also made their way to certain circles in America.
I also imagine that I create a story, in part, with someone with whom I share sensibilities and dreams, even though between us is an exhilarating distance of more than 120 years.

El Rey que no quería ser Rey

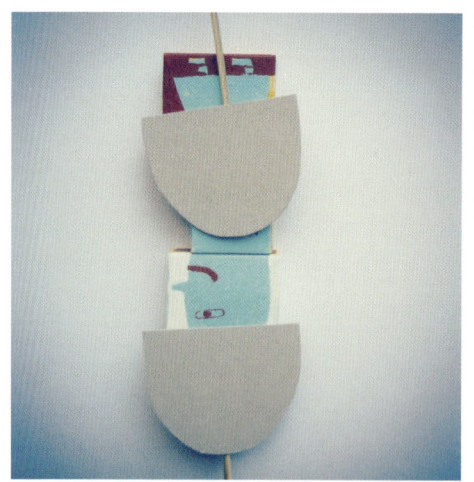

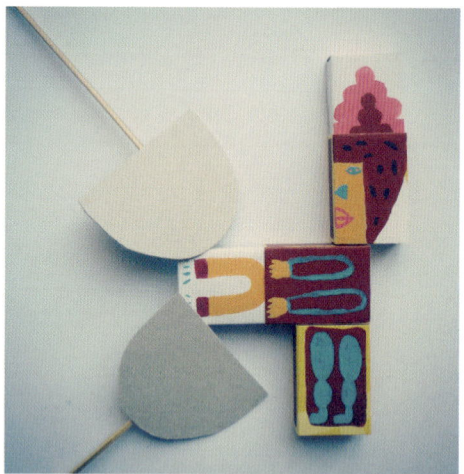

Miguel Ángel Pérez Arteaga

Veo Veo
en el aire

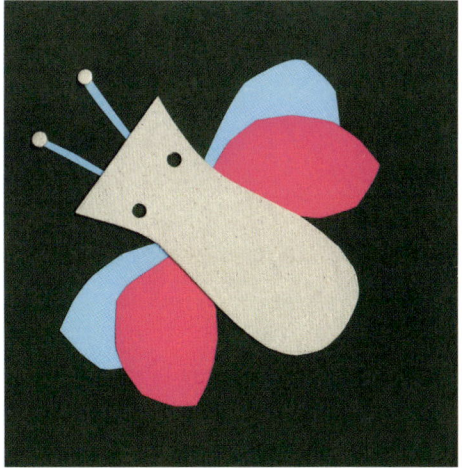

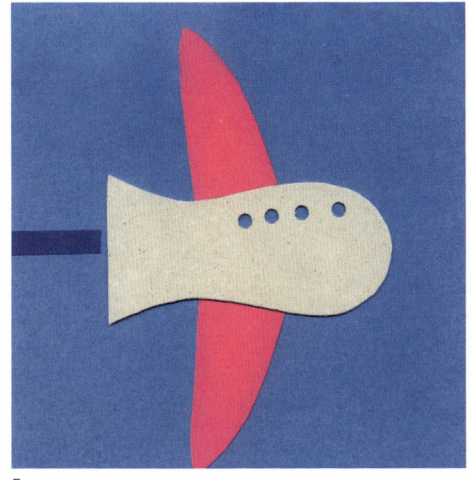

Miguel A. Pérez Arteaga

ediciones
el naranjo

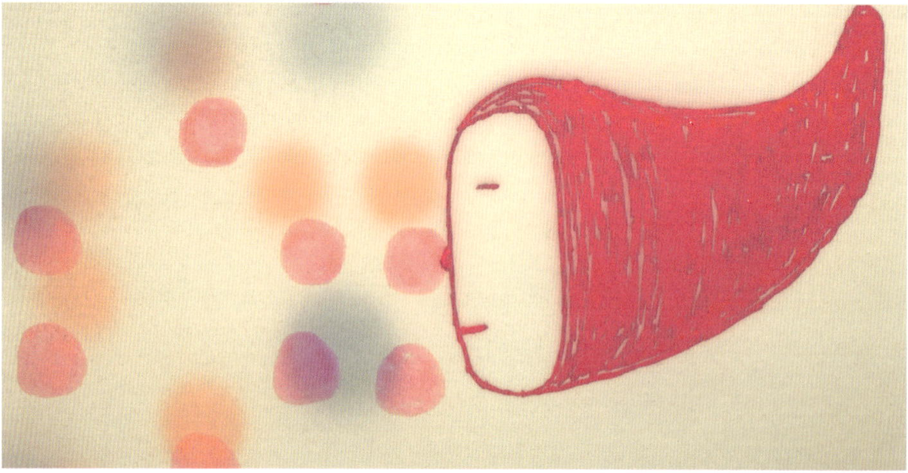

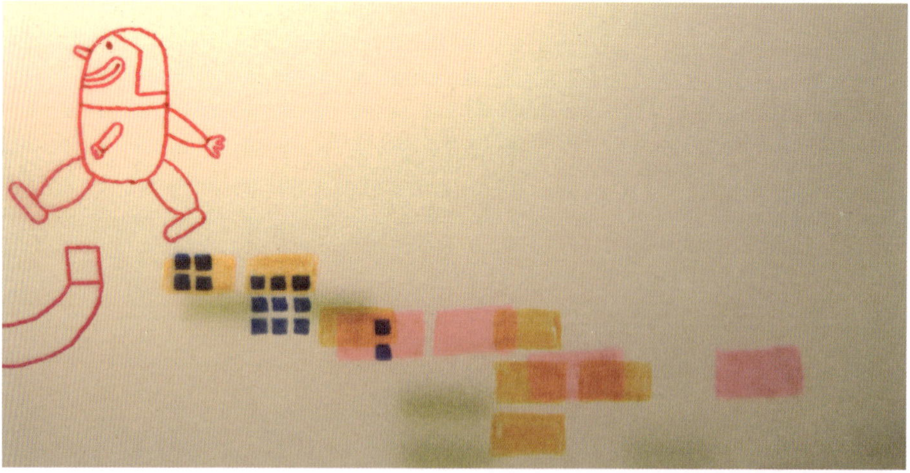

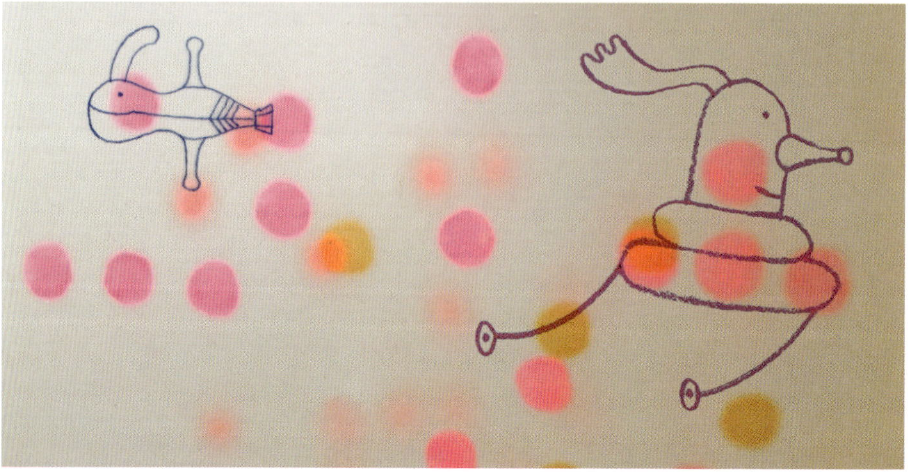

7

"Over time, I've come to realize that each of my books stems from a concept linked in some way to educational issues. I've always been interested in education. I've taught at different educational levels and I'm deeply concerned about such things as creativity and its loss as we advance through school. For that reason, I like to create stories for really young kids. I don't mind doing drawings that aren't highly elaborate and stylized. An illustration with mistakes, intentionally imperfect, made from found or recycled materials can be far more powerful.

    I like to encourage children to create their own stories. I use any means I can to try and speak their language. I use wood, stones, matchboxes, clay, ink stains, spackling and cardboard cutouts. Anything to communicate ideas with a certain beauty, poetically, and with a bit of humor."

"I try and make the different projects feed off each other. Sometimes I use the same ideas, the same graphic elements slightly modified to communicate very different things. I like to use aesthetics related to contemporary art for advertising posters and children's stories; or use languages from a child's world to communicate with an adult audience. Being able to move from stories to exhibitions, or from advertising to packaging, is what makes this job so unpredictable and unique for me."

1. *Bosu the Lizard and the Plants That Never Die*, Milrazones, 2015.
2. Folititon.com. Illustrated wallpaper and decorative elements website, 2022.
3. *Albarrazin. Inventario*, Texts by Grassa Toro, Fundación Santa María de Albarracín, 2016.
4. *The King Who Didn't Want To Be King*, Milrazones, 2015.
5. *I Spy In The Air*, Ediciones El Naranjo, 2012.
6. *Los sueños*, unpublished.
7. Poster *La noche en blanco*, Government of Aragon, 2020.
8. Poster *Ley de derechos culturales*, Government of Aragon, 2022.

Simone Rea

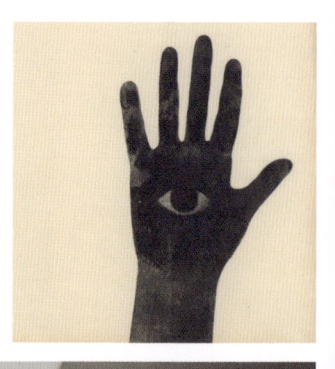

"I started drawing when I was three years old and I've never stopped. Still I decided to set out on this amazing adventure almost by accident. I studied photography and graphic advertising at an art institute and then attended the Academy of Fine Arts in Rome, in the decoration department because there was a professor, Gino Marotta, who I'd heard was a great painter. And I definitely wanted to paint. Then, one day by accident, I found myself at an exhibition in Rome featuring work from an illustration school in northern Italy. I immediately felt at home. I still remember that sensation and what I thought: 'I could follow that path'.

The need to communicate has always been inside me. Illustration is a very powerful means of communication. What better tool than a book to tell stories?

I think that book illustration is only communicative if it respects the texts with which it interacts and only if it leaves the reader room for imagination."

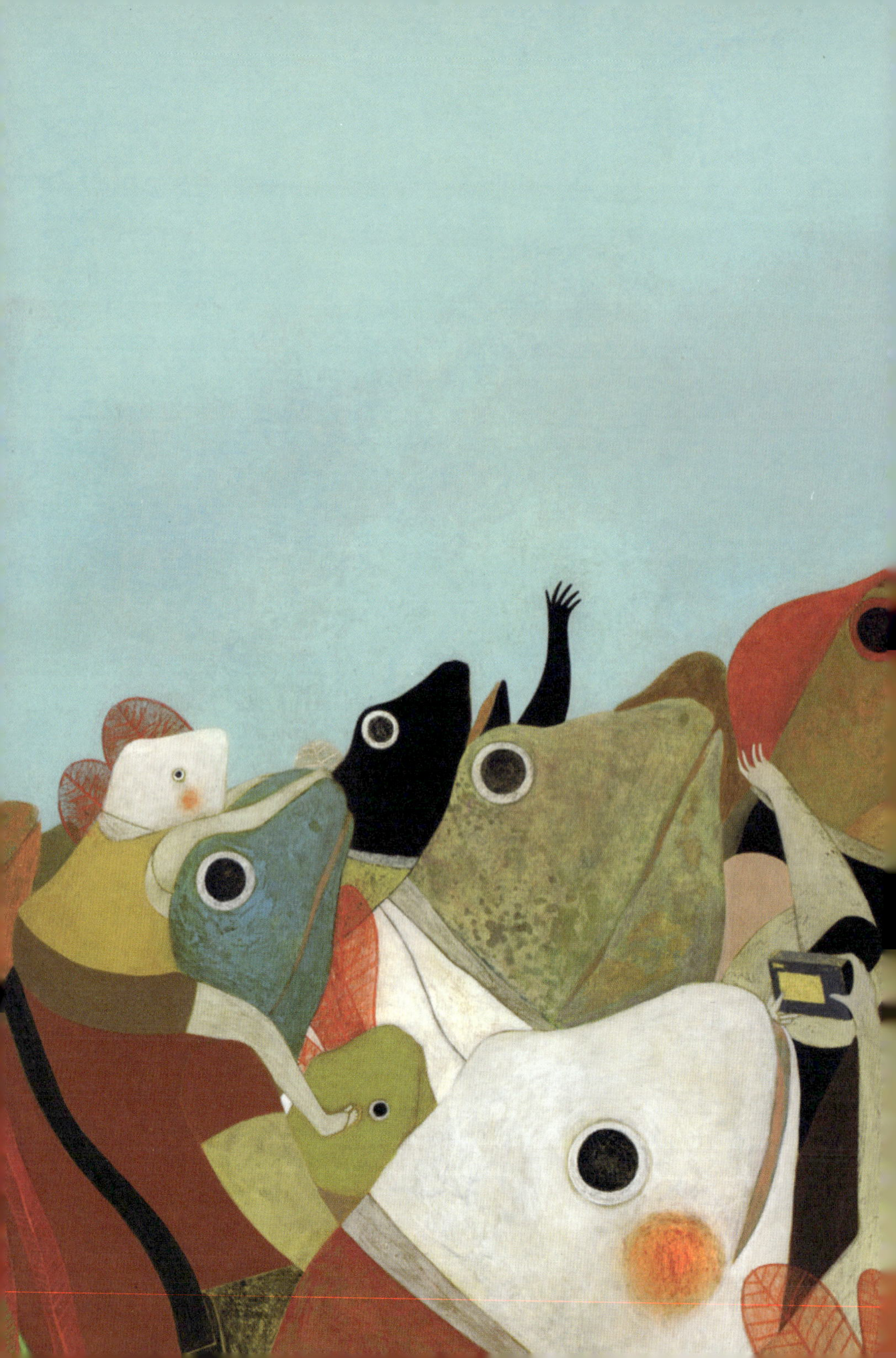

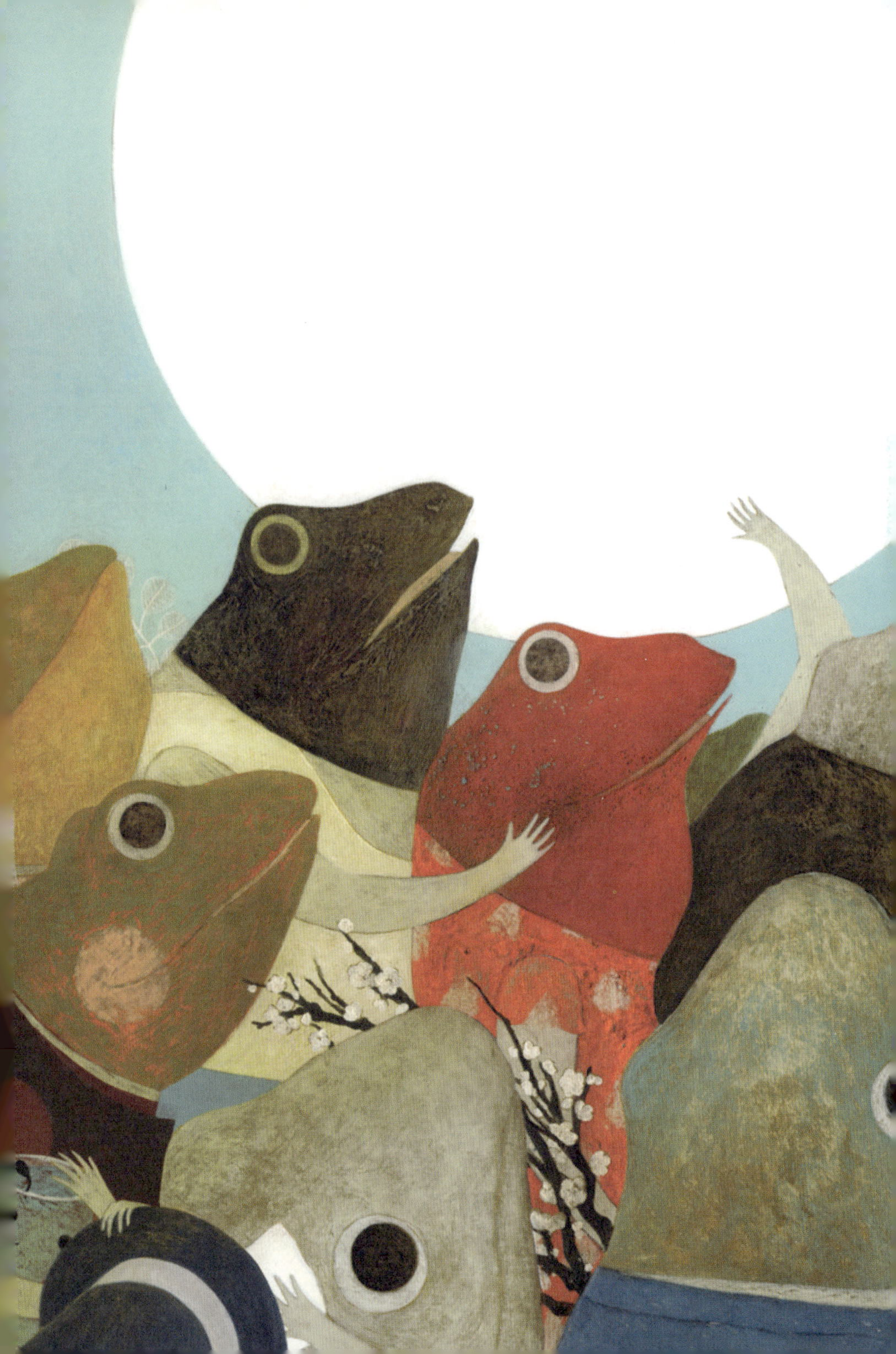

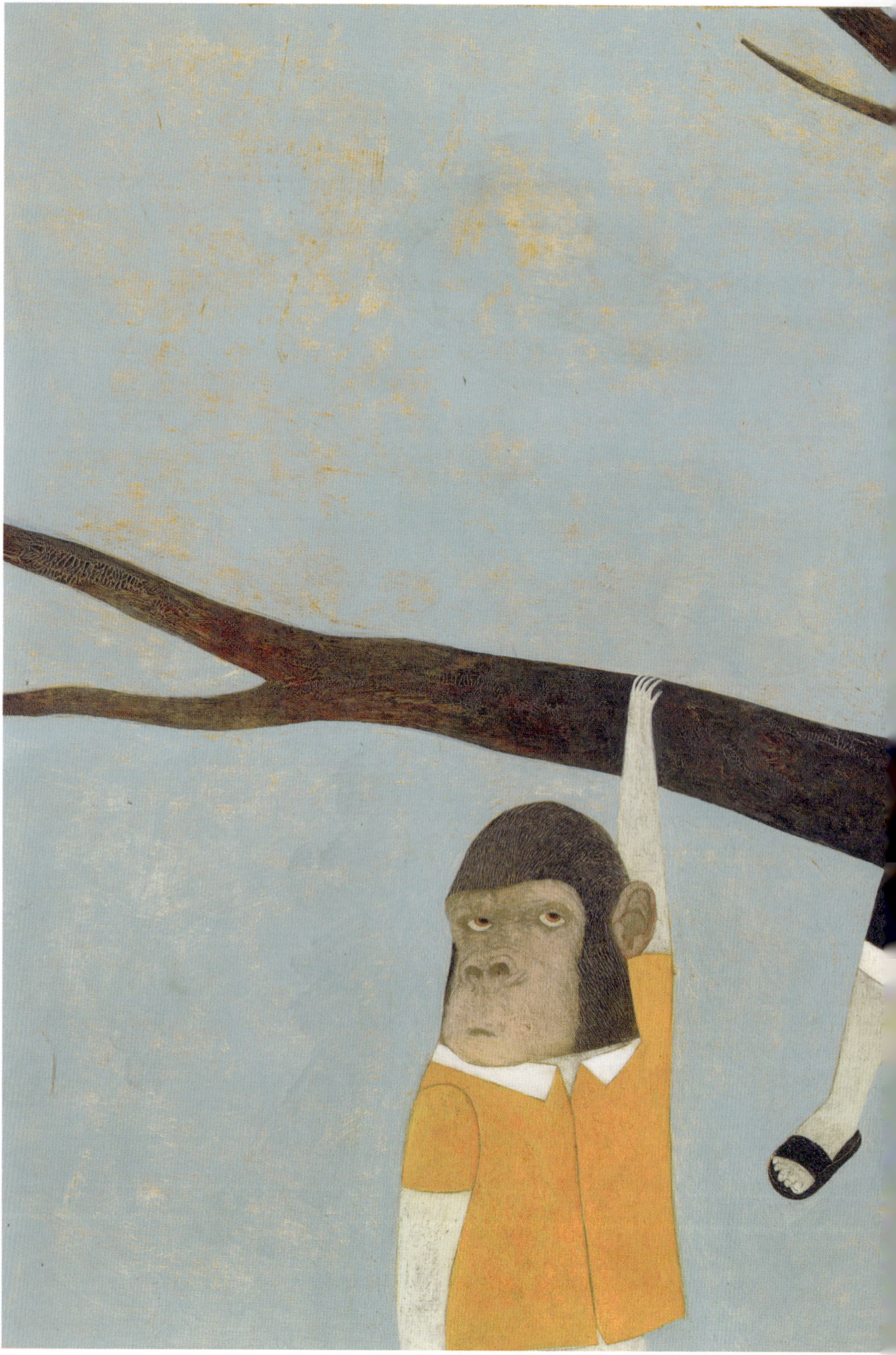

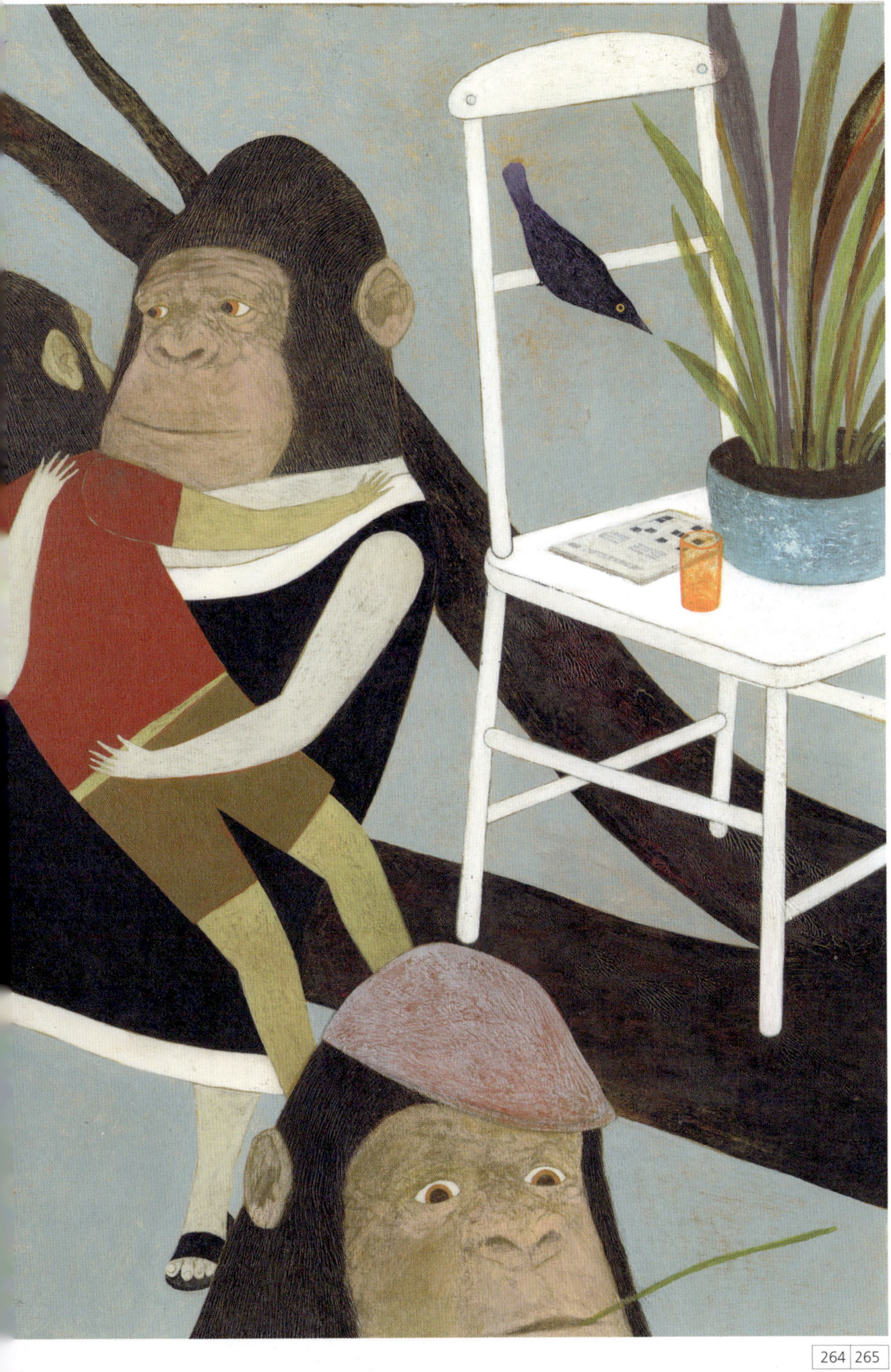

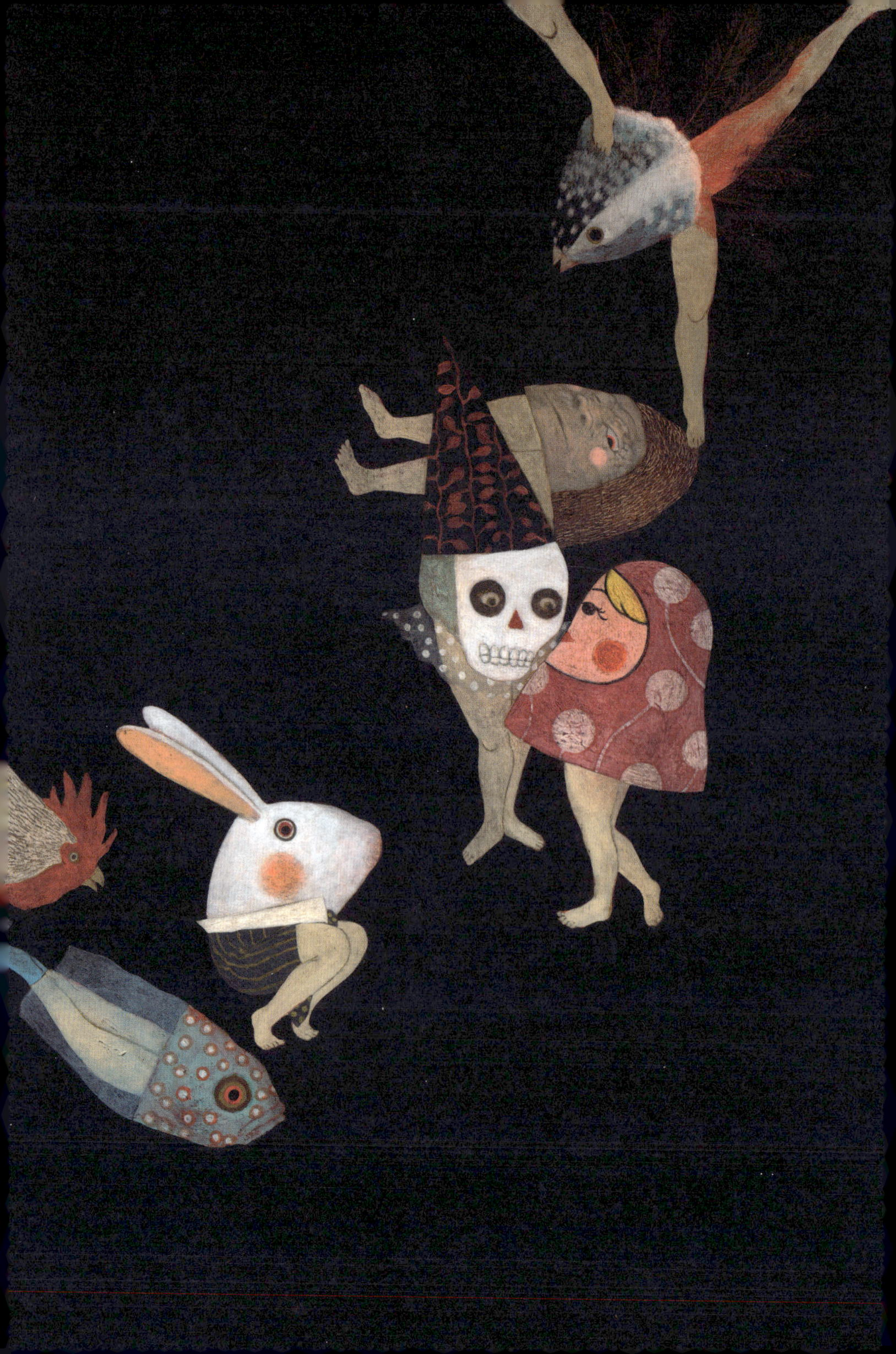

"I think my illustrations are sincere. I always try to adapt to the text without going against my nature. A good book isn't bound by time. It doesn't have an objective, and, of course, it doesn't have to please the viewer. A good picture book doesn't age, and it speaks to everyone, to people young and old.

I have about thirty books to my credit. The publishers I work with and have worked with are: Topipittori, A Buen Paso, Rizzoli, Orecchio Acerbo, Seuil Jeunesse, Didier Jeunesse, Cambourakis, Vanvere Editore, la Margherita Editore, Einaudi Ragazzi, Franco Cosimo Panini and Il Castoro Editore.

I'm very fortunate to be able to work with stories. Each book is an ecosystem, and this gives me the opportunity to be inspired, to imagine always different situations, compositions, colors. It's very stimulating work. You could say my work is more like research: What does this story need? What kind of search do I need to do to get the best result? Which technique should I use to best represent this text? What to tell and not to tell with images?"

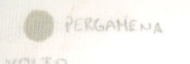

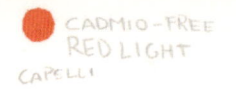

PERGAMENA   ● CADMIO-FREE   BIANCO DI ZINCO
VOLTO   RED LIGHT   VESTITO   OIL
                CAPELLI   OCCHIO   TERRA
                                                  D'OMBRA
                                                  NATURALE

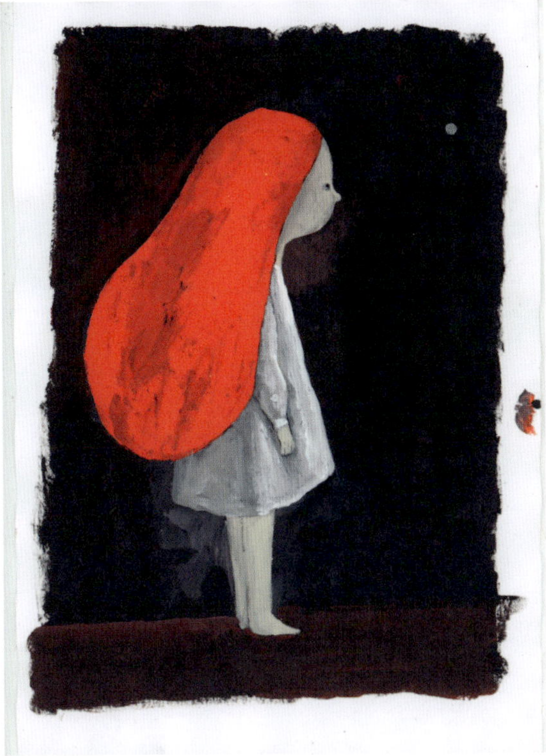

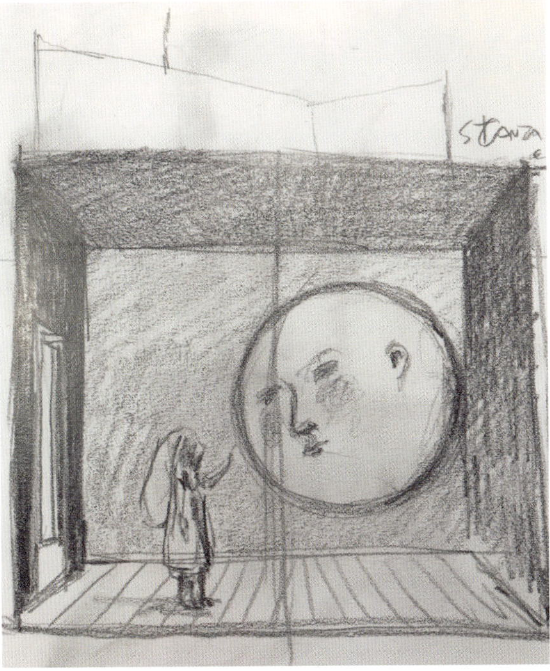
STANZA

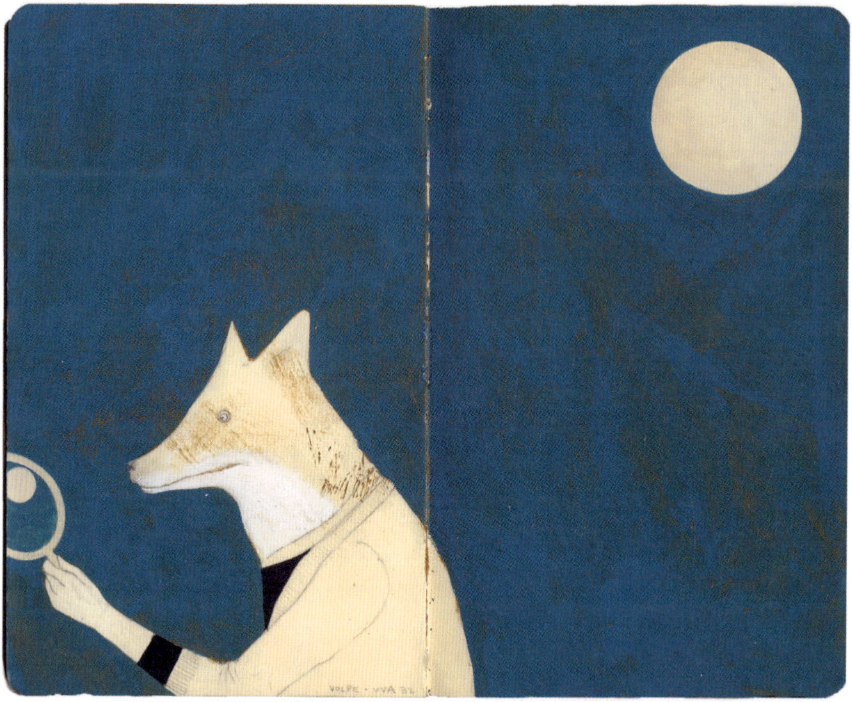
VOLPE - VVA 32

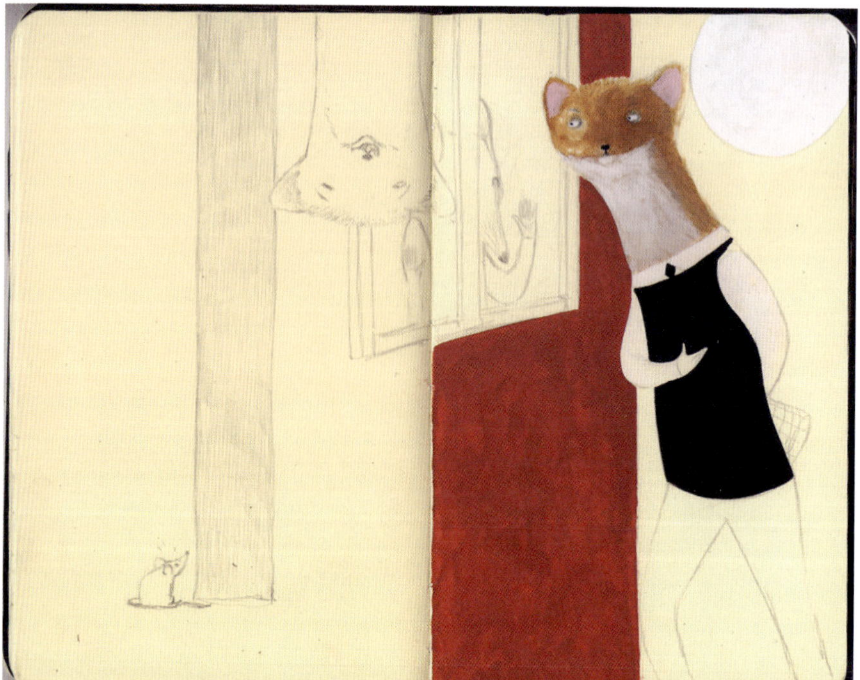

Observe before drawing

"My ideas come from reality. I like to look for shapes, forms, to recover objects from the real world. I observe my surroundings: animals, houses, landscapes, atmospheres. Everything that intrigues me becomes a source of inspiration. I'm also very inspired by the graphic arts, stop-motion, and cinema in general.

I don't usually make storyboards; I only draw a kind of sketch on the final sheet of paper. If I'm satisfied with this, I move on to coloring. Over time, I realized that this focus helps me to be more expressive, less organized, more direct, less rigid, more communicative. But I've also realized that to work in this way, my ideas at least have to be clear, and this doesn't always happen so quickly. Sometimes I feel overwhelmed. On those days I can't draw. Probably I'm tired. I go out. I go for bike ride and I try not to think about work. I distract myself and wait. I don't think there's anything else to do but wait until I've regained my strength."

"When I was a child, for a brief period of time, I wanted to learn to play the guitar. But every time I went to guitar lessons I felt like I was wasting my time. I always thought about drawing. For me, drawing is like playing, and play is a serious thing."

Tom Schamp

Photography: Eveliene Deraedt

OUTSIDE

studio / atelier / illustratoria

"My wood studio, with a garden, located in a peaceful neighborhood in Brussels, is the place where I prefer to spend my time working on projects as diverse as possible. Alternating between assignments for companies, whether or not submitted through advertising or communication agencies, book publishers or private clients, suits me particularly well. Thanks to the help from my partner Katrien, I don't have to worry about the business side, which frees my head to focus on the creative work.

Imagination, acrylic paint, cardboard and a set of good headphones are my primary tools. I never lack the first; fear of the blank page is completely foreign to me. My imagination is sparked in particular by the everyday things that cross my path or by what I read or hear on the radio. Humor is also essential to my creative process I suppose. Over the past few years, my images have become more popular, which often leads to a snowball effect: potential clients often explicitly request illustrations that keep viewers/readers/buyers busy for a while.

Today, I paint all my illustrations by hand. Still, I often paint the different elements of my illustrations on cardboard, which I later scan and join digitally. This mix of craftsmanship and technology seems to be the right recipe for my brain. During my creative process, one idea leads to another. While preparing the two semi-encyclopedic children's books – with a third in the making – published in the last few years, I did a lot of Google searches, which is rather unusual for me, since I usually prefer to rely on pure imagination."

CADEAULALA!
↑NORD↑
JOUETS
Ich möchte ein Eisbär sein
EISBAR
Céleste
BIG BEN
МОСКВА
Chocolate Chips
Ski in the Sky!
A WHOLE LOT of LOVE
GALERIES LAFAYETTE
TORTUGA
SHOPPING
Cadeaulala!
GALERIES
LAFAYETTE
Père Noël
Père Noël
LAFAYETTE
MARTIN
métro
les 2 alpes
Y avait-il des palmiers au Pôle-Sud?
SUD

1

CAP sur la COUPOLE
En avant la musique!
le papa pinguin
GALERIES LAFAYETTE
Y avait-il des palmiers au Pôle-Sud?

MEXICO
PUEBLO MAGICO
LUCHA LIBRE
FRIDA
la CAJA de PAPEL
BANCO MATIC
la Fiesta de las luces
CASA AZUL
SAN CRISTOBAL de las CASAS (de PAPEL)
LA LUZ
DEL SUR
JAGUAR
OAXACA
NOËL
XOCOLALA
LUCES
T M

VIVA MEXICO
PUEBLO MAGIC
El Siglo de las Luces
Fiesta
LUCHA LIBRE
MEXICO
LA LUZ
DEL SUR
OAXACA
XOCOLALA
mama
papa
SAMSON
NIGHT
VIVA ZAPATOS
San Cristobal
de las Casas de Papel
LIGHT

"I don't usually do sketches. Rather I start by outlining the most important elements with white pencil on poster board. Once I start painting, I let myself be swept away by the abundance of colors. Acrylic paint allows me to paint opaque and translucent layers.

Since I don't like to differentiate between a work of art for children or adults, I fill my children's work with hints and references that fathers, grandfathers and whoever else reads them can appreciate.

The assignments I like the most are ones where the client, after an initial description of the commission, has total faith in my line of thinking without wanting to make too many changes. In general, book publishers fit this profile. A good example is the Belgian-Dutch publishing house Lannoo with which I've published seventeen children's books over the years. During the work process, consultations are rare; I've never been asked to make major changes or move in a different direction. This gives me peace of mind."

MODEMUSEUM
ZOOT SUITE!
MODEBOOT
UP
academie
MIX & MATCH!
EXPO
DRAMA QUEEN
BLIJFT de RAF!
permanente
A→Z
Kant & Klaar
MoMu Café
Cotton Club
MODE
WOOL

278 | 279

MONUMENT

MUSEUM MATERNITE

mr

NEVER EVER be CLEVER

En effet!

4

"I started illustrating books around 2000, and I've published a total forty-five since. My most recent books are also available in other languages, in addition to English and Spanish.

I've done commercial assignments in recent years for the French galleries Lafayette. They asked me to create illustrations in which the decoration was based on the 2021 Christmas display windows for their international chain of stores. I've also done work for the Japanese hypermarket Umie in Kyoto, for which I've been creating illustrations for various sales events over the past five years. And also for the Belgian Fashion Museum in Antwerp, for which I designed some *merchandising* items.

To escape from work from time to time, a bike ride and a cold beer usually do the trick. As a Belgian, I have a lot of options in the case of the latter."

1. 2D illustration and its 3D version. Christmas at Galeries Lafayette, Paris (France), 2020.
2. Painted elements and digital composition. Christmas at Galeries Lafayette, Paris, 2020.
3. MOMU Fashion Museum, Antwerp (Belgium), 2021.
4. A selection from my multipurpose and endless collection of letters, m&e.

Hervé Tullet

Self-portrait

"I'm an author and illustrator of children's books. Or better yet I'm a designer of books to be read to children and babies. I say 'baby' because I've always been fascinated by the relationship that can be established with infants through different languages, in addition to words. In my books, I've tried to play with these different languages and communicate with babies. I'm guided by a kind of belief that I've worked out for myself: since babies don't know anything, they can always learn something. The unknown doesn't frighten them.

I also believe that each child is connected to the sensations she or he had when they were babies and that babies themselves are connected to the sensations of prehistoric humans. In a way, sometimes I imagine that I'm a prehistoric man reading my latest creation to a child in a cave lit by a flickering flame casting dramatic shadows on the walls. It helps me find the strength of expression in its archaic simplicity and in a visual expression, because in all these characters there are actually few who know how to read. In addition, this image seems to me to be filled with the mystery and magic that I find in the first silent movies.

I'm lucky that I don't know how to draw very well. As a result, since my first book, I've tried to navigate this problem and find the power of ideas that are stronger than pretty images. Also in the case of prehistoric man, the child and the unpolished artist have been a deep source of inspiration to me through the commitment they have to, and which they possess in, the act of drawing, to express what they need to say directly, without any filters or effects."

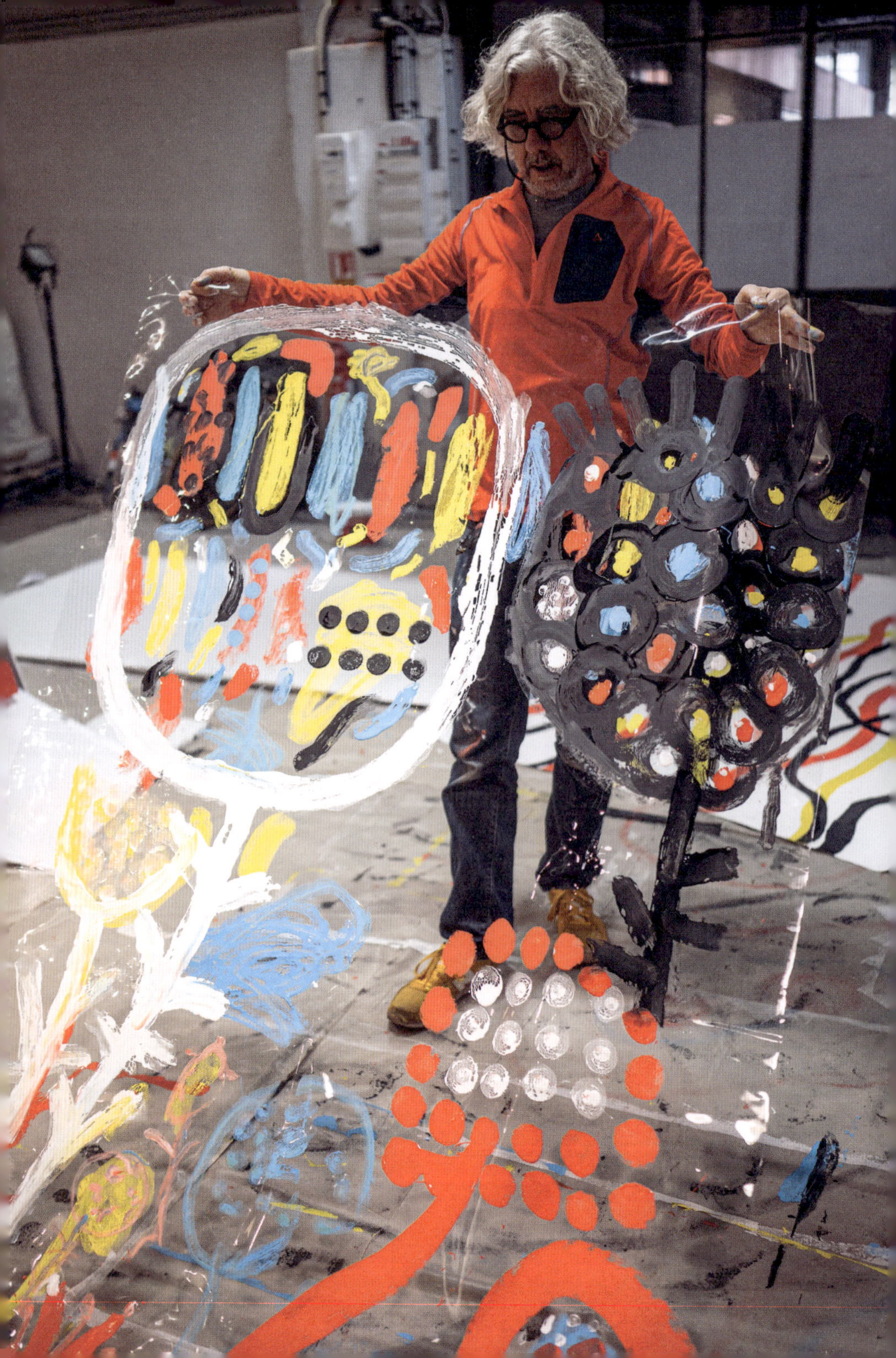

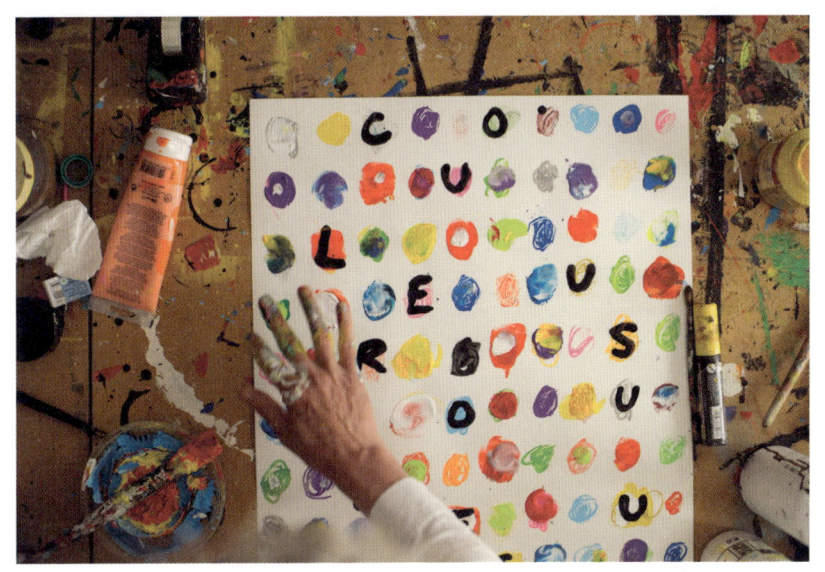

Photography: Jake Green

"I understood very early that I worked for and with the reader, that I had to grant them their place and their space so that they could play with me, the author of the book. I also realized quickly that there were two readers: one that knows how to read and another who doesn't, and that this combination is very interesting.

I had the good fortune to understand early on that my books could have a purpose, thanks to people deeply involved with and committed to the welfare of children, especially in places where there are a lot of problems. I felt a sense of commitment, a soldier for creation, for experimentation who will provide material to spice up the daily life of these amazing teachers, librarians and everyone else involved in this field.

I strive to be a good soldier, one who defends the book, who helps to provide access to books, who believes that books can save the world or at least some lives, the same way that books have saved me.

Basically what interests me most is that children learn to engage actively with the world, so that they can transform it someday. This is how I understand the role of an idea, and it's why I like to search for ideas."

Photography: Grégoire Deroulède

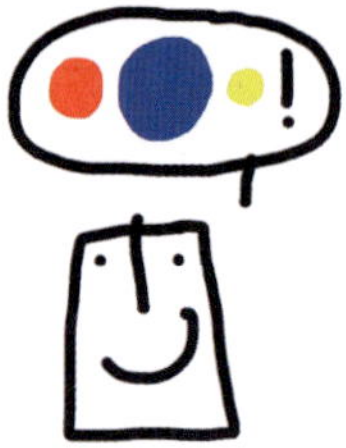
!
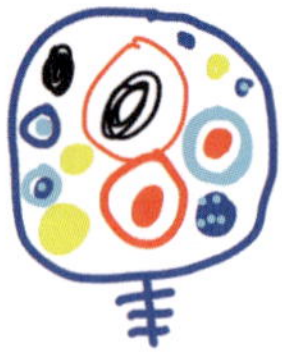
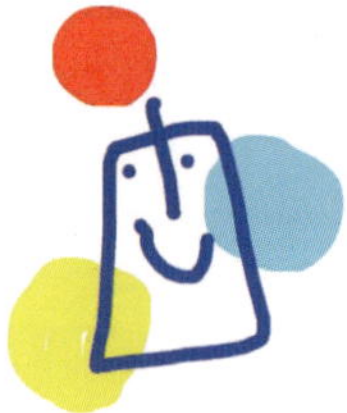
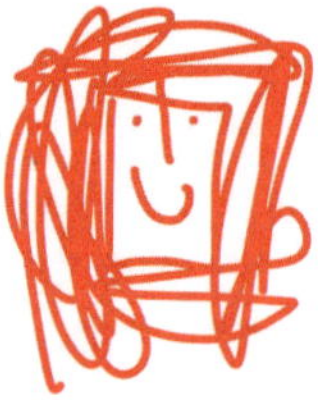
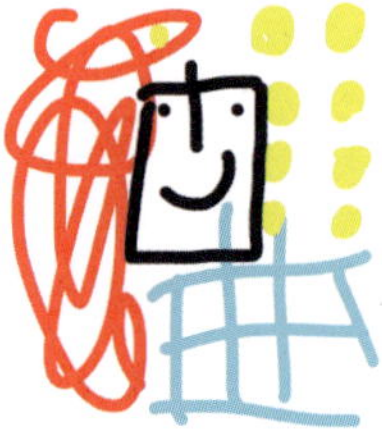
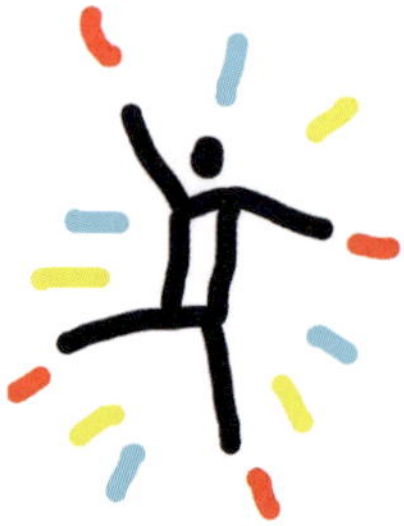
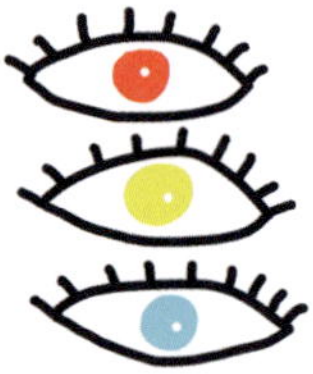
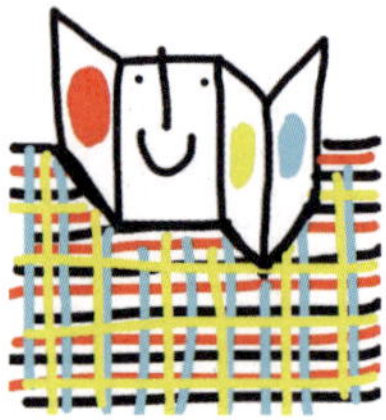
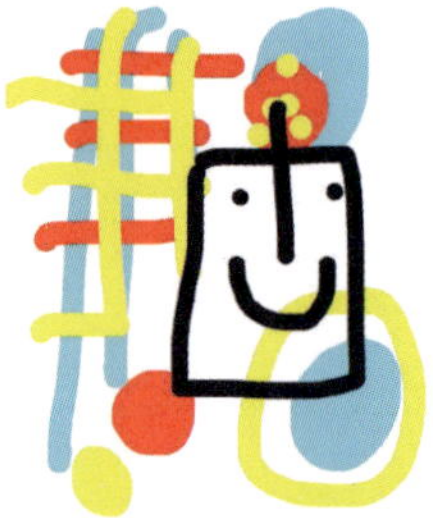
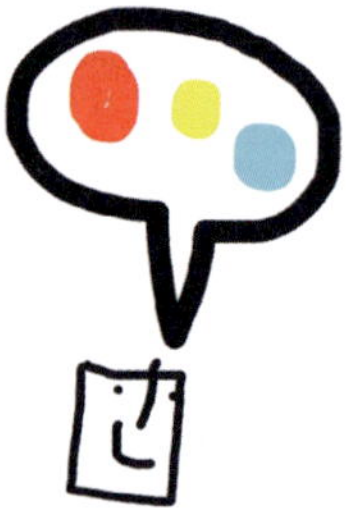
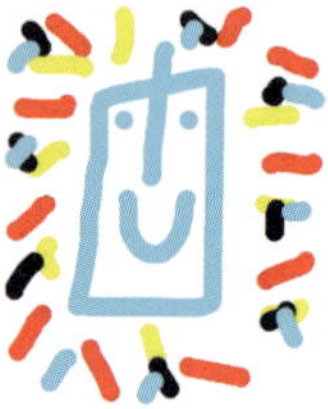
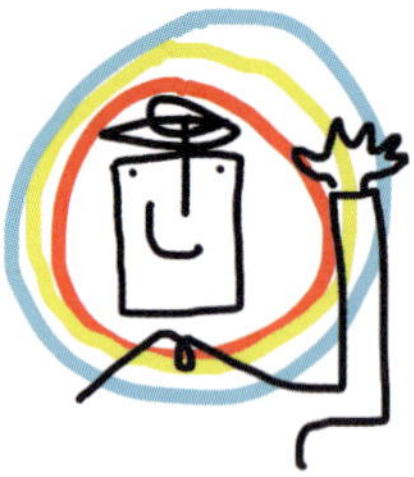
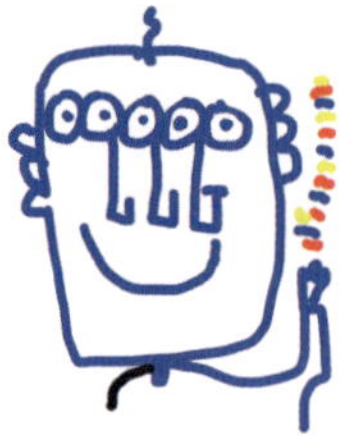
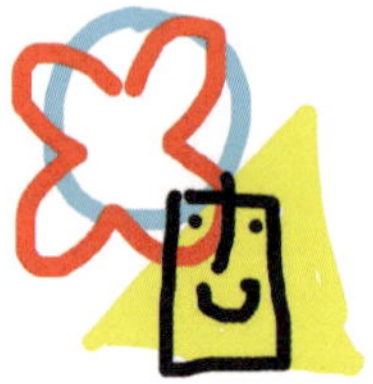
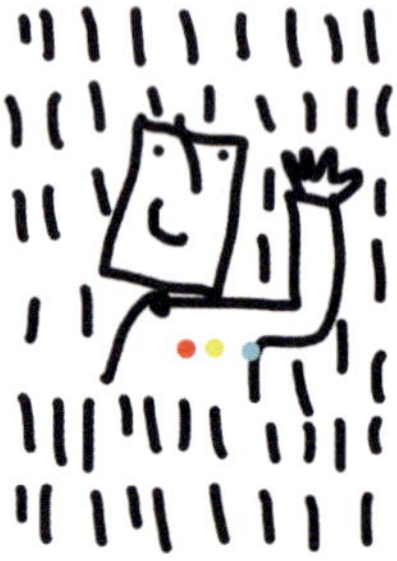
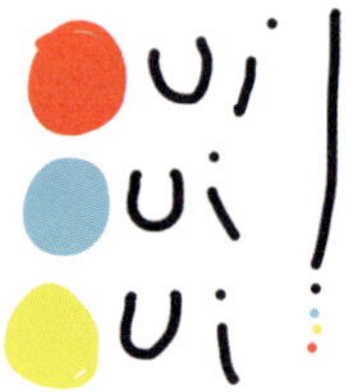
ui
ui
ui
!

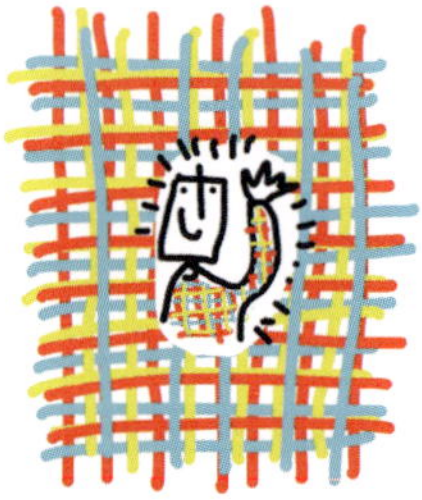
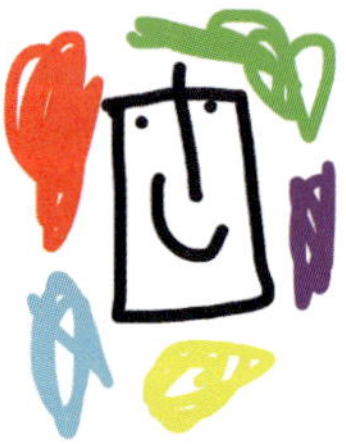
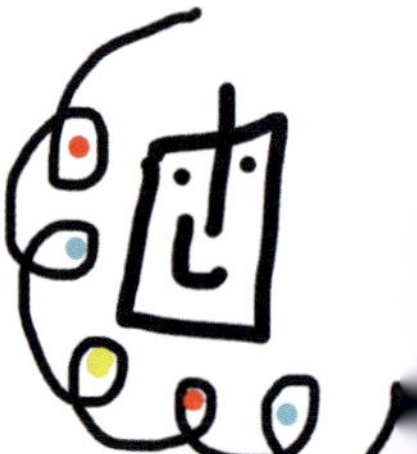

Connected

"Social networks have completely changed my relationship with people who follow my work. I receive messages every day in which people talk to me about a book, showing me a workshop that was given or an amazing exhibition. These are people whom I used to meet only at talks I gave or at book signings.

Social networks have increased the number of conversations, always with joy and sincerity. Each message is important to me. I need it to feel like it's me who answers these messages personally so that even there on a social network, it feels like a human is at the center of it all and not an algorithm or an assistant who responds.

Yes. I'm very interested in this.

So I developed a kind of an image bank, which I call my *emojis,* and which I send according to my mood or frame of mind. Images that have discovered their identity. Blue, yellow, red, black, like a Hervé Tullet signature. Simple enough to be seen in a small format like a mobile phone. Pretty enough to be printed on a t-shirt like some people do. An idea, a message in an image so that children and people's whose language I don't know can understand them.

I also usually send personalized messages. On the iPad or iPhone. It's easy, fast and fun. And it's a genuine pleasure. Often it's the start of a conversation. In a way, responding to these messages in images is my usual way of drawing."

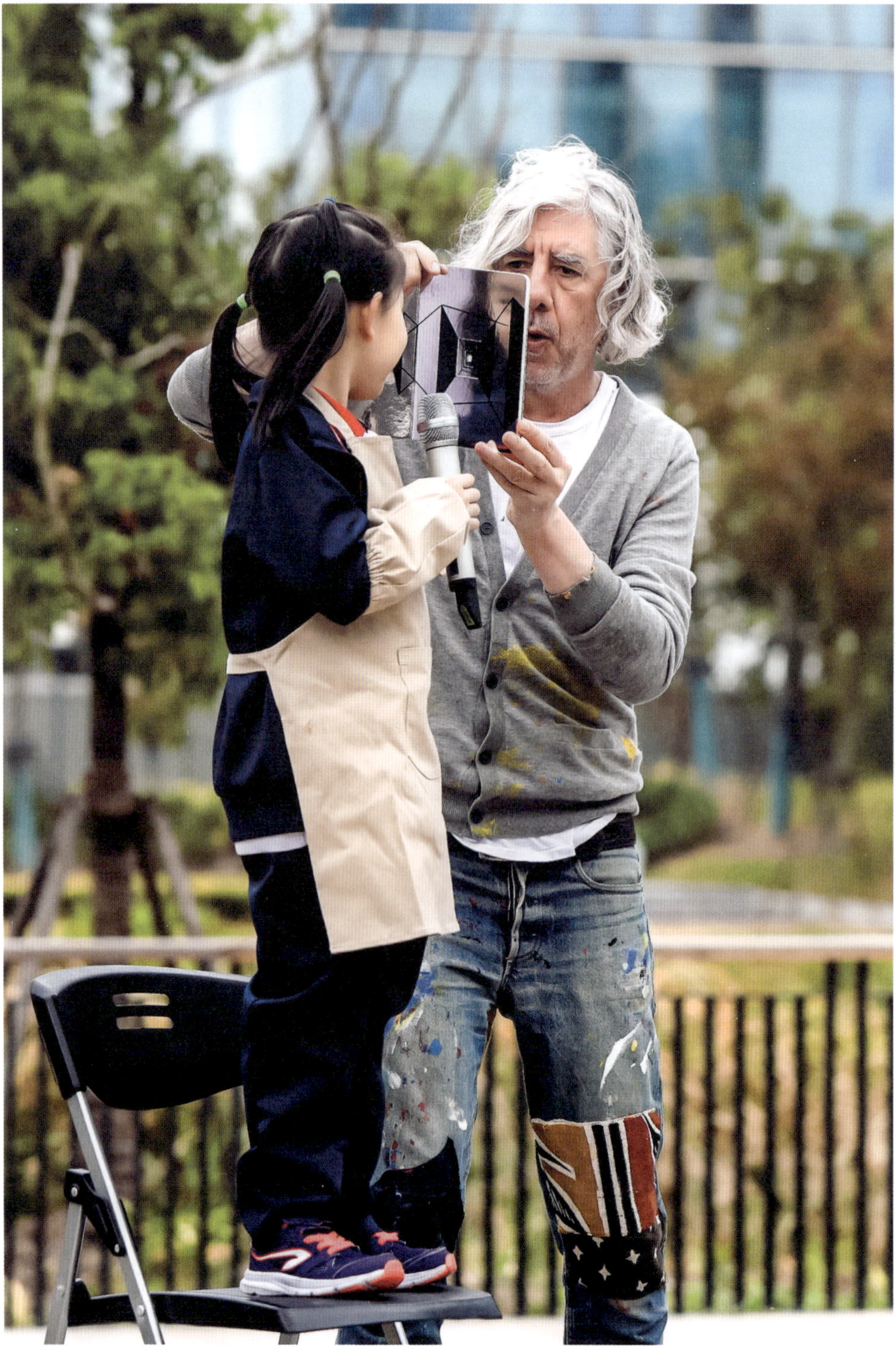

"I search. I go in circles. I don't find. I go on tip-toe. I miss the turn. I know I have to pass by this. I go back and look again. But what?"

Ideas

"I like to say, 'If you don't look, you don't find'. It seems more accurate, a tad less arrogant and bit more uplifting than Picasso's 'I don't look. I find'.

I go in circles to nowhere, to emptiness, to boredom.
Boredom it seems to me is inevitable. I have to go through it. For this reason I like to be bored. I know my ideas are born from boredom. So when one day I think I have one, I feel the energy of the idea and the joy of escaping this boredom, to locate the energy of the idea.

When this happens, I pick out a pretty notebook. I have a collection of them ready for this day.

I write.

The words and the images come quickly.

It's a bit like writing in shorthand, quickly, out of fear that the idea will escape. If I reach the end of the dictation, it means that I have an idea that will probably become a book, an image or an exhibition one day, and if not... Well, I start again."

Valerio Vidali

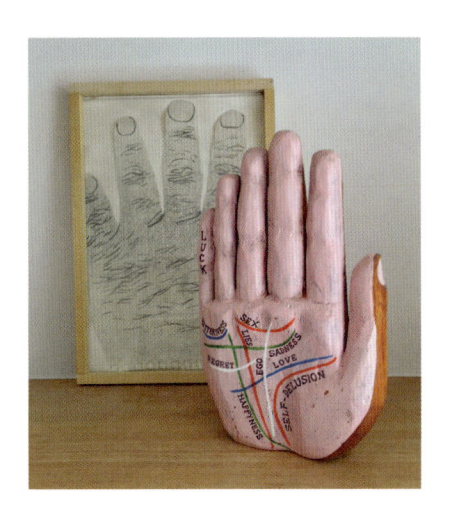

"My work is the result of the constant struggle between my love of simplicity and my natural tendency to draw complicated and busy images. Like any other author, my contribution to a project is my point of view, which is shaped by my interests, what's important to me, my education and my professional path. As an illustrator, I value above all else the idea behind a project and the way it tells a story.

The book *The Forest* (León Encantado, 2018), the result of a collaboration with Violeta Lopiz, represents the longest and most challenging project I've ever had the pleasure to take part in; it's especially dear to me. It's a visual metaphor about the adventure of life, captured through die-cuts, reliefs, cut-outs and gatefolds. It required seven years of hard work and a very courageous and uncompromising editor. In 2018, it was rated the best picture book of the year by *The New York Times*.

The book *Hundert* (Kein & Aber, 2018) was nominated for the German Children's Literature Prize and has been translated into eighteen languages.

In 2020, I illustrated for Enchanted Lion the first English edition of *Telephone Tales,* by Gianni Rodari. Now it's also published by Einaudi Ragazzi in Italy as an edition celebrating the 60th anniversary of Rodari's masterpiece.

As for my parallel interests, I've always liked to build things, to make small sculptures and toys, especially out of wood. For the last few years, I've been studying traditional furniture making. I'm just an amateur, but I have a small workshop at home and it brings me a lot of joy."

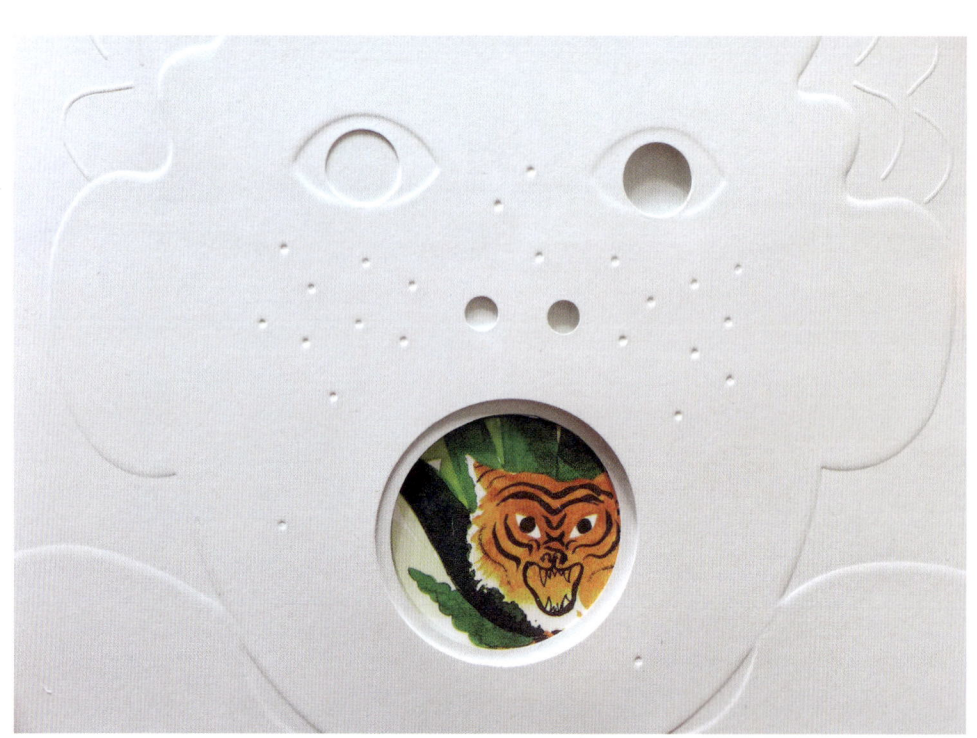

1

292 | 293

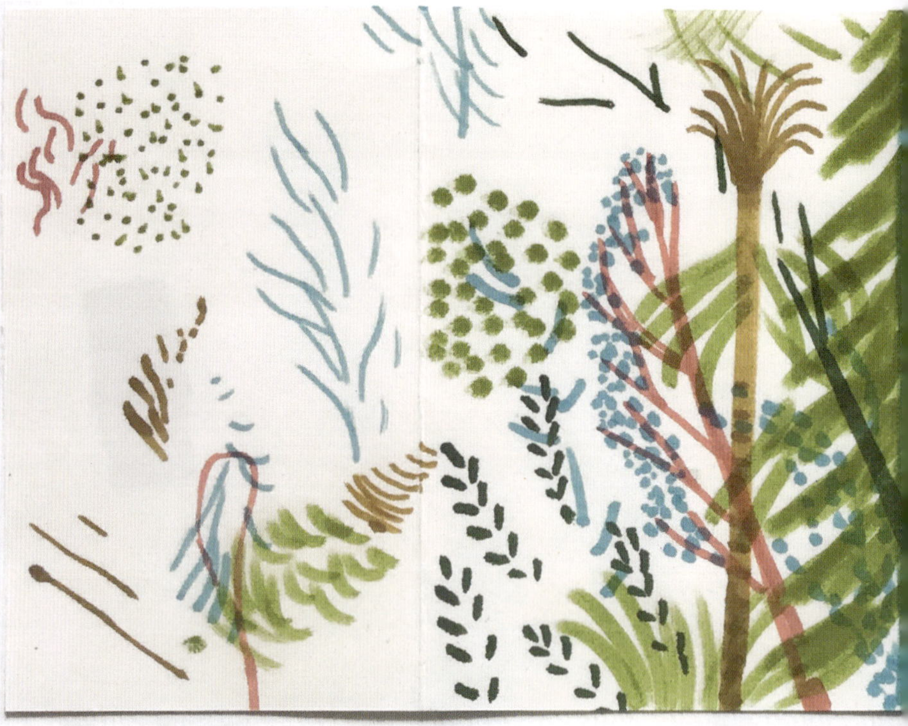

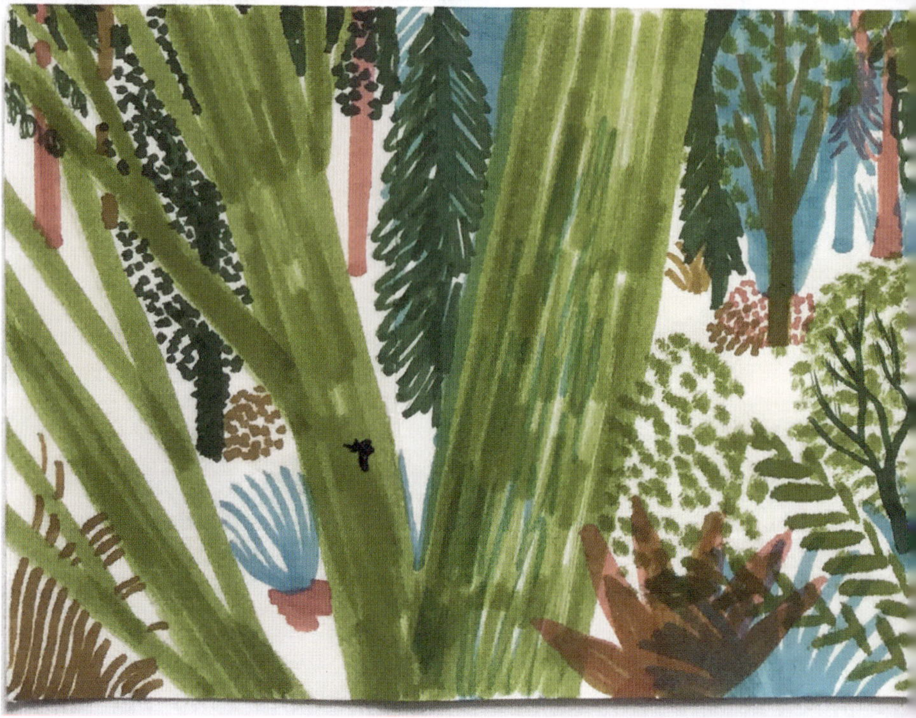

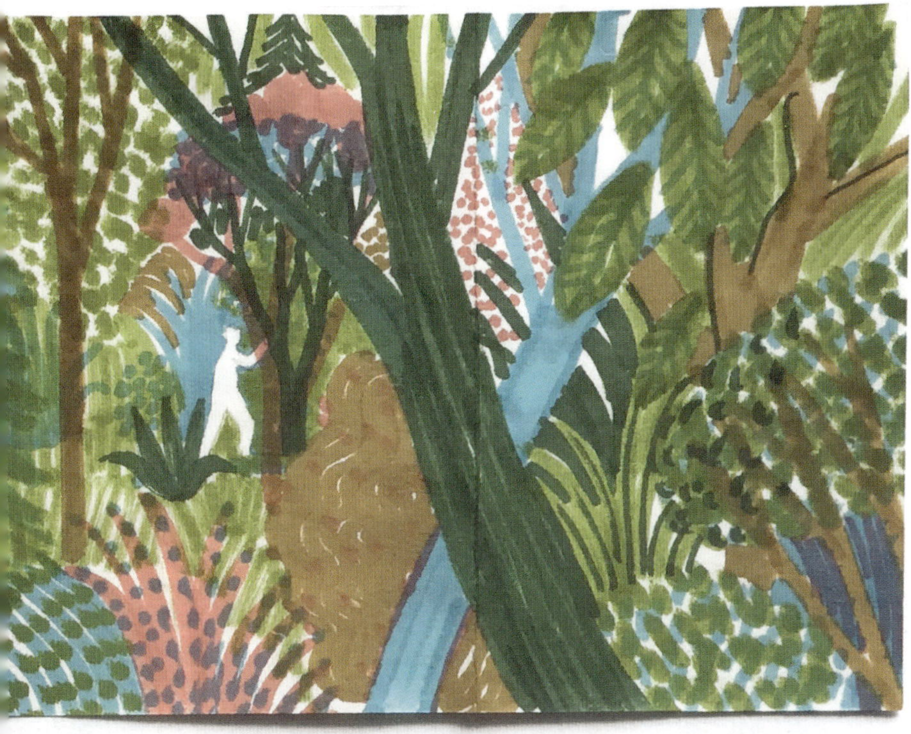

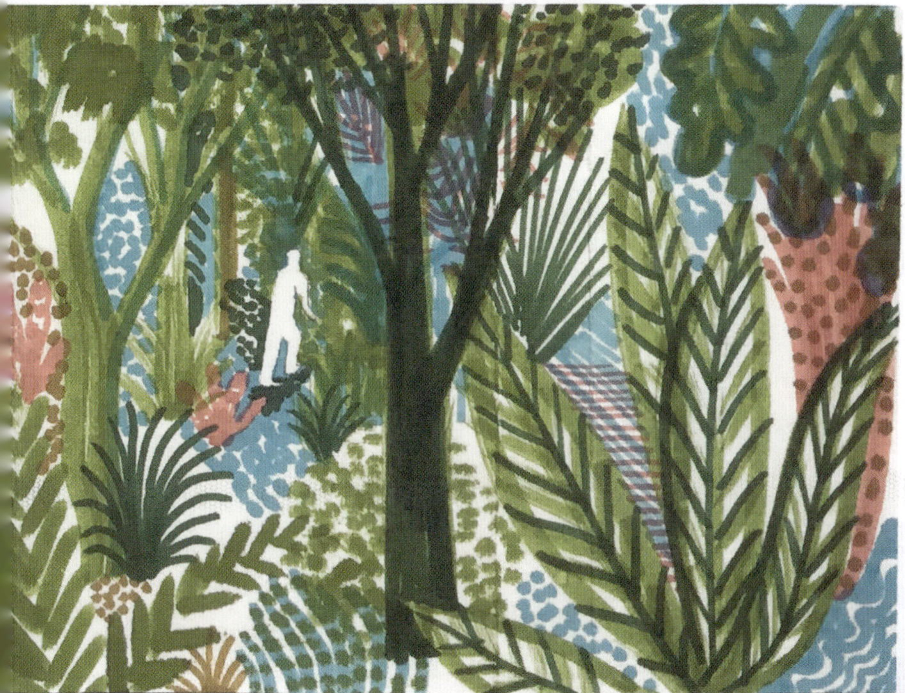

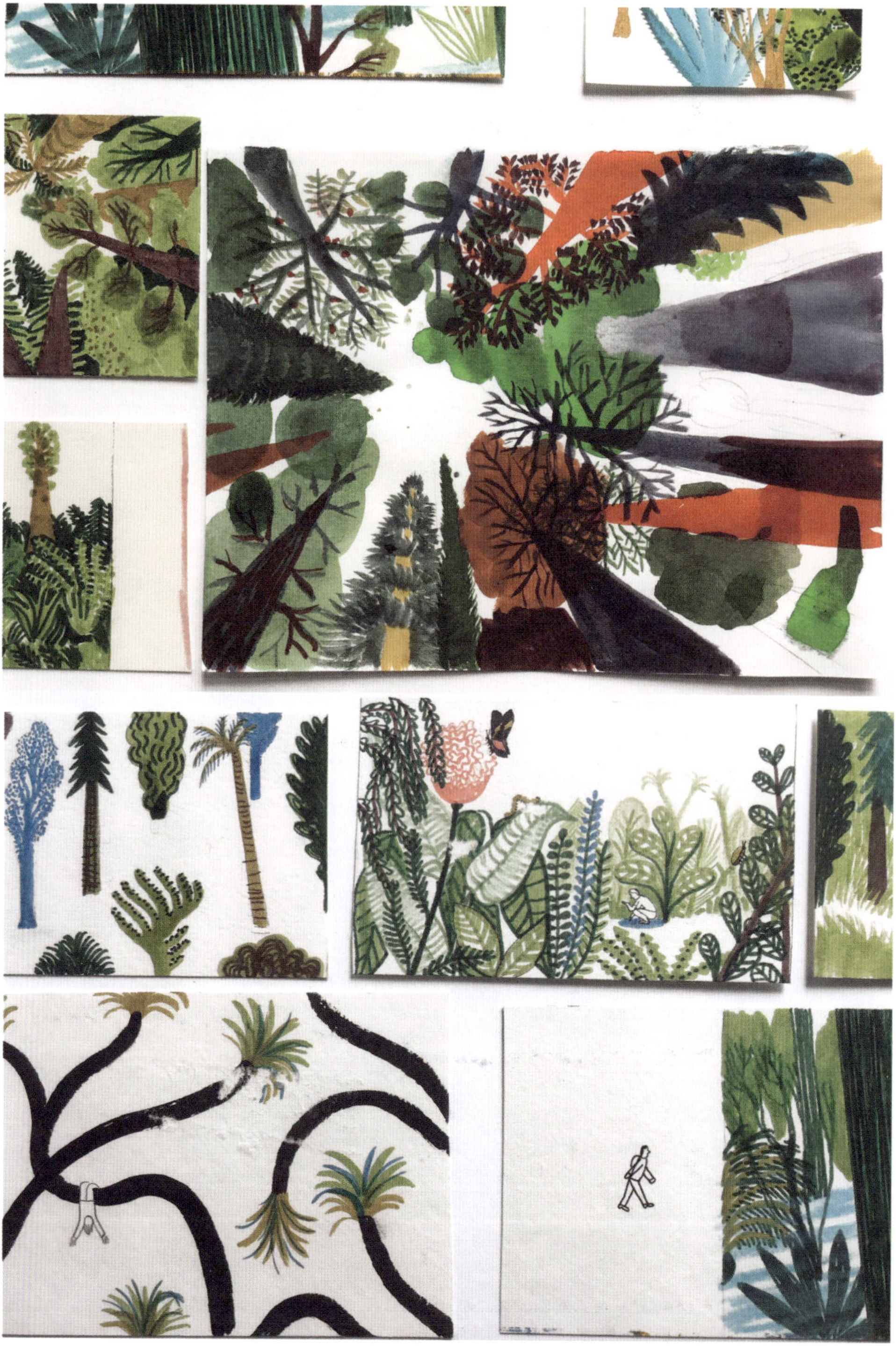

"The secret to being a good illustrator is to try and enjoy and value each and every one of the stages of the creative process, even the unpleasant parts. To be thoughtful and genuine. As Milter Glaser once said: 'Fail more. Fail better.'"

"Creativity is one of the tools we have as human beings to express our individuality and our value as part of society. I think it's subconsciously rooted in our need to be loved. When you create a nice drawing, you're saying more or less: 'Hey, everybody! Look at me. Look at what I've made. Now praise me!' Creativity is also what makes us human. It's the driving force behind our evolution as a species.

Ideas are everywhere around us. Literally, they're in everything we make (and everything that nature makes, too). And they're as contagious as a virus. They duplicate and mutate endlessly. To be creative, all you have to do is pay attention to what's going on around you and be willing to be affected by it. Creativity is like a muscle: the more you use it, the stronger it gets. But it's even more important to cultivate a critical eye and a guiding philosophy.

What inspires me most is the sincerity and uniqueness that certain books possess. The total coherence between a particular idea and the tools used to communicate it. I like when a project isn't just beautiful or clever but uncompromising and thoughtful, down to the smallest detail.

Play and creativity are two sides of the same coin. It's what my hands do to help my brain think. They move things around, scribble on paper and help me flesh out an idea.

Mistakes are the byproduct of all the fun, and they're just as important. They bring the spontaneity and brilliance to a project that only accidents can produce."

1. *The Forest*, León Encantado, 2018.
2. *The Forest*. Sketches.
3. Mobiles and wood sculptures.

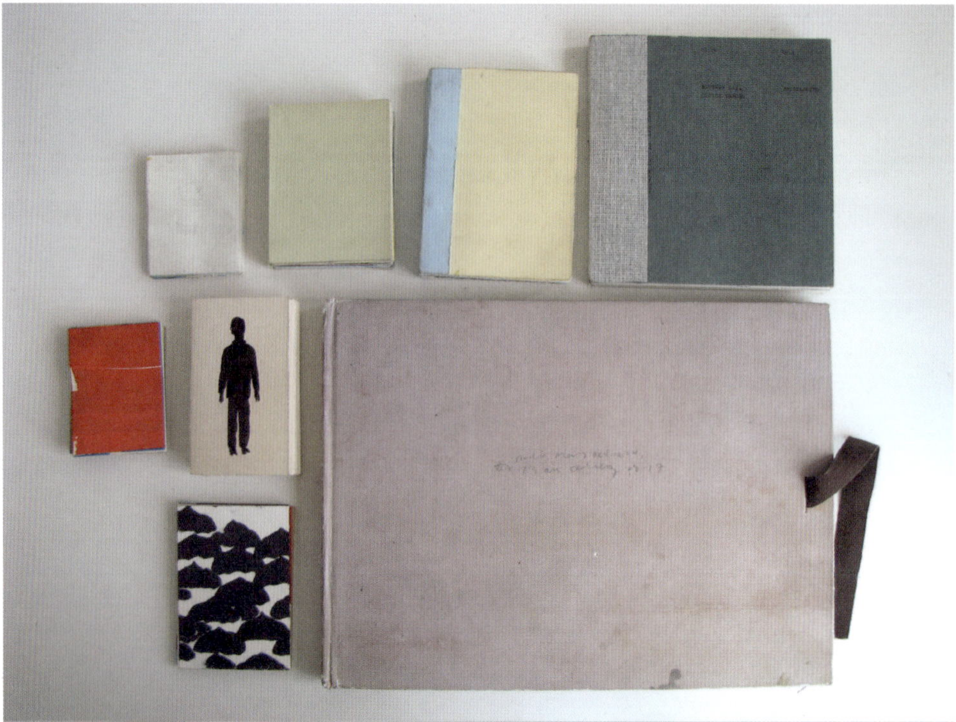

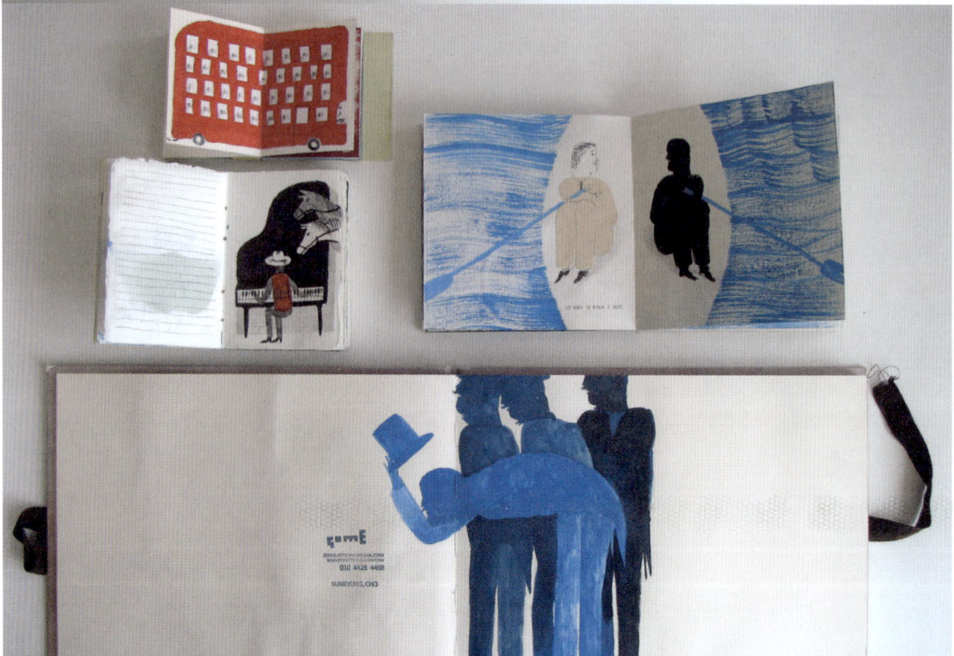
010 4428 4408

298 | 299

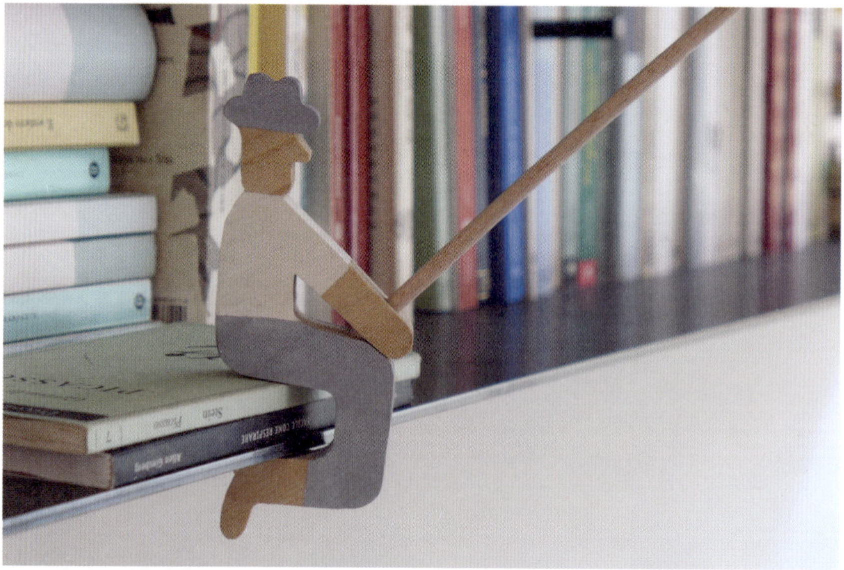

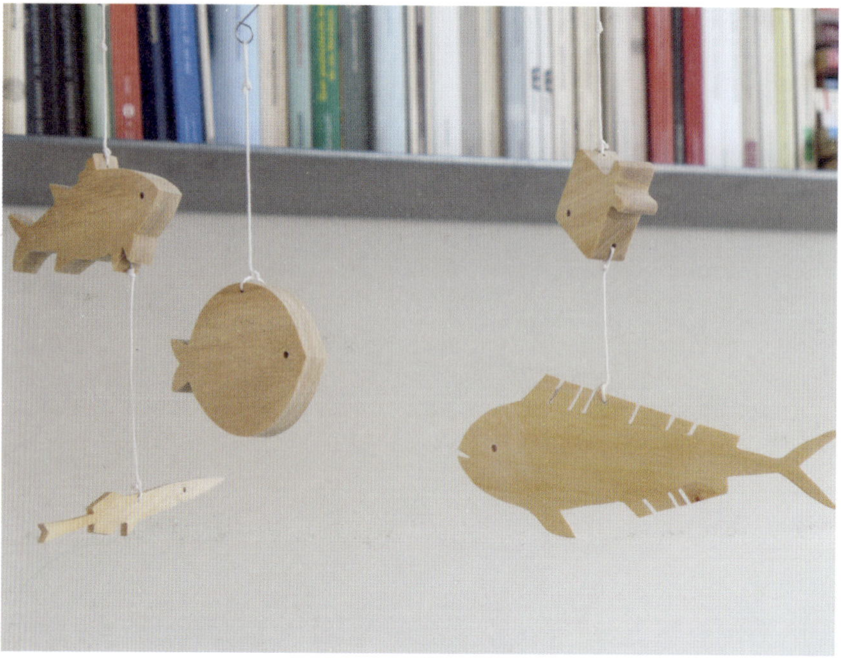

3

300 | 301

Artists

Elisa Arguilé

Pablo Auladell
www.pabloauladell.com
@pabloauladell

Gary Baseman
www.garybaseman.com
@garybaseman

Katie Benn
www.katiebenn.com
@katie_benn_

Ana Biscaia
www.anabiscaia.com
@anabiscaia

Serge Bloch
www.sergebloch.com
@serge.bloch

Pep Carrió
www.pepcarrio.com
@pepcarrio

Carolina Celas
www.carolinacelas.com
@carolina.celas

Jesús Cisneros
@jesus.cisneros.ilustrador

Lisa Congdon
lisacongdon.com
@lisacongdon

Fanny Dreyer
fannydreyer.blogspot.com
@fanny_dreyer

Delphine Durand
delphinedurand.blogspot.com
@delphine.durand

Isidro Ferrer
www.isidroferrer.com

Guridi
@guridi_

Yoshiko Hada
www.yoshikohada.com
@yoshiko_hada

Elizabeth Haidle
@ehaidle

Chris Haughton
www.chrishaughton.com
@chrishaughton

Isol
isolisol.blogspot.com
@isolmisenta

Martin Jarrie
martinjarrie.com
@martinjarrie

Anita Kunz
www.anitakunz.com
@anitakunz

Manuel Marsol
www.manuelmarsol.com
@manuel_marsol

Flavio Morais
www.flaviomorais.net
@_flavio_morais

Pérez Arteaga
www.batidoradeideas.com
@perez_arteaga_ilustrador

Simone Rea
@simone_rea_official

Tom Schamp
www.tomschamp.com
@tom.schamp.illustrator

Hervé Tullet
www.herve-tullet.com
@hervetullet

Valerio Vidali
www.valeriovidali.com
@vidalivalerio

About the author

Miguel Ángel Pérez Arteaga

Miguel Angel Pérez Arteaga works in graphic design and advertising communication as Batidora de Ideas.

He is the author and illustrator of ten children's stories published in Spain, Mexico and Brazil. His books have been recognized by the National Reading Program, the Reading Promotion Program of the State of Serena and the National Library Program in Mexico; by the Ministry of Education of Chile; the Banco del Libro of Venezuela; the Sistema d'Adquisició Bibliotecària of the Regional Government of Catalonia and the Libraries of the Community of Madrid (Spain).

He is the author of the books *How Ideas Are Born: Graphic Designers and Creative Processes, Isidro Ferrer: About Nothing*, published by Hoaki Books, and *Creativity: Curiosity, Motivation and Play* published by Prensas de la Universidad de Zaragoza.

He participated in the exhibitions "Ready to Read. Book design from Spain", a selection of the best books published in Spain (New York, Washington, Mexico, Buenos Aires, São Paulo, Madrid and Lisbon) and "Ilustrísimos: Overview of Children and Young Adults Illustration in Spain" at the Bologna Book Fair.

He was a Finalist in the Daniel Gil Awards (Spain) and in the Biennial of Illustration of Amarante (Portugal). He has held numerous solo and group painting, photography and illustration exhibitions.

He is a professor in the Marketing Department of the University of Zaragoza (Spain).